Discourses of Disorder

Discourses of Disorder

Riots, Strikes and Protests in the Media

Edited by Christopher Hart
and Darren Kelsey

EDINBURGH
University Press

Edinburgh University Press is one of the leading university presses in the UK. We publish academic books and journals in our selected subject areas across the humanities and social sciences, combining cutting-edge scholarship with high editorial and production values to produce academic works of lasting importance. For more information visit our website: edinburghuniversitypress.com

Edinburgh University Press Ltd
The Tun – Holyrood Road
12(2f) Jackson's Entry
Edinburgh EH8 8PJ

Typeset in 11/13pt Adobe Garamond Pro by
Servis Filmsetting Ltd, Stockport, Cheshire
printed and bound in Great Britain.

A CIP record for this book is available from the British Library

ISBN 978 1 4744 3541 3 (hardback)
ISBN 978 1 4744 3542 0 (webready PDF)
ISBN 978 1 4744 3543 7 (epub)

Contents

Notes on Contributors

Matt Davies is Senior Lecturer in English Language in the Department of English at the University of Chester. His research includes discourse and ideology in the news media, exploring conflicts and controversies in English language and linguistics, and corpus linguistic approaches to the analysis of song lyrics. He is the author of *Oppositions and Ideology in News Discourse* (Bloomsbury, 2012) and is currently conducting further research into the power of syntactically constructed oppositions.

Rania Elnakkouzi has recently completed her PhD in the Department of Linguistics and English Language at Lancaster University. Her research focuses on the argumentative techniques, narratives and metaphors involved in the legitimation of past actions.

Christopher Hart is Professor of Linguistics at Lancaster University. His research focuses on the relationship between discourse, cognition and social action. He is author of *Critical Discourse and Cognitive Science: New Perspectives on Immigration Discourse* (Palgrave, 2010) and *Discourse, Grammar and Ideology: Functional and Cognitive Perspectives* (Bloomsbury, 2014).

Darren Kelsey is Head of Media, Culture, Heritage in the School of Arts and Cultures at Newcastle University. He researches mythology and ideology in contemporary media, culture and politics. He is author of *Media, Myth and Terrorism: A Discourse-Mythological Analysis of the 'Blitz Spirit'* (Palgrave, 2015). His most recent work, *Media and Affective Mythologies* (Palgrave, 2017), synergises approaches to critical discourse studies with the work of Carl Jung, Joseph Campbell and other mythologists.

Gerrit Kotzur recently passed his viva voce in the Department of Humanities, Northumbria University Newcastle. His PhD thesis explored the resistant discourse of visually impaired people in the context of employment.

Andrea Mayr is a lecturer in the School of Arts at Queen's University Belfast. Her research is in the area of critical discourse studies and media analysis, with a particular focus on (digital) media in relation to exclusion and citizenship. Together with David Machin, she is author of *The Language of Crime and Deviance: An Introduction to Critical Linguistic Analysis in Media and Popular Culture* (Continuum, 2011) and *How to Do Critical Discourse Analysis: A Multimodal Introduction* (Sage, 2012).

Rotsukhon Nophakhun was an English Language research assistant and Visiting Lecturer at the University of Chester. Since then, she has taught at Manchester Metropolitan University and is currently teaching English Language and Literature at King's Leadership Academy, Warrington.

Serjoscha Ostermeyer is a researcher at Otto-von-Guericke-University Magdeburg. His research explores urban and cultural studies. He lectures on Cultural Engineering and has co-edited books on interdisciplinary discourse.

Carolina Pérez-Arredondo is an Adjunct Lecturer in the Language Department at Universidad Bernardo O'Higgins, Chile. Her research explores media representations of student movements and their motives. She is one of the editors of the book *Discourses from Latin America and the Caribbean: Current Concepts and Challenges* (Palgrave, in press).

Boitshwarelo Rantsudu is a research student in the Centre for Language and Communication Research at Cardiff University. Her research explores the interplay between evaluative stance and objectivity in hard news reporting.

Juhani Rudanko is a Professor Emeritus in the English Department of the University of Tampere, Finland. He is the author of several books, including *Discourses of Freedom of Speech* (Palgrave, 2012).

David Sittler completed his PhD at Erfurt University in 2015. His research explored the urban street as a mass medium. He is scientific coordinator of the research lab of the a.r.t.e.s. Graduate School for the Humanities Cologne at Cologne University. He is a co-editor of *Infrastructuring Publics: Making Infrastructures Public* (Springer, 2018).

Introduction

Christopher Hart and Darren Kelsey

Instances of civil disorder in the form of organised riots, strikes and protests are a significant part of the political process. Riots, strikes and protests serve to highlight fissures in society, express discontent, and stimulate public debate. Ultimately, riots, strikes and protests aim to challenge and effect change in existing social and economic structures and policies. The 'success' of such instances of civil disorder depends heavily on media treatments of the social actors and actions involved, including whether events are labelled as 'riots', 'strikes' or 'protests'.[1] Since, as Lee points out, most instances of civil disorder take place in highly specific times and places, witnessed first-hand by only relatively small numbers of people, 'the capability of protests to communicate their messages and achieve the desired outcomes depends on whether and how they are portrayed by the mass media' (2014: 2725). It is through positive and prominent media coverage that social movements can gain traction, galvanise public support and thus influence governmental authorities (Gamson and Wolfsfeld 1993). However, mainstream media, for reasons of political economy, tend to marginalise, delegitimise and undermine riots, strikes and protests, presenting them as illegitimate acts of non-conformity or criminality that constitute a 'threat' to civil society. Research on media representations of civil disorder points overwhelmingly to a tendency among mainstream media to focus on the violent and/or disruptive consequences of riots, strikes and protests rather than addressing the structural conditions and political cause(s) that motivated the action (Boykoff 2006; Di Cicco 2010; Gitlin 1980; Glasgow Media Group 1976, 1980, 1982; Hackett and Zhou 1994; Leung 2009; McLeod and Hertog 1992; Shoemaker 1984; Small 1995; Xu 2013). The media, in other words, typically adhere to a discourse of deviance (Hall 1973; Murdock 1973) and report riots, strikes and protests within a violence 'frame' (Entman 1993; Gamson and Modigliani 1989).[2] Chan and Lee (1984) describe this pattern of representation as 'the protest paradigm'.

For example, Hackett and Zhou (1994) analysed US press coverage in the first two weeks following the start of the Gulf War and found the dominant frame to be an 'Enemy Within' frame, which positioned anti-war protesters as the violent and/or treasonous internal Other. In an analysis of prominent US newspapers' coverage of the World Trade Organization protests in Seattle in 1999, Boykoff (2006) found that nearly 63 per cent of news stories featured the violence frame with more than 50 per cent of accounts focusing on violent protesters. McLeod and Hertog (1992) similarly highlight that within the violence frame it is typical for protesters to be presented as aggressors while the police are presented as responding appropriately to restore order. Murdock (1981) shows that violence was a major theme in newspaper coverage of anti-Vietnam War demonstrations in the UK, even though very little violence actually occurred. Murdock (1981) suggests that this persistent media framing arises because a protest's violence, however limited, is what gives it newsworthiness. This, in turn, as Gamson observes, can lead to a form of 'bartering' between protest movements and the media in which 'to keep media attention, challengers are tempted to ever more extravagant and dramatic actions regardless of contribution to the challenger's goals' (1989: 465).

A number of ideological consequences arise from this media practice. For example, as Boykoff (2006: 204) points out, frames of violence are at odds with frames of peace and justice which protest movements may be seeking to highlight. McLeod (1995) suggests that reporting within violence frames typically transfers the intended targets of protest movements from governments or corporate agencies to the police and that, since challenging governments is a form of political action while challenging the police is a form of criminal action, this further serves to delegitimise protesters by depoliticising their actions and equating them with criminals. Boykoff (2006) similarly shows how protesters get equated with terrorists, either through enthymematic argument in which protesters and terrorism are mentioned in close textual proximity to one another or through a vocabulary of (mainly guerrilla) warfare.

The research discussed above has effectively delineated the patterns of representation through which protest movements are portrayed as deviant but it has not addressed the impact that this strategy may have on audiences. McLeod (1995) uses experimental methods to empirically demonstrate the effects of such portrayals on media audiences. McLeod showed two television news stories about the same protest to two groups of experimental subjects.

The two (fabricated) stories shared some common characteristics of protest stories, including a focus on violence rather than the issues at stake. However, there were a number of differences between the stories so that one was typical of media coverage in marginalising the protesters while the other was more balanced and empathic towards the protesters. One crucial manipulation was the degree of agency ascribed to the police. In the typical news story, violent scenes were presented as one-sided (*A few demonstrators also hurled rocks and other debris at Minneapolis police who were standing by*) while in the more sympathetic version the violence was presented as two-sided (*Angry marchers threw rocks as police charged them with mace*). Attitudes towards police and protesters were then measured through a series of multi-item scales in a post-stimulus questionnaire. The results of the experiment showed that subjects who saw the typical, one-sided story were significantly less critical of the police and significantly more critical of protesters compared with subjects who saw the more sympathetic version. Similar effects have been demonstrated for differences in photographic representations of protests. Arpan et al. (2006) showed different groups of subjects a news report about a protest which included a photograph of the event. They manipulated the degree of conflict depicted in the photograph and found that subjects' evaluations of protests and protesters were more negative when photos depicting higher levels of conflict were shown.

Much of the research discussed above is based in media and mass communication studies and relies on traditional methods of quantitative content analysis. While content analysis is undoubtedly a useful paradigm for identifying salient topics, themes or 'frames' in media texts, it fails to discern the precise linguistic or other semiotic resources involved in the articulation of stanced discourses and, as a result, may miss some of the more subtle means by which texts communicate values, which can only be illuminated through close textual analysis (van Dijk 1988). Content analysis is sometimes therefore criticised for being unsystematic and impressionistic (van Dijk 1988).

One approach to social research which aims to overcome the shortcomings of content analysis is critical discourse studies (Fairclough 1995a, 1995b; Fowler 1991; Richardson 2007; van Dijk 1991; Wodak et al. 1999). Critical discourse studies (CDS) is an approach to social research which focuses on social identities, norms, values, inequalities and power relations as they are reflected in, and enacted through, the micro-level, semiotic 'choices' that are routinely presented in texts. It explicitly theorises the instrumentality of textual practice (Fairclough 1989, 1992, 1995a, 1995b, 2003) and has developed a unique set of tools for analysing the various micro-level features of texts which play a part in discursively constructing and sustaining social realities (for overviews, see Flowerdew and Richardson 2017; Hart and Cap 2014; Wodak and Forchtner 2017; Wodak and Meyer 2016). CDS is not a single theory but a perspective characterised by a broad range of methods and approaches aimed at analysing the different ideological meaning-making properties of texts. Researchers in CDS are variously concerned with the lexical items, grammatical structures, semantic categories, argumentative moves, narratives, myths and metaphors, *inter alia*, that play a part in the reproduction of ideology and the legitimation of action.

Taking a discourse perspective on media representations of the 1984–5 British Miners' Strike, Montgomery (1995) contrasted reports from the *Daily Mail* and the *Telegraph* with those from the *Morning Star* (a socialist newspaper with much smaller circulation figures and more specific reader demographics). While all three papers adhered to the protest paradigm by focusing on violence on the picket line, Montgomery found 'differences in the way that the respective roles of participants were actually constructed in the syntax of different newspaper accounts' (1995: 241). In the *Daily Mail* and the *Telegraph*, when police were focused on in the subject of a clause, this tended to be as a patient in a passive voice construction (*a police dog handler was kicked on the ground*). When picketing miners occurred in the subject of a clause this was as agents in active voice constructions (*pickets bombarded the police with bricks, stones, sticks*). By contrast, in the *Morning Star*, when the police appeared in the focal subject position this was typically as agents in active clauses (*police attacked isolated groups of miners*). When miners appeared in the subject position this was either as patients in passive constructions (*several miners were hit with truncheons*) or as agents in intransitive processes involving movement or change of location and therefore no physical or material consequence (*3,000 pickets yesterday gathered outside Cortonwood Colliery*). The analyses showed that the actions of police and pickets were represented in quite different ways, involving contrasting patterns of linguistic choice. Montgomery concluded that 'particular linguistic choices (in this case those of transitivity and voice) make sense of, and give significance to, the phenomenon of picketing in strikingly different ways' (1995: 245). Montgomery went on to suggest that 'the more widely and pervasively a structure circulates, especially in privileged communicative contexts such as mass circulation daily newspapers, the more difficult it becomes to select differently – and hence to see and think differently about the depicted events' (1995: 245).

Fang (1994) analysed representations of foreign protests in the Chinese state newspaper *Renmin Ribao*. They found lexical and syntactic distinctions which depended on whether the country in which the action was taking place had a friendly or more inimical relationship with China. In countries that are more hostile towards China, actions tended to be described as 'demonstrations', 'struggles' or 'protests' whereas similar mass actions in countries more aligned with China were typically described as 'clashes' or 'riots'. This contrast in lexical choice not only serves to legitimise or delegitimise the movements in question but further serves to legitimise or delegitimise the responses of authorities so that the response of governments and police forces in countries politically closer to China is constructed as legitimate. This process went further in the syntactic structuring of sentences. For inimical countries police action was largely described in the active voice, thereby emphasising police violence, while for friendly countries any police action that was reported tended to be reported in the passive voice, thus de-emphasising their role. Fang further found that when reporting injuries or deaths of protesters, the newspaper favoured the active voice with police as agent for hostile countries (*The police killed three men*), thus explicitly assigning responsibility to the police. By contrast, in the case of friendly countries, either intransitive verbs (*12 people have died, and 61 sustained injuries in the clashes*) or agentless passive constructions (*Thirty people were killed*) were preferred. Both intransitive verbs and agentless passive constructions avoid mention of the police and suggest instead that the 'riots' themselves were the cause of deaths or injuries.

Hart (2013a, 2013b) analysed media representations of the 2009 G20 and 2010 Student Fee protests in the UK. He found that while both right-wing and left-wing newspapers stuck to the protest paradigm in focusing on violence between police and protesters, the right-wing press tended to present a one-sided version of events while the left-wing press presented a more two-sided interpretation. One of the ways this contrast manifested was in the use of regular transitive verbs (*attack, strike, hit*), which make a distinction between an agent and a patient in the interaction, versus reciprocal verb constructions (*clash with, trade punches with, exchange blows with*) in which both groups of participants are encoded as agentive. Hart further found that when the police were presented as agentive by the right-wing press their actions were described euphemistically through the semantic category of motion (*Police moved in on the climate camp*).

In a follow-up study, Hart (2016) showed experimentally that the use of transitive versus reciprocal verbs affects blame assignment and perception of aggression in discourse on political protests. Hart conducted a between-subjects design similar to McLeod (1995). Two experimental groups were presented with a media report about a recent protest in the fictional city of Southfield. The report was identical across conditions except for the use of transitive versus reciprocal verbs in describing violent interactions between police and protesters. Subjects in the transitive condition (in which protesters were the agent) were more likely to assign blame for the violence exclusively to the protesters. By contrast, subjects in the reciprocal condition were significantly more likely to assign blame equally to both police and protesters. Subjects also perceived protesters as more aggressive in the transitive condition compared with the reciprocal condition while police were perceived as more aggressive in the reciprocal condition than in the transitive condition (in which they were patients).

A further finding from CDS points to the importance of metaphor in making sense of riots, strikes and protests (Charteris-Black 2017; Fridolfsson 2004, 2008; Hart 2014a, 2014b, 2017; Hawkins 2014). Here, metaphors in discourse are understood to invoke a cognitive process of frame-projection in which a more familiar area of knowledge and experience provides a template for understanding another less-known and more complex area. Metaphor is thus an important framing device. In discourses of disorder, a number of salient metaphors are identified. For example, Fridolfsson (2004, 2008) analysed Swedish press coverage of alternative globalisation protests at an EU summit in Gothenburg in 2001 and found the metaphor DEMONSTRATION IS WAR to be a recurrent structuring feature reflected in expressions like 'the battle of Gothenburg', 'besieged city', 'guerrilla warfare' and 'regular street combat'. Marked references to 'peaceful demonstrations', Fridolfsson suggests, served to imply and enhance the antagonistic, war-like nature of non-peaceful demonstrations. Hart (2014a) similarly found the DEMONSTRATION IS WAR metaphor in media reports of the G20 protests in the UK where 'a band of demonstrators' were described as 'storming' a Royal Bank of Scotland branch and interactions between police and protesters were described as 'running battles' or 'skirmishes'. This metaphor accentuates the violent characteristics of protest, dramatises the narrative presented and has consequences in constructing a particular normative response. As Fridolfsson points out, 'the use of war metaphors establishes the plausibility for military intervention when dealing with political protest. Unruly natural phenomena are also something that reasonably only can be controlled by forceful intervention' (2008: 138). As an example of naturalising metaphor, Hart (2014b) identified the metaphor RIOT IS FIRE to be a salient feature in media coverage of the 2011 London Riots. Within this metaphor, the death of Mark Duggan is described as the 'spark' that 'ignited' the riots, which 'raged' over days and 'spread' to other cities. Among the potential ideological or rhetorical effects of this metaphor is that, since the conventional way of controlling fire is with water, it suggests the plausibility of using water cannon as a means of controlling similar events in the future. Hart (2017) tested this hypothesis in an experimental setting by giving subjects a news article reporting unrest in a fictitious city which the local police responded to using water cannon. The article was mocked up to look and feel like a genuine online news article. Subjects were then asked to rate the appropriateness of the police response on a perceived legitimacy scale. Subjects were given the article with one crucial manipulation: either making use of the RIOT IS FIRE metaphor or describing the event in equivalent literal terms. A further manipulation related to photographs presented in the text. Articles were either presented with images involving fire, images not involving fire or with no images at all. The results showed that images of fire in photographs significantly enhanced support for the use of water cannon regardless of the metaphor manipulation. The RIOT IS FIRE metaphor was shown to have a similar effect in facilitating support for the use of water cannon but only in the absence of incongruent photographs (i.e. those not involving fire). It seems that non-fire images in a multimodal news text inhibit the potential effects of fire metaphors in language. The study points to the role of metaphor in creating mental imagery which functions in a similar way to equivalent concrete images in shaping attitudes towards social actors and actions. It thus justifies attention to metaphor in CDS. Alongside studies such as Arpan et al. (2006), it also evidences the fundamental part played by images in the news in discursively constructing public opinion on matters of policing and public order.

Kelsey (2015) also analysed press coverage of the 2011 England riots. He analysed discursive constructions of social class, morality, the 'mob', and perceptions of a 'sick society' that reflected ideological tensions during and after the riots. He showed how the initial depoliticised actions of rioters were redefined as a politicised problem, symbolic of a 'sick society' that could be 'cured' by Conservative social policy. By exploring various discursive nuances, Kelsey proposed the concept of *paradoxical persuasion* to explain how press coverage appeared to print contradictory stories whilst maintaining a broader, consistent, ideological position. Kelsey concluded that 'ideological consistencies operating beyond the foreground and immediacy of individual texts can override the appearance of discursive contradiction across longitudinal contexts' (2015: 243).

CDS has traditionally focused on examining textual choices made in the linguistic modality where it is shown that linguistic representation is not objective or inevitable but that, rather, linguistic representation is always representation from a particular ideological point of view (Fowler 1991: 66). More recently, however, there has been a multimodal turn within CDS with some existing frameworks being extended to account for meaning-making processes common to linguistic and visual communication as well as new frameworks emerging to handle the unique affordances of visual and multimodal platforms

(Lassen et al. 2006; Machin 2007, 2013; Machin and Mayr 2012; Stocchetti and Kukkonen 2011). Abousnnouga and Machin state:

> As we can study lexical and grammatical choices in language to reveal discourses so we can study choices of visual semiotic resources. This approach allows us to describe what kind of resources are available to visual designers and show how these can be used to persuade and legitimise. (Abousnnouga and Machin 2011: 327)

Based on Kress and van Leeuwen's (2006) 'grammar of visual design', Hart (2014b) analysed transitivity patterns in news photographs of political protests. He observed that, as in language, participants can be shown as agents or patients in different types of process. Hart (2014b: 84) suggested that if protesters are typically presented as agents in transitive processes while police are depicted as patients (and agents only in intransitive processes), then this asymmetry would contribute visually to constructing a discourse of deviancy in which protesters are seen as perpetrators of violence while the police are legitimised as peaceful or restrained. Metaphor and analogy too may be realised cross-modally. For example, Fridolfsson notes of media coverage of protests in Gothenburg that news photographs were 'charged with visual references to war aesthetics like people hunching down in the streets or frightened faces taking protection in a smoky environment' (2008: 137). Hart (2014b: 85–96) further considered the ideological functions of contrasting points of view in news photographs of political protests. Differences on the horizontal plane, for example, are analysed as inviting the viewer to 'take different sides' as they are positioned in line with one group of participants while in opposition to the other or else are encouraged to adopt a more neutral stance when they are positioned at right angles with both sets of participants in the scene.

CDS has also taken a more quantitative turn in recent times (Baker and McEnery 2015; Baker et al. 2008; Gabrielatos and Baker 2008; Mautner 2005). Traditionally, CDS is qualitative in nature where, as van Dijk observes:

> as long as computer programs cannot take over such precise microanalyses, [CDS] is limited to small amounts of data. Large-scale investigations of hundreds or thousands of media texts must still be complemented with a more superficial and more limited type of content analysis. (Van Dijk 1988: x)

However, the development of corpus linguistics has allowed precisely computer-aided identification and analysis of the kind of micro-level features of interest in CDS as they occur across large quantities of texts – although, as yet, this approach is limited to the linguistic modality with visual features currently beyond the reach of automated processes (Carter and Adolphs 2008). Corpus linguistics enables researchers to show that patterns of representation identified in qualitative analysis occur frequently enough across large numbers of texts to be significant. However, corpus linguistics also enables researchers to detect patterns of representation or evaluation which are not immediately discernible from analyses of single or smaller numbers of texts. By examining the 'collocates' of words denoting different social groups, for example, one can see the qualities and values that are regularly attributed to those groups and with which, as a consequence, they become associated. Similarly, one can see the semantic and valence associations that a word may subtly carry in a particular context based on its behaviour in a standard reference corpus. Corpus linguistics, further, facilitates systematic and reliable contrastive analysis as features can be compared for their frequency and use across a variety of context divisions. Wong (2017) used corpus methods to analyse representations of a recent political protest in Hong Kong, Occupy Central, in English-language newspaper articles from *China Daily* and the *South China Morning Post* (*SCMP*). Analysis of the ten most frequent collocates of the word *police* showed that in *China Daily* the police were constructed as calm and professional while in *SCMP* they were associated with excessive use of force. For example, collocates in *SCMP* included *fire*, *pepper*, *tear* and *gas*. These words did not show up as frequent collocates in *China Daily* where instead collocates included *used*, *restraint* and *support*.

Multimodal and quantitative approaches to CDS are in part motivated by the advent of digital media which, arguably, has created a more multimodal and pervasive media environment (KhosraviNik and Unger 2016). Certainly, digital media has brought about new media ecologies, the dynamics of which scholars in CDS are only now beginning to explore (e.g. KhosraviNik 2014, 2017; KhosraviNik and Unger 2016).[3] Digital media, in the form of websites, blogs, social media platforms like Twitter and Facebook, as well as 'below-the-line' comment spaces on the websites of major newspapers, has altered the flow of texts and changed the binary status of, and relationship between, text producers and text consumers (KhosraviNik and Unger 2016). Digital media gives a public voice to a much wider array of people. Consequently, it is sometimes seen as providing a democratic space in which citizens can participate in a deliberative political process (Castells 2015; Gerbaudo 2012; Harlow and Harp 2013). From this perspective, digital media is characterised as an emerging site of discursive struggle (KhosraviNik 2014) where hegemonic discourses can be challenged and resisted (Fozdar and Pedersen 2013; Kelsey and Bennett 2014; Macgilchrist and Böhmig 2012). As Fozdar and Pedersen state, digital media can provide 'a counter to media convergence' which allows 'alternative positions to be voiced and heard, and hence real dialogue to occur' (2013: 3). Digital media, for example, has allowed 'alternative' news sources and outlets to flourish, no longer having to rely on hand-to-hand distribution (Castells 2015; Hands 2011). As Jansson and Lindell put it: 'What we are witnessing is thus more than a technological and representational transition; it is a multi-layered spatial transition that can be described as a shift from mass media textures to trans-media textures' (2015: 79).

Given these cultural and technological shifts, researchers of riots, strikes and protests in the media have noted that contemporary news media exhibit a more complex and nuanced relationship with the politics of protest than suggested by the protest paradigm (Cottle 2008: 859). The negative bias of the media should therefore be treated as a variable that depends on factors including the type of protest or issue at stake and, crucially, the type of media (Boyle et al. 2012; Lee 2014; Weaver and Scacco 2013). Digital media not only creates a space for discursive expressions of dissent but through the connectivity it affords, digital media enables social movements to be more readily formed and maintained and their message to be more widely disseminated (Hands 2011; Tufekci 2017). For example, digital media, especially social media, played an important role in the Occupy movement and the Arab Spring (Castells 2015; Gerbaudo 2012). Finally, digital media is not only used to organise mass street events, it also provides for new online forms of activism such as Facebook campaigns.

Although digital media is often celebrated as a venue for political engagement, some scholars are less optimistic about the extent to which it facilitates a more participatory form of politics. For example, Morozov (2011) argues that the internet has not provided the freedoms hoped for and authoritarian regimes have exploited digital communication networks to extend their power and control over citizens. Fuchs (2015) takes a Marxist perspective in criticising the political economies that have been exacerbated by social media landscapes. Other researchers have critiqued online communication from sociological and anthropological perspectives to note a preoccupation with self-presentation (manifested in linguistic markers of stance). Myers suggests of blogging that 'the emphasis on individual voice . . . does not have the focus on a shared social project that would be needed for deliberative discussion. It is not the same as participatory citizenship' (2010: 264). Other researchers have similarly remarked on the lack of deliberation in digitally mediated contexts. Richardson and Stanyer found commenting on online newspaper sites to be 'the preserve of the blindly opinionated, who used the opportunity to voice their own hobby horse issues and gave little indication that they were open to the possibility of having their opinion changed by the standpoint and reasoning of others' (2011: 1000). Digital media may also stifle more vociferous forms of protest as people are content to express their dissatisfaction by posting something online. There are further concerns that digital platforms may actually provide a medium through which hegemonic discourses are proliferated as they are dominated by a minority of users who recapitulate the same topics and agendas as traditional media (Poell and Borra 2012; Vicari 2013). Poell and Borra (2012) analysed a corpus of tweets, photos and videos that constituted user-driven social media accounts of protests against the 2010 G20 summit in Toronto, Canada. They found the reporting to have a significant event-oriented focus that mirrored mainstream media practices for reporting protests.

Research on digital media, then, offers mixed views as to its utility in fostering more participatory forms of democracy and facilitating political change. Nevertheless, it is a fundamental part of the new media ecology which cannot be ignored. To fully understand the dynamics of media representation in relation to riots, strikes and protests all forms of media, including digital media, must be considered. The analytical methods of CDS, however, as well as its largely top-down conception of power, are only recently becoming attuned to the new digital environment. There is yet to be any consolidated framework or agreed upon disciplinary norms for analysing digitally mediated discourse from a critical perspective. Several chapters in this volume analyse discourse produced in digital media contexts, most notably chapters by Carolina Pérez-Arredondo and Andrea Mayr who analyse representations of protest movements in online alternative media and on Facebook respectively. Other chapters consider news produced by mainstream national newspapers as part of their online content. These chapters, thus, contribute to development in this area. However, it is worth noting that digital media is a relatively recent addition to the media landscape. In a volume that covers a time span starting with the 1812 Baltimore riots, the majority of chapters in this volume remain focused on traditional forms of media.

What this Introduction has aimed to do is highlight the space for studying media representations of riots, strikes and protests from a discursive perspective, paying particular attention to the micro-level semiotic features of texts and their context-bound social functions. All of the chapters in this volume take a discursive approach of one form or another and all converge in understanding media discourses of disorder as sites of ideological struggle and reproduction. However, the chapters adopt different methods and analytical frameworks in targeting different features, modalities and genres of discourse. The volume also spans time and place to consider media discourses of disorder in different temporal and geo-political contexts.

The book is divided into two parts. Part I addresses representations in language. In the first chapter, Juhani Rudanko analyses narratives of the 1812 Baltimore riots. In analysing alternative narratives in two different newspapers, the chapter addresses 'spin' in early American print news practices. In Chapter 2, Darren Kelsey analyses mythology, metaphor and ideology in moral storytelling during the 2011 England riots. Kelsey shows how the public were represented as victims and heroes through the myth of the Blitz before analysing representations of rioters in discourses that used a 'sick society' metaphor. In Chapter 3, Carolina Pérez-Arredondo analyses representations of the Chilean student movement. She explores the different strategies used to construct and attribute motivation to the Chilean student movement demonstrators in the alternative press from 2011 to 2013. In Chapter 4, Gerrit Kotzur analyses perspectivisation in German newspaper reporting of the Stuttgart 21 protests. Kotzur argues that perspectivisation as a discursive strategy indexes a story's news values – making it theoretically distinguished both from perspective as a purely cognitive phenomenon and from explicit evaluation in text. In Chapter 5, Boitshwarelo Rantsudu discusses the various ways that reported speech is included within news reports covering a public sector workers' strike in two Botswana newspapers. Rantsudu argues that while the inclusion of attributed content in the news is often associated with a neutral way of reporting, the framing of the quoted content is indicative of strategic stance-taking under the guise of objectivity. In Chapter 6, Matt Davies and Rotsukhon Nophakhun show how trade union endorsed strike action is systematically demonised in news reports in the UK press, despite public opinion not reflecting this level of antagonism towards industrial action. They argue that one consistent strategy used to (mis)represent strikers is to relate this form of protest to threats of intimidation and violence by using militarised discourse.

Part II addresses representations which extend beyond the linguistic modality to include imagery in the form of photographs, videos and political cartoons. In Chapter 7, Christopher Hart analyses news photographs and cartoons to show how metaphorical war framings featured in multimodal media representations of the 1984–5 British Miners' Strike. From a critical semiotic standpoint, Hart argues that the conceptualisations invoked by these framing efforts served to 'otherise' the miners, whilst simultaneously legitimating the actions of the government and the police during the strike. In Chapter 8, Rania Elnakkouzi analyses Arab Spring political cartoons as a type of visual or multimodal argumentation advanced by cartoonists to defend and justify their standpoints. Elnakkouzi shows how Arab cartoonists strategically manoeuvre by appealing to universal principles and values such as freedom of speech, social justice and liberty in their endeavour to address international audiences and mobilise support. In Chapter 9, Andrea Mayr analyses a Brazilian Facebook campaign that was launched by young people in protest against an incidence of police violence shortly before the World Cup in 2014. The ethnographic and multimodal analysis suggests that social media can be an important platform for denouncing human rights abuses, but it also points to its limited potential to mobilise change in a society with rampant social and racial inequality. Finally, in Chapter 10, Serjoscha Ostermeyer and David Sittler extend the notion of multimodality further to consider the body as a semiotic resource. Ostermeyer and Sittler analyse stills from the live television broadcast of an attack during the 1992 Los Angeles riots. They argue that rioting always means to act bodily and at the same time to perform symbolically in public. They show how rioters draw on a repertoire of body 'moves' sourced from mediatised popular culture activities like American football and breakdance. They thus show how body movement can be integrated into frameworks for multimodal CDS.

It is hoped that this book will be of interest to scholars in critical discourse studies but also those working in media and social movement studies and those concerned more broadly with semiotics and social practice.

Notes

1. Riots, strikes and protests, then, are not objective or discrete categories of action. Although strikes specifically involve the withdrawal of labour, this is typically in protest against wages or working conditions, and events on the picket line are often characterised as 'riotous' when they turn violent. Rather, then, which lexical item is applied constitutes a subjective assessment of the situation which serves to evoke different moral evaluations or emotional reactions and assign lesser or greater levels of legitimacy to the events in question (Fang 1994).
2. Frames are the 'interpretive packages' through which a news story is presented and made sense of (Entman 1993; Gamson and Modigliani 1989). Frames select and make salient certain aspects of a perceived reality 'in such a way as to promote a particular problem definition, causal interpretation, moral evaluation, and/or treatment recommendation for the item described' (Entman 1993: 52).
3. CDS has previously been criticised for a 'reluctance to embrace the web of all media' (Mautner 2005: 809).

References

Abousnnouga, G. and D. Machin (2011), 'Visual discourses of the role of women in war commemoration: A multimodal analysis of British war monuments', *Journal of Language and Politics*, 10 (3), pp. 322–46.

Arpan, L. M., K. Baker, Y. Lee, T. Jung, L. Lorusso and J. Smith (2006), 'News coverage of social protests and the effects of photographs and prior attitudes', *Mass Communication and Society*, 9 (1), pp. 1–20.

Baker, P., C. Gabrielatos, M. KhosraviNik, M. Krzyzanowski, T. McEnery and

R. Wodak (2008), 'A useful methodological synergy? Combining critical discourse analysis and corpus linguistics to examine discourses of refugees and asylum seekers in the UK press', *Discourse & Society*, 19 (3), pp. 273–305.

Baker, P. and T. McEnery (eds) (2015), *Corpora and Discourse: Integrating Discourse and Corpora*, Basingstoke: Palgrave Macmillan.

Boykoff, J. (2006), 'Framing dissent: Mass-media coverage of the global justice movement', *New Political Science*, 28 (2), pp. 201–28.

Boyle, M. P., D. M. McLeod and C. L. Armstrong (2012), 'Adherence to the protest paradigm: The influence of protest goals and tactics on news coverage in U.S. and international newspapers', *International Journal of Press/Politics*, 17 (2), pp. 127–44.

Carter, R. and S. Adolphs (2008), 'Linking the verbal and visual: New directions for corpus linguistics', *Language and Computers*, 64 (1), pp. 275–91.

Castells, M. (2015), *Networks of Outrage and Hope: Social Movements in the Internet Age*, Cambridge: Polity Press.

Chan, J. M. and C. C. Lee (1984), 'Journalistic paradigms on civil protests: A case study of Hong Kong', in A. Arno and W. Dissanayake (eds), *The News Media in National and International Conflict*, Boulder, CO: Westview Press, pp. 183–202.

Charteris-Black, J. (2017), *Fire Metaphors: Discourses of Awe and Authority*, London: Bloomsbury.

Cottle, S. (2008), 'Reporting demonstrations: The changing media politics of dissent', *Media, Culture & Society*, 30 (6), pp. 853–72.

Di Cicco, D. T. (2010), 'The public nuisance paradigm: Changes in mass media coverage of political protest since the 1960s', *Journalism and Mass Communication Quarterly*, 87 (1), pp. 135–53.

Entman, R. M. (1993), 'Framing: Towards clarification of a fractured paradigm', *Journal of Communication*, 43, pp. 51–8.

Fairclough, N. (1989), *Language and Power*, London: Longman.

Fairclough, N. (1992), *Discourse and Social Change*, Cambridge: Polity Press.

Fairclough, N. (1995a), *Critical Discourse Analysis: The Critical Study of Language*, London: Longman.

Fairclough, N. (1995b), *Media Discourse*, London: Edward Arnold.

Fairclough, N. (2003), *Analysing Discourse: Textual Analysis for Social Research*, London: Routledge.

Fang, Y.-J. (1994), '"Riots" and demonstrations in the Chinese press: A case study of language and ideology', *Discourse & Society*, 5 (4), pp. 463–81.

Flowerdew, J. and J. E. Richardson (eds) (2017), *The Routledge Handbook of Critical Discourse Studies*, London: Routledge.

Fowler, R. (1991), *Language in the News: Discourse and Ideology in the Press*, London: Routledge.

Fozdar, F. and A. Pedersen (2013), 'Diablogging about asylum seekers: Building a counterhegemonic discourse', *Discourse & Communication*, 7 (4), pp. 1–18.

Fridolfsson, C. (2004), 'Politics, protest and the threatening outside: A discourse analysis of events at an EU summit', *Distinktion: Journal of Social Theory*, 5 (1), pp. 79–92.

Fridolfsson, C. (2008), 'Political protest and metaphor', in T. Carve and J. Pikalo (eds), *Political Language and Metaphor: Interpreting and Changing the World*, London: Routledge, pp. 132–48.

Fuchs, C. (2015), *Social Media: A Critical Introduction*, London: Sage.

Gabrielatos, C. and P. Baker (2008), 'Fleeing, sneaking, flooding: A corpus analysis of discursive constructions of refugees and asylum seekers in the UK press 1996–2005', *Journal of English Linguistics*, 36 (1), pp. 5–38.

Gamson, W. A. (1989), 'Reflections on the strategy of social protest', *Sociological Forum*, 4, pp. 455–67.

Gamson, W. A. and A. Modigliani (1989), 'Media discourse and public opinion on nuclear power: A constructionist approach', *American Journal of Sociology*, 95, pp. 1–37

Gamson, W. A. and G. Wolfsfeld (1993), 'Movements and media as interacting systems', *Annals of the American Academy of Political and Social Science*, 528, pp. 114–25.

Gerbaudo, P. (2012), *The Tweets and the Streets: Social Media and Contemporary Activism*, London: Pluto.

Gitlin, T. (1980), *The Whole World Is Watching*, Berkeley, CA: University of California Press.

Glasgow Media Group (1976), *Bad News*, London: Routledge & Kegan Paul.

Glasgow Media Group (1980), *More Bad News*, London: Routledge & Kegan Paul.

Glasgow Media Group (1982), *Really Bad News*, London: Writers and Readers Publishing Cooperative.

Hackett, R and Y. Zhou (1994), 'Challenging a master narrative: Peace protest and opinion/editorial discourse in the US press during the Gulf War', *Discourse & Society*, 5 (4), pp. 509–41.

Hall, S. (1973), 'A world at one with itself', in S. Cohen and J. Young (eds), *The Manufacture of News: Deviance, Social Problems and the Mass Media*, London: Constable, pp. 147–56.

Hands, J. (2011), *@ Is for Activism*, London: Pluto.

Harlow, S. and D. Harp (2013), 'Collective action on the web', *Information, Communication & Society*, 15 (2), pp. 196–216.

Hart, C. (2013a), 'Event-construal in press reports of violence in political protests: A cognitive linguistic approach to CDA', *Journal of Language and Politics*, 12 (3), pp. 400–23.

Hart, C. (2013b), 'Constructing contexts through grammar: Cognitive models and conceptualisation in British newspaper reports of political protests', in J. Flowerdew (ed.), *Discourse and Contexts*, London: Continuum, pp. 159–84.

Hart, C. (2014a), 'Construal operations in online press reports of political protests', in C. Hart and P. Cap (eds), *Contemporary Critical Discourse Studies*, London: Bloomsbury, pp. 167–88.

Hart, C. (2014b), *Discourse, Grammar and Ideology: Functional and Cognitive Perspectives*, London: Bloomsbury.

Hart, C. (2016), 'Event-frames affect blame assignment and perception of aggression: An experimental case study in CDA', *Applied Linguistics*, amw017, <https://doi.org/10.1093/applin/amw017> (last accessed 1 May 2018).

Hart, C. (2017), '"Riots engulfed the city": An experimental study investigating the legitimating effects of fire metaphors in discourses of disorder', *Discourse & Society*, 29 (3), pp. 279–98.

Hart, C. and P. Cap (eds) (2014), *Contemporary Critical Discourse Studies*, London: Bloomsbury.

Hawkins, S. (2014), 'Teargas, flags and Harlem shake: Images of and for revolution in Tunisia and the dialectics of the local in the global', in P. Werbner, M. Webb and K. Spellman-Poots (eds), *Global Protest: The Arab Spring and Beyond*, Edinburgh: Edinburgh University Press, pp. 31–52.

Jansson, A. and J. Lindell (2015), 'News media consumption in the transmedia age: Amalgamations, orientations and geo-social structuration', *Journalism Studies*, 16 (1), pp. 79–96.

Kelsey, D. (2015), 'Defining the sick society: Discourses of class and morality in British right-wing newspapers during the 2011 England riots', *Capital & Class*, 39 (2), pp. 243–64.

Kelsey, D. and L. Bennett (2014), 'Discipline and resistance on social media: Discourse, power and context in the Paul Chambers "Twitter Joke Trial"', *Discourse, Context and Media*, 3, pp. 37–45.

KhosraviNik, M. (2014), 'Critical discourse analysis, power and new media discourse', in M. Kopytowska and Y. Kalyango (eds), *Why Discourse Matters: Negotiating Identity in the Mediatized World*, New York: Peter Lang, pp. 287–306.

KhosraviNik, M. (2017), 'Social media critical discourse studies (SM-CDS)', in J. Flowerdew and J. E. Flowerdew (eds), *The Routledge Handbook of Critical Discourse Studies*, London: Routledge, pp. 582–96.

KhosraviNik, M. and J. Unger (2016), 'Critical discourse studies and social media: Power, resistance and critique in changing media ecologies', in R. Wodak and M. Meyer (eds), *Methods of Critical Discourse Studies*, London: Sage, pp. 206–33.

Kress, G. and T. van Leeuwen (2006), *Reading Images: The Grammar of Visual Design*, London: Routledge.

Lassen, I., J. Strunck and T. Vestergaard (eds) (2006), *Mediating Ideology in Text and Image: Ten Critical Studies*, Amsterdam: John Benjamins.

Lee, F. L. F. (2014), 'Triggering the protest paradigm: Examining factors affecting news coverage of protests', *International Journal of Communication*, 8, pp. 2725–46.

Leung, L. (2009), 'Mediated violence as "global news": Co-opted "performance" in the framing of the WTO', *Media, Culture & Society*, 31 (2), pp. 251–70.

Macgilchrist, F. and I. Böhmig (2012), 'Blogs, genes and immigration: Online media and minimal politics', *Media Culture & Society*, 34 (1), pp. 83–100.

Machin, D. (2007), *An Introduction to Multimodal Analysis*, London: Bloomsbury.

Machin, D. (2013), 'What is multimodal critical discourse studies?', *Critical Discourse Studies*, 10 (4), pp. 347–55.

Machin, D. and A. Mayr (2012), *Critical Discourse Analysis: A Multimodal Approach*, London: Sage.

McLeod, D. M. (1995), 'Communicating deviance: The effects of television news coverage of social protest', *Journal of Broadcasting & Electronic Media*, 39 (1), pp. 4–19.

McLeod, D. M. and J. K. Hertog (1992), 'The manufacture of public opinion by reporters: Informal cues for public perceptions of protest groups', *Discourse & Society*, 3, pp. 259–75.

Mautner, G. (2005), 'Time to get wired: Using web-based corpora in critical discourse analysis', *Discourse & Society*, 16 (6), pp. 809–28.

Montgomery, M. (1995), *An Introduction to Language and Society*, 2nd edn, London: Routledge.

Morozov, E. (2011), *The Net Delusion: How Not to Liberate the World*, London: Penguin.

Murdock, G. (1973), 'Political deviance: The press presentation of a militant mass demonstration', in S. Cohen and J. Young (eds), *The Manufacture of News: Deviance, Social Problems and the Mass Media*, London: Constable, pp. 206–25.

Murdock, G. (1981), 'Political deviance: The press representation of a militant mass demonstration', in S. Cohen and J. Young (eds), *The Manufacture of News: Deviance, Social Problems and the Mass Media*, Beverly Hills, CA: Sage, pp. 206–25.

Myers, G. (2010), 'Stance-taking and public discussion in blogs', *Critical Discourse Studies*, 7 (4), pp. 263–75.

Poell, T. and E. Borra (2012), 'Twitter, YouTube, and Flickr as platforms of alternative journalism: The social media account of the 2010 Toronto G20 protests', *Journalism*, 13 (6), pp. 695–713.

Richardson, J. E. (2007), *Analysing Newspapers: An Approach from Critical Discourse Analysis*, Basingstoke: Palgrave Macmillan.

Richardson, J. E. and J. Stanyer (2011), 'Reader opinion in the digital age: Tabloid and broadsheet newspaper websites and the exercise of political voice', *Journalism*, 12 (8), pp. 983–1003.

Shoemaker, P. J. (1984), 'Media treatment of deviant political groups', *Journalism & Mass Communication Quarterly*, 61, pp. 66–75.

Small, M. (1995), *Covering Dissent*, New Brunswick, NJ: Rutgers University Press.

Stocchetti, M. and K. Kukkonen (eds) (2011), *Images in Use: Towards the Critical Analysis of Visual Communication*, Amsterdam: John Benjamins.

Tufekci, Z. (2017), *Twitter and Tear Gas: The Power and Fragility of Networked Protest*, London: Yale University Press.

van Dijk, T. A. (1988), *News Analysis: Case Studies of International and National News in the Press*, Hillsdale, NJ: Lawrence Erlbaum.

van Dijk, T. A. (1991), *Racism and the Press*, London: Routledge.

Vicari, S. (2013), 'Public reasoning around social contention: A case study of Twitter use in the Italian mobilization for global change', *Current Sociology*, 61 (4), pp. 474–90.

Weaver, D. A. and J. M. Scacco (2013), 'Revisiting the protest paradigm: The Tea Party as filtered through prime-time cable news', *International Journal of Press/Politics*, 18 (1), pp. 61–84.

Wodak, R., R. De Cilla, M. Reisigl and K. Liebhart (1999), *The Discursive Construction of National Identity*, 2nd edn, Edinburgh: Edinburgh University Press.

Wodak, R. and B. Forchtner (eds) (2017), *The Routledge Handbook of Critical Discourse Studies*, London: Routledge.

Wodak, R. and M. Meyer (eds) (2016), *Methods of Critical Discourse Studies*, 3rd edn, London: Sage.

Wong, M. L.-Y. (2017), 'Analysing aggression of social actors in political protests: Combining corpus and cognitive approaches to discourse analysis', *Journal of Aggression, Conflict and Peace Research*, 9 (3), pp. 178–94.

Xu, K. (2013), 'Framing Occupy Wall Street: A content analysis of *The New York Times* and *USA Today*', *International Journal of Communication*, 7, pp. 2412–32.

PART I
LANGUAGE

1

Representations of the Baltimore Riots of July 1812: Political Spin in the Early American Republic

Juhani Rudanko

Introduction and Historical Background

After the ratification of the American Constitution the political divide in the early American Republic was between Federalists, especially strong in New England, and Republicans, with Virginia as their power base. With respect to foreign policy, Federalists tended to place an emphasis on good relations with Great Britain, while Republicans tended to have an orientation towards France. Thomas Jefferson and James Madison were leading Republicans, while leading Federalists included John Adams and Alexander Hamilton.

During Jefferson's tenure as president from 1801 to 1809 relations with Great Britain tended to be strained, for instance because of the impressment of American citizens to serve in the British navy during Napoleonic wars. An uneasy peace continued to prevail in the early years of the Madison administration, but a new factor was introduced with the arrival of what have been termed 'War Hawks' in the Twelfth Congress in 1811, mostly from Southern and Western States. Here is a description of the atmosphere in the United States:

> The picture of Royal Marines abducting American sailors under the color of impressment infuriated the West and South as well as the rest of the country. The rhetoric of the War Hawks insisting that American honor was at stake on the high seas should not be dismissed as empty bluster, for the people of that time regarded the reputations of persons and communities as important signs of their worth and weight. (Heidler and Heidler 2002: 4–5)

President Madison, the Father of the American Constitution and the Bill of Rights, was no firebrand and certainly not eager for war, but on 1 June 1812 he sent a war message to Congress, and Congress passed a declaration of war against Great Britain on 18 June 1812. Both Houses of Congress approved the declaration, but not unanimously. The margins were 79 to 49 in the House of Representatives and 19 to 13 in the Senate (Hickey 2012: 43). Support for the measure came mostly from Republicans, while Federalists tended to oppose the measure.

As regards the State of Maryland, the Southern part of the state tended to be Federalist, but the city of Baltimore was strongly Republican. Baltimore was the third largest city in the United States, with a population that approached 50,000 by 1814. Here is a description of the city:

> The explosive growth of Baltimore resulted from the unbounded economic opportunity that characterized the era. Profits in commerce were being matched by those in stock and land speculation. Everything about the city was new and somewhat raw. Its people were mostly immigrants from Europe, from other parts of Maryland, or from other states. Thousands had been born in foreign countries; Germans, Scotch-Irish, Scots, and French crowded the city's streets. Even in this early period ethnic groups struggled to maintain their identities by forming separate churches, private societies, and militia companies. (Cassell 1975: 241)

Anti-British feeling in Baltimore ran strong, and '[t]he many French, Irish, and Germans in the population hated Great Britain, and so too did most of the native-born Americans' (Hickey 1989: 56). However, in Baltimore there were also some spirited Federalists, including Alexander Contee Hanson, described as the 'most radical of the young Federalists' in the city (Cassell 1975: 243). He was an editor, along with Jacob Wagner, of the *Federal Republican*, a stridently Federalist newspaper in Baltimore. On 20 June 1812 the newspaper published a strong attack on the declaration of war. Here is an extract:

(1)   . . . it [the war] is unnecessary, inexpedient, and entered into from partial, personal, and as we believe, motives bearing upon their front marks of undisguised foreign influence, which cannot be mistaken. (*Federal Republican*, 29 June 1812)

The appearance of the 20 June 1812 issue of the newspaper provoked the first episode in the Baltimore riots: a mob of citizens of Baltimore attacked the office of the *Federal Republican* in Baltimore, but there were no deaths or injuries to people. Hanson and others working for the newspaper then moved out of town, to the District of Columbia nearby, continuing to publish their newspaper from there.

About a month later, on 20 July 1812, Wagner rented a house in Charles Street in Baltimore, and in the course of the following days Hanson and his friends established themselves in the house. On the morning of 27 July 1812 a new issue of the *Federal Republican* appeared in Baltimore (Hickey 2012: 56). The issue had been previously printed in the District of Columbia, but it carried the address of the house in Charles Street on its mast head (Hickey 2012: 56), creating the impression that it was printed in Baltimore. The issue contained criticism of the declaration of war on Great Britain, of Republicans in Congress, and the Mayor of Baltimore, especially for failing to protect the newspaper the previous month. This led to the second episode of the Baltimore riots.

The second episode was far more serious than the first. Hanson and his friends had collected firearms into the house they had rented, and a group of some thirty supporters made the house into an armed camp. A group of people gathered round the house in the evening of 27 July, started throwing stones and breaking windows, then broke down the front door. Those inside fired into those coming in, with at least three of the intruders being severely wounded. Those who were coming in retreated outside the house, but did not leave the area. Those inside continued to fire into the crowd, and one person, Dr Thaddeus Gale, died from the shots. Some militia units arrived outside the house, and the crowd outside procured a cannon but were unable to fire it. By the morning of the following day, 28 July 1812, city officials reached an arrangement between those inside and the crowd, whereby those inside were taken into the city jail for their own protection. There were some militia guarding the jail during the day on 28 July but they were dismissed by the evening, and in the evening a crowd gathered around the jail. The Mayor tried to disperse them but was brushed aside, and the crowd broke into the jail. Some of the Federalists were able to escape in the confusion but several were beaten severely, with one of them, General Lingan, dying from his wounds. Dr Richard Hall, a physician and a Republican, then persuaded the crowd to leave, and turned the cell into a makeshift hospital the morning of 29 July. This effectively marked the end of the second episode of the Baltimore riots.[1]

The purpose of this chapter is to examine the way in which the events of the second episode were reported and commented on in a Federalist and a Republican newspaper. The Federalist newspaper selected is the *Federal Republican*. It was published in Baltimore up until 20 June 1812, and from then onwards in the District of Columbia nearby. This newspaper was chosen because it was a leading Federalist newspaper at the time (Humphrey 1996: 93) and because it was at the centre of the unrest and therefore paid considerable attention to the unrest. The Republican side is represented by the *National Intelligencer*. This newspaper was selected because it was a prominent newspaper also published in the District of Columbia and because it had close ties to the Republican party (see Pasley 2001: 203, 208). The overall objective of this study is to find out how the events were constructed and represented in the two newspapers in the days immediately following the second episode. The method is to consider and to compare the descriptions and motives of the actors involved and the descriptions of what the actors did at key stages of the events as they unfolded. A central issue is whether the notion of 'spin' may be applicable to the newspaper accounts published in the immediate aftermath of the events. The term 'spin' is a modern one,[2] and it is sometimes understood to refer to the 'way in which a government, any government, seeks to present its actions in the most favorable light' (Moore 2006: 1). However, a broader interpretation of the concept is more fruitful for the present study:

> Spin, or selective interpretation, is the intentional slanting of ambiguous political events and situations to promote an interpretation favorable to one's own side. Although short of overt lying or propaganda, the term has a negative connotation akin to deceiving, twisting, or biasing in a preferred direction. (Schaefer and Birkland 2007: 272)[3]

The broader interpretation is helpful in the present study because the American government of the day did not stage the riots, and if there was spin in presenting the incidents, it was undertaken by the newspapers in accordance with their political agendas, not directly by the government as such. Each of the two newspapers had a political agenda, and the unrest in Baltimore in July 1812 was a highly charged incident, with potential political implications for both Republicans and Federalists at the time. It is thus of interest to examine whether signs of slanting in the presentation of the unrest in Baltimore can be found at that early point in the history of the American press, and if so, in what ways they might manifest themselves.

Comparing Two Narratives of the Unrest in Baltimore

This study focuses on narratives of what happened on 27 and 28 July 1812. On the Federalist side, the main source is the account of the unrest in the issue of 3 August 1812 of the *Federal Republican*, and as regards the Republican side, corresponding account in the issue of 1 August 1812 of the *National Intelligencer* is the main focus of attention. Neither story is on the front page, but the account in the *Federal Republican* is clearly longer, covering parts of pages 2 and 3 of the paper, while the account in the *National Intelligencer* covers part of page 2. The titles of the stories also show a significant difference. In the *Federal Republican* the headline of the story is 'The Massacre at Baltimore', and in the *National Intelligencer* the heading of the story is 'Dreadful Commotion'. The former headline, featuring the word 'massacre', clearly conveys the events in question in a more serious, and even sinister, light than the latter headline, which has the bland and vague word 'commotion' in it. The difference is also an indication of how the reporting of an incident was not necessarily kept separate from commentary on the incident in newspapers in the early American Republic.

To give some structure to the rest of this investigation, a number of separate issues are identified to serve as a basis of the discussion. First, a comparison is offered of how the character, motivation and actions of the two protagonists were described prior to the start of the unrest on 27 July 1812. The two protagonists here were those inside the house in Charles Street, termed 'those inside', and those outside in the street, termed 'those outside'. A second issue to be considered is the question of how the actions of two protagonists are depicted after unrest began in the evening of 27 July and continued during the following night. Third, the narratives of what happened in the jail during the evening of 28 July and the following night are compared. In each case attention is paid to what is present and what is highlighted in the newspaper reports of the incidents. In addition, it is also relevant to pay attention to gaps, to what might have been present in the newspaper reports but was not, and to compare the newspapers from this point of view. (On paying attention to what is not present in a newspaper text but could have been present, see, for example, Richardson 2007: 38.)

The gathering of a group of men and the collecting of weapons in the house in Charles Street is featured in both the Federalist and the Republican newspapers. A description of those inside is given in the *Federal Republican* on 3 August 1812:

> Admonished by the manner in which our office was first destroyed, that no support to our rights was to be expected from the civil or military authorities, whose duty it was to afford it; we had no alternative but to prepare to defend ourselves, on the establishment of the paper on Monday. In our last we stated that with this view we had seasonably provided the dwelling house of one of the proprietors, with defensive means, and that we were honored with the voluntary aid of a band of heroes, some of whom had imparted lustre to distinguished stations in the army of our revolution. It would be no easy task to find in an equal number engaged in a similar undertaking, so much public and private worth—so many virtues, which adorn the patriot of mature years, and which afford to the younger the best pledge of rivalling him. (*Federal Republican*, 3 August 1812)

The actions of those inside the house were thus planned in advance, and the first episode of unrest in June 1812 was put forward as the rationale for collecting weapons and men in the house. The arming of those inside is presented as the only course of action available to them. The paper also emphasises the outstanding nature of the men defending the house. The group are described as a 'band of heroes', with mention made of the service of some of them in the revolution.

As for depicting the other side in the confrontation, the *Federal Republican* writes:

> As was not unexpected, in the night of the day when the first number of the paper appeared, after five weeks suspension, occasioned by the former destruction, the mob made its appearance, . . . (*Federal Republican*, 3 August 1812)

Other, more colourful terms are used in the *Federal Republican* narrative a little later (see below), but the initial description is here limited to terming the crowd a 'mob'. The same word is also used in the narrative of the Republican *National Intelligencer* (see below), but that newspaper also uses the terms 'body of people' or 'party' to refer to the people outside.

The question of why a 'body of people' collected around the house in Charles Street that evening is treated at much greater length in the *National Intelligencer* than in the *Federal Republican*. The latter does not engage at this point in the chronological sequence with the question of what motivated people to gather around the house, and merely observes that the appearance of what it terms a 'mob' was as expected: 'As was not unexpected, . . . the mob made its appearance'. However, the *National Intelligencer* devotes considerably more attention to the question:

> Whether it was that this re-publication of this paper conveyed fresh matter of offence to those who first took umbrage at it; whether an association of the people had sworn the extermination of this print; or whether their indignation was principally aroused by the garrisoning of an armed citadel in the midst of their city, we cannot say. But on the evening a body of people collected around the house, wherein one of the Editors (the other remaining, as we understand, at Georgetown) had taken up his residence, in a tumultuous manner, the mob being chiefly of boys at first, but encreasing as the scene acquired greater interest. (*National Intelligencer*, 1 August 1812)

No one motive is identified as decisive in the newspaper for those outside, but as regards the putative motives of the crowd mention is made of the possibility that 'their indignation was . . . aroused by the garrisoning of an armed citadel in the midst of their city'. The characterisation of the house as an 'armed citadel in the midst of their city' suggests that what those inside the house had done and were doing was exceptional, abnormal and objectionable, serving to provide a rationale of sorts for the people outside to do something about it, to restore normalcy in a city. More generally, the very discussion of motives may suggest that those outside had some rational reason for being there, and it is therefore not an accident that the Federalist narrative left a gap by ignoring the question of rational motives, while the Republican paper, representing views that those outside the house had sympathies with, took it up in considerable detail. The difference stands out all the more because overall the account of the unrest in the Republican newspaper is considerably shorter.

Proceeding to the violent confrontations between those inside and those outside but attempting to enter the house, here is the narrative of the *Federal Republican*:

> the mob made its first appearance and soon assaulted the house, with the most formidable missiles. In an instant, the windows and front door were demolished, and the mob attempted to rush in. Under these circumstances, when a moment's delay would have been the destruction to those who were on the defensive, and after a cautionary notice had been afforded to the assailants, orders for firing were given to the party appointed to protect the lower story, which was done to the number of 7 or 8 muskets. Here ensued a partial suspension of hostilities by the mob. Had the party in the house continued to fire till they retreated and pursued them till they dispersed, as might lawfully have been done, and which as most men think, ought to have been done, the persons and lives of our friends would have remained safe, the property unmolested, and a lesson been given to the disorderly which would not soon have lost its force. The laws of nature and of society sanctioned the employment of the means which were in our hands of prostrating some hundreds of the miscreants, assembled for the purpose of plunder, murder, and the subversion of the most precious constitution privileges; but the suggestions of humanity prevailed with the veterans who commanded, and they paid the price of their clemency with life itself. The mob gaining fresh spirit from the comparative impunity with which they had hitherto acted, upheld by a reinforcement of desperadoes and a further supply of arms, continued the siege during the night. (*Federal Republican*, 3 August 1812)

The account of these events in the *National Intelligencer* is much briefer:

> The persons in the interior of the house, after warning the assailants (as they state them to have been, but as others deny, saying that mere curiosity drew them together) fired upon them, killed one person (Dr. Gale, the Electrician) and wounded from 20 to 30, some dangerously. The populace, it is said, then retired, but thirsting with a desire to revenge the death of the unarmed persons whom design or curiosity had first assembled, returned to

the attack with a piece of artillery. Before, however, this could be brought to bear on the garrison of the house, the persons who composed it, under the persuasion of the civil authority, surrendered themselves and were marched to the jail as a place of security, . . . (*National Intelligencer*, 1 August 1812)

These narratives are remarkable for a number of reasons. First of all, they offer further clues to the way the authors wanted to conceptualise the two sides. In the Federalist narrative those outside the house are characterised as assailants, and even more negatively as 'miscreants' and 'desperadoes'. In the context of such terms the motivation of those outside is then described as 'plunder, murder, and the subversion of the most precious constitution privileges'. On the Republican side, the term 'assailant' is also used, but neither *miscreant* nor *desperado* is used to refer to those outside. Instead, the word 'populace' is brought into the discourse. Sense 1 of the word in the *Oxford English Dictionary* (*OED*) is given as follows:

1. Ordinary people, as opposed to the titled, wealthy, or privileged classes; people generally. Also (*derogatory*): the mob, the rabble, the masses. (OED Online 2008)

The word may thus carry a negative semantic prosody, but there is also some ambiguity in the sense of the word, and it seems less definitely negative than 'miscreant' or 'desperado'.

Apart from the choice of individual words, it is noteworthy that the narrative in the *Federal Republican* fails to mention the killing of Dr Gale in its narrative of the chronological sequence of events. (The death of Dr Gale is mentioned in the article in the *Federal Republican*, but this is done much later in the story; see below.) By contrast, this first casualty of the confrontation, which occurred on the side of those outside, is given prominence in the chronological account of the events in the Republican newspaper.

It is also worth noting how the order for firing the muskets is constructed and conceptualised. In the Federalist paper, the key sentence is 'orders for firing were given to the party appointed to protect the lower story, which was done to the number of 7 or 8 muskets'. The sentence invokes the concept of protection as a rationale for the shooting, which serves to mitigate the act of firing on those coming in. It is also worth noting that both the main clause 'orders for firing were given' and the relative clause 'which was done to the number of 7 or 8 muskets' are in the passive, with the agent omitted. The main clause predicate 'give (the order for firing)' and the predicate 'to do something' in the relative clause are both agentive. Agentivity is here taken to mean that the predicates express actions that someone (some individual or group) undertakes volitionally and deliberately, that someone is in control of and that someone is responsible for.[4] However, while the predicates are agentive, they are in the passive. The passive has been termed an 'agent-back-grounding construction' by itself (Wanner 2009: 113), but what is even more important here is that there is no *by* phrase with the two passives and that the agent is not expressed. Here it is of interest to quote van Oosten on one of the uses of agentless passives: 'The speaker wishes to leave the identity of the agent vague, for such reasons as politeness or expediency, or, sometimes, to reduce the assertion of responsibility for the agent' (1984: 14). The omission of the agent backgrounds and obscures not only the identity but also the agency of the person or persons responsible for giving the order for firing (see also Trew 1979: 98–9; Fowler 1991: 78). Opening fire on one's political opponents is hardly a creditable act, and the grammatical choices made in the *Federal Republican* are not random. Instead, they are significant in constructing a narrative that minimises the embarrassment to the Federalist side.

By contrast, in the Republican newspaper the key sentence is in the active 'The persons in the interior of the house . . . fired upon them, killed one person . . .'. In this sentence, the agent is explicitly spelled out. This way of depicting the event gives prominence to the agency and agentivity of those inside in the action of killing Dr Gale. The scene is constructed in such a way that the 'persons in the interior of the house' are represented as undertaking the action volitionally, as being in full control of the action and as being responsible for the action, to invoke the key ingredients of agentivity. The explicit reference to the killing of Dr Gale further underlines the nature and extent of their responsibility. The grammatical construction chosen encodes a narrative that is suited to maximise the embarrassment to the Federalist side.

It is also worth noting how the very act of killing people is expressed with a euphemism in the Federalist newspaper: 'employment of the means which were in our hands of prostrating some hundreds of the miscreants'. The predicate 'to prostrate someone' is a more abstract and a milder term than 'to shoot someone'. The non-specificity of the noun phrase 'the means which were in our hands' is also worth noting, used instead of a more concrete noun phrase of the type of 'weapon' or 'musket'.

Further, the actions of those in the house are presented as something that was milder than what they would have been entitled to. The 'laws of nature and of society' are invoked to argue that they would have sanctioned 'prostrating', that is, killing, 'some hundreds' of those on the other side. Since a much smaller number was killed, namely, one person, the killing of that one person is downplayed when it is claimed that those in the house had the right to kill 'some hundreds' of the other side. Further, it bears repeating that not even that one fatality is mentioned in the chronological narrative of the events in the *Federal Republican*.

Moving on to the events in the jail, the last part of the Baltimore unrest, here is how the *Federal Republican* describes them:

> Through the day, demonstrations were given of a positive determination in the mob to break the prison, and massacre the gentlemen, who were placed there for safety. This occasioned a militia force to be called out for its protection, which in the evening, when most necessary, was withdrawn and dismissed by the brigadier general. Every man, we believe, will make the same comment upon this proceeding of the person upon whom alone, the best blood of the country, disarmed and rendered defenceless at his instance, depended for security from massacre at the hands of an unbridled rabble, of whose rage and ferocity the occurrences of the last twenty four hours were a continued evidence. Left to prosecute their avowed intentions, without restraint, the issue was as horrible as the anticipation had been infallible. The prison was entered by the murderers, and all whom address, stratagem or fortune did not favor, were assassinated and thrown into an heap as dead carcasses. But when the help of man failed, and cannibal fury walked hand in hand with death, the interposition of providence was most remarkable. In the heap of apparently dead bodies, which the populace ceased to mangle and deform, from fatigue and the fullest belief, that not a lingering spark of life remained in the mass, only one was really dead—the amiable, the venerable, the gallant General Lingan, of Montgomery, from his youth the defender of liberty, the soldier of the revolution, the delight of patriotism, the indispensable prop of a numerous family, & the idol of a whole county. (*Federal Republican*, 3 August 1812)

The account of what happened in the jail in the Republican *National Intelligencer* is much shorter:

> The mob reassembled in great numbers, and well prepared with instruments for the purpose, broke open the jail, rushed into the apartment where the prisoners were confined, and with clubs and other weapons assailed them, killed one person (Gen. Lingan of this neighbourhood) and dangerously wounded several, of whom it is reported that one (Gen. Harry Lee, of Virginia) has since died of his wounds. Some of those who were in confinement escaped unhurt, and others slightly wounded, and have gone from Baltimore, some of them having passed through this city. (*National Intelligencer*, 1 August 1812)

The narrative in the *Federal Republican* contains graphic descriptions of what happened, as in 'thrown into an heap as dead carcasses'. For its part, the *National Intelligencer* does not seek to rationalise the mob action in any way here either, and instead confines itself to a much briefer report of the incident. A noteworthy gap in the Republican newspaper is the omission of any mention of the dismissal of the militia from the scene. It is also noteworthy that the paragraph concludes with the point that some 'escaped unhurt, and others slightly wounded'. The account in the *Federal Republican* also implies that some escaped, but the point about some surviving is presented from the point of view of those who perished: 'all whom address, stratagem or fortune did not favor, were assassinated . . .'. For its part, the *National Intelligencer* mentions the death of General Lingan and the wounding of others, but the paper also gives prominence to the survivors, which mitigates the darker side of the narrative of what happened at the jail to some extent.

In concluding sections of their narratives, the two papers also differ. As regards the *Federal Republican*, the paper seeks to explore the broader implications of what the paper had called 'The Massacre at Baltimore'. Here is an extract:

> Let us reverse this for a moment, by supposing federalists capable of suppressing the freedom of speaking and writing—what would then become of the minority in New-England; or confining ourselves to our own state, what would be the condition of the democrats of Montgomery, Charles, St. Mary's, Somerset, &c.?—If 'the expression of sentiments obnoxious to the people' be a crime in Baltimore, 'courting destruction,' so is it every where, and were retaliation admissible in a government of laws, would work the extermination of half the citizens. (*Federal Republican*, 3 August 1812)

The issue of the *National Intelligencer* of 1 August 1812 does not comment on the question of freedom of the press, but the issue of 13 August 1812 offers this comment, under the title 'Mobs and Riots':

> We trust we never shall be, as we never have been, the advocates of riots, mobs, or any other illegal assemblies of people, nor of violence of any description, but more especially of that which is directed against the freedom of the press. This is one of those unalienable rights which, as republicans, we will always support; and, as conductors of a press, if attempted to be violated thro' us, we will not cease to defend to the last extremity. This is a doctrine we have always maintained, and we defy any man, be he friend or foe, to exhibit a line from our pen breathing a thought to the contrary.
>
> Entertaining these sentiments, we have cordially united with all good citizens in deprecating the events which have lately taken place at Baltimore; but our sympathies have not been of that convenient character that expands or contracts, as the enormities by which they are attracted assume one or another political hue. (*National Intelligencer*, 13 August 1812)

The comments here unambiguously condemn 'violence of any description'. In the second paragraph the paper highlights the consistency with which Republicans had defended the freedom of the press. This serves to remind readers of the Sedition Act during the Federalist Adams administration, when Federalists had enacted the Sedition Act against the vehement opposition of Republicans, and strictly enforced it against their opponents.

Towards the end of the article of 3 August 1812, the *Federal Republican* comes back to what happened at the house, mentioning the killing of Dr Gale by those inside the house in Charles Street:

> No part of the defense was more conspicuous, than the patience with which the assault of the mob was borne. Not till the door and windows were demolished, was the blow returned, and not then till warning was given, and the experiment of blank firing tried, without success.—We have flattered ourselves, that not even a member of the mob would be hardy enough to deny this. Gale was killed, boldly entering the front door at the head of a party, after it had been beat open. (*Federal Republican*, 3 August 1812)

The mention of the death of Dr Gale in the *Federal Republican* thus comes only after the depiction of the bloody incident at the prison, where a Federalist was killed. This way of presenting the deaths reverses the chronological order in which the incidents occurred. In the actual sequence of events the killing of Dr Gale came before the killing of General Lingan, giving fresh impetus to the mob. When the *Federal Republican* mentions the death of Dr Gale after the death of General Lingan, it removes any suggestion or possibility of a causal link between them, which might be made by an implicature, that is, that the killing of Dr Gale may have excited the crowd to take revenge. By reversing the order of the actual events, the narrative of the *Federal Republican* makes the killing of General Lingan even more reprehensible.

Here is an extract from the concluding part of the *Federal Republican* narrative 'The Massacre at Baltimore':

> We have suffered much in person and property, but our grievances are lightened by the reflection, that our sufferings will redound to the public good, by laying open the true character of those who are laboring to strangle the liberty of the people, and to subvert the independence of the country. (*Federal Republican*, 3 August 1812)

The *Federal Republican* thus attempts to link the Republican party, or at least the Republican party in Maryland, to the riots. There is no evidence that the rioting was instigated by the Republican party in Maryland, let alone the national Republican party, but the rioters assailing the Federalists in the house in Charles Street unquestionably had Republican sympathies, and the argument might be termed 'guilt by association', which in fallacy theory may be viewed under the fallacy of *ad hominem*.[5] In the present case, it might be presented as follows (see Walton 1998: 257):

> The actions of the rioters assailing the Federalists were reprehensible.
> The rioters had Republican sympathies.
> Therefore Republicans are reprehensible.

The comments in the *National Intelligencer* of 13 August 1812, quoted above, were a response to the 'guilt by association' argument of the Federalist newspaper, and condemned the rioting in Baltimore.

Here is how the *National Intelligencer* concludes its report in its issue of 1 August 1812:

> Such a scene of violence, we believe, is unprecedented in the annals of the Republic. Long may it be before we witness its repetition! (*National Intelligencer*, 1 August 1812)

The *National Intelligencer* thus did not seek to defend the indefensible, the July riots in Baltimore, including the events at the jail.

For its part, the *Federal Republican* also looked to the future, in trying to associate the Republican party with the riots and with an effort to suppress the liberty of the people, and thus attempting to persuade people to shift their allegiances to Federalists. Here is an extract from a later issue:

> A period has arrived that calls on you to act a part worthy of you. The Liberty of the Press is tarnished.—There was a time in this State when she had her temples among us. Now they are destroyed, and her votaries murdered by robbers and assassins.—Compelled to fly from the despotism of a mob, she has sought an asylum where her name is still sacred, & where murder and plunder not yet virtues. On the banks of the Potomac she raises her ravishing song. (*Federal Republican*, 26 August 1812)

To some extent there was a backlash against the Republican administration over the unrest in Baltimore. One sign of it was that Hanson, one of the editors of the *Federal Republican*, was soon elected to Congress and that Federalists made gains in state elections in Maryland in late 1812. For its part, the city of Baltimore remained Republican.

Conclusion

The Baltimore riots of 1812 were no 'massacre', but they were something more serious than a 'commotion'. This study is mainly based on reports and comments on the riots in two newspapers, the *Federal Republican*, on the Federalist side, and the *National Intelligencer*, on the Republican side. The former called the riots, or the second riot, 'the massacre at Baltimore', while the latter paper called the same incidents a 'dreadful commotion'. The difference here is one indication of a difference in perspective between the two papers.

This study showed that while the two newspapers were partisan, there was some common ground between them, for both emphasised their support for freedom of the press and their rejection of violence and mob rule. However, a number of differences were identified in their accounts of the events of 27 and 28 July 1812, apart from the titles of the stories. The Federalist paper devoted little or no attention to looking for a rational motive for why people had gathered around the house in Charles Street. Instead, the paper devoted a great deal of effort to depicting the high moral character of those inside the house, also emphasising the caution, in Federalist eyes, that they had exercised before opening fire. Further, as regards the coverage of what happened at the house, the killing of Dr Gale was awkward from a Federalist perspective, and the newspaper omitted his death completely from that part of the story. As far as the events at the jail are concerned, the Federalist newspaper depicted them in graphic and gruesome detail, also devoting a great deal of space to praising the character of the one casualty, General Lingan.

As for the Republican newspaper, the sympathies of the crowd were unquestionably with Republicans, and the *National Intelligencer* offered some comments on why people gathered around the house in Charles Street. The killing of Dr Gale did not reflect credit on Federalists, and the Republican paper presented the event much more directly than the Federalist paper, with the language of the Republican paper assigning responsibility for the killing directly to those inside the house. By contrast, the mob attack on the jail, with the subsequent death of General Lingan, was an incident that could not be defended. Given the Republican sympathies of the mob at the jail, the incident was an embarrassment for the Republican newspaper, and the account of the incident was much briefer than in the Federalist newspaper. For its part, the *National Intelligencer* gave prominence to the fact that other Federalists escaped from the jail unhurt or with minor injuries, and the newspaper also unambiguously condemned the rioting in its issue of 13 August 1812.

The Baltimore riots had an impact on Maryland politics, favouring Federalists in elections in late 1812, and they also had some effect on sentiment in New York and New England (Hickey 2012: 65), but they did not grow into a major national embarrassment for the Republican party. Republicans should thank the physician at the jail in helping bring the incident to a close before more loss of life occurred. The repudiation, by Republicans, of the unrest, as in the 13 August 1812 issue of the *National Intelligencer*, served to counter the broader Federalist criticism that freedom of speech was under threat, particularly because the repudiation was coupled with a pointed reminder that Republicans had a history of consistently defending freedom of speech against partisan excesses during the Adams administration. Additionally, when there was the threat of further unrest in Baltimore after the appearance of the 3 August 1812 issue of the *Federal Republican*, the Republican authorities in Baltimore acted quickly: a crowd gathered near the post office in Baltimore apparently to prevent the distribution of the paper, but the militia 'easily' dispersed the crowd (Hickey 2012: 62).

The study of the coverage of the riots in the two newspapers reveals that features of political spin in response to incidents involving unrest can be found in the press even in the early American republic. Such features of spin included differences in the newspapers on what is reported and what is not reported, or is only reported briefly. Deviations from the chronological sequence of events may sometimes also be features of spin, as for instance when the *Federal Republican* fails to mention the killing of Dr Gale, an embarrassing incident from a Federalist point of view, in the chronological sequence of events. Lexical choices were seen to differ depending on the party affiliation of the newspaper, and it makes a difference, for instance, whether an incident is construed as a 'massacre' or as a 'dreadful commotion'. More grammatical features of spin included the use of passives without expressed agents to background those aspects of the events in accounts of the incidents that were disadvantageous for one's own side. A further feature of spin identified here was the attempt to make use of the technique of 'guilt by association' in order to tarnish one's political opponents.

Naturally, the present chapter invites further work on political spin in the reporting of other controversial and politically charged incidents involving unrest in American history and in the history of other countries with a free press.

Notes

1. For fuller accounts of the unrest, see Tucker (1954: 139–42); Cassell (1975: 247–56); Hickey (2012: 56–60).
2. The earliest example of the use of the noun *spin* in the relevant sense in the OED is from 1977: 'Pertschuk is accused of . . . being too ardent a consumer advocate, of "lobbying" members of the committee on behalf of things he thinks are good, of putting his own philosophical "spin" on options' (*The Washington Post*, March 1977).
3. The OED (2008) definition of the relevant sense of 'spin' is also worth noting: 'A bias or slant on information, intended to create a favourable impression when it

is presented to the public; an interpretation or viewpoint. Frequently in phr. *to put a positive (negative, etc.) spin on. colloq.* (chiefly *U.S. Politics*).'

4. The three concepts listed in the text as prototypical properties of agentivity – volition, control and responsibility – are prominent, for instance, in Hundt's work (Hundt 2004: 49; see also Rudanko 2015: 20–1). Dowty (1991) is an important earlier contribution to work on agents and agentivity, and while the three properties highlighted here do not exactly match the properties of what he termed the 'Agent Proto-Role', it may be noted that the related notion of 'volitional involvement in the event or state' is also featured prominently in his work (1991: 592). For the notion of control, see also Berman (1970). As for the notion of responsibility, its quasi-legal flavour is also of interest because this study inquires into issues of presentation and public relations.

5. Here is a textbook definition of a fallacy in informal logic: 'It is customary in the study of logic to reserve the term "fallacy" for arguments that are *psychologically* persuasive but *logically* incorrect; that *do* as a matter of fact persuade but, given certain argumentative standards, *shouldn't*. We therefore define "fallacy" as a type argument that *seems* to be correct but that proves, on examination, not to be so' (Copi and Burgess-Jackson 1996: 97; original emphasis).

References

Berman, A. (1970), 'Agent, experiencer and controllability', in S. Kuno (ed.), *Mathematical Linguistics and Automatic Translation*, Report NSF-24, Cambridge, MA: Harvard University Press, pp. 203–37.

Cassell, F. A. (1975), 'The great Baltimore riot of 1812', *Maryland Historical Magazine*, 70 (3), pp. 241–59.

Copi, I. and K. Burgess-Jackson (1996), *Informal Logic*, 3rd edn, Upper Saddle River, NJ: Prentice Hall.

Dowty, D. (1991), 'Thematic proto-roles and argument selection', *Language*, 67, pp. 547–614.

Fowler, R. (1991), *Language in the News: Discourse and Ideology in the Press*, London: Routledge.

Heidler, D. S. and J. T. Heidler (2002), *The War of 1812*, Westport, CT: Greenwood Press.

Hickey, D. (1989), *The War of 1812: A Forgotten Conflict*, Urbana, IL: University of Illinois Press.

Hickey, D. (2012), *The War of 1812: A Forgotten Conflict*, bicentennial edn, Urbana, IL: University of Illinois Press.

Humphrey, C. S. (1996), *The Press of the Young Republic, 1783–1833*, Westport, CT: Greenwood Press.

Hundt, M. (2004), 'Animacy, agentivity, and the spread of the progressive in Modern English', *English Language and Linguistics*, 8, pp. 47–69.

Moore, M. (2006), *The Origins of Modern Spin*, Basingstoke: Palgrave Macmillan.

OED Online (2008), Includes full text of *The Oxford English Dictionary*, 2nd edn (1989) and the 3 Additions, <http://www.oed.com> (last accessed 3 May 2018).

Pasley, J. (2001), *'The Tyranny of Printers': Newspaper Politics in the Early American Republic*, Charlottesville: University of Virginia Press.

Richardson, J. (2007), *Analysing Newspapers: An Approach from Critical Discourse Analysis*, Basingstoke: Palgrave Macmillan.

Rudanko, J. (2015), *Linking Form and Meaning: Studies on Selected Control Patterns in Recent English*, Basingstoke: Palgrave Macmillan.

Schaefer, T. and T. Birkland (2007), *Encyclopedia of Media and Politics*, Washington DC: CQ Press.

Trew, T. (1979), 'Theory and ideology at work', in R. Fowler, B. Hodge, G. Kress and T. Trew (eds), *Language and Control*, London: Routledge & Kegan Paul, pp. 94–116.

Tucker, G. (1954), *Poltroons and Patriots*, Indianapolis: Bobbs-Merrill.

van Oosten, J. (1984), *On the Nature of Subjects, Topics, and Agents*, Dissertation, University of California, Berkeley.

Walton, D. (1998), *Ad Hominem Arguments*, Tuscaloosa, AL and London: University of Alabama Press.

Wanner, A. (2009), *Deconstructing the English Passive*, Berlin: Mouton de Gruyter.

2

Moral Storytelling during the 2011 England Riots: Mythology, Metaphor and Ideology

Darren Kelsey

Introduction

This chapter analyses moral storytelling in media responses to the England riots. Case one analyses the myth of the Blitz (Calder 1991; Ponting 1990; Kelsey 2015a) through the diachronic–synchronic discursive tensions of national narration, popular memory and British identity. I argue that these mechanisms operated ideologically to provide metaphors of war and morality with intertextual scope and dialogical salience through public and political discourse. In doing so, case one analyses victim and hero archetypes in representations of the general public through examples of moral storytelling that invoked the myth of the Blitz. Case two then analyses representations of rioters. It considers the ideological operations and *paradoxical persuasions* (Kelsey 2015a, 2015b) that operated through moral discourses and a sick society metaphor. The latter shows how moral discourses oscillated precariously between constructions of rioters transcending the social class system whilst paradoxically operating through discourses of blame aimed at the welfare state. I have selected these two cases because they reflect moral constructions of Britain in past and present contexts through attempts to understand what happened during the riots.[1] Both cases concern forms of mythology that draw on visual and linguistic metaphors of war and social sickness. But before I go any further, let us recap what happened during the riots and some of the political responses that others have commented upon since then.

Riots under Review

On 4 August 2011 a 29-year-old black male was shot dead by police in Tottenham. On 6 August a peaceful protest took place in Tottenham against the shooting. When police in Tottenham attempted to disperse the protest violent clashes occurred as large groups also responded by setting fire to police and public properties. From 7 August onwards, these acts of violence and civil disobedience spread across London and other cities in England with riots and looting taking place in sixty-six locations. Whilst these were not necessarily instances of protest violence following the events in Tottenham, they were clearly reactions mobilised by the riots that started a day earlier. Five people died in the riots, which lasted until 10 August and are estimated to have involved up to 15,000 people and cost the country up to half a billion pounds (Bridges 2012: 2).

Initial responses to the riots sought to explain why they were happening. Whilst issues of race were represented as partly relevant to begin with, widespread looting and rioting across the country had clearly taken on a less identifiable or common cause for violence than those on the initial evening following the protest against the police. Bridges has examined some of the responses from politicians following the initial unrest in Tottenham:

> [David] Lammy was one of the first politicians, standing before cameras on Tottenham High Road the following day, to describe the rioters as 'mindless, mindless people', to which he has subsequently added the epitaphs of nihilistic and hedonistic. In this, Lammy gave the lead to other political leaders in their characterisation of the riots as 'criminality, pure and simple' (Prime Minister David Cameron), 'needless and opportunist theft and violence' (Deputy Prime Minister Nick Clegg) and the product of 'a feral underclass' (Justice Secretary Kenneth Clark). (Bridges 2012: 3)

These responses demonstrated a tendency among political sources to depoliticise, criminalise and delegitimise voices that sought to provide deeper, sociological and economic analysis of the riots. In the aftermath of the riots many commented, often critically, on the initial responses of political and media sources, whilst often trying to gain a more informed and complex understanding of why they happened (Cavanagh and Dennis 2012; Fuchs 2012; Taylor 2012; Milburn 2012; Benyon 2012; Younge 2011; Reicher and Stott 2011; Cavalcanti et al. 2012; Angel 2012; Bridges 2012; Ball and Drury 2012; Jefferson 2012; Lagrange 2012; Lea and Hallsworth 2012; Palmer 2012; D. Waddington 2012; P. A. J. Waddington 2012). For example, Younge argues that the context of the riots held a political substance, even if the immediate actions did not appear to be explicitly political:

> Insisting on the criminality of those involved, as though that alone explains their motivation and the context is irrelevant, is fatuous. To stress criminality does not deny the political nature of what took place, it simply chooses

to only partially describe it. They were looting, not shop-lifting, and challenging the police for control of the streets, not stealing coppers' hubcaps. When a group of people join forces to flout both law and social convention, they are acting politically. (The question, as yet unanswered, is to what purpose.) (Younge 2011)

As psychologists Steve Reicher and Cliff Stott (2011) have commented, the language of 'mindlessness' and simplistic descriptions of the 'mob' are dangerous, misleading and unhelpful since they detract from the deeper understandings that are needed in explaining why these events occur. It is also worth noting that the Riots Communities and Victims Panel, set up by the coalition government with a cross-party make-up, was reluctant to acknowledge structural factors in society or courses of poverty, deprivation and family issues that it implied were contributing factors in a 'culture of poverty':

> Its final report . . . resonates with the Victorian values and underlying notions of the 'deserving' and 'undeserving' poor found in David Lammy's book. Both are also reminiscent in their analysis of the type of 'culture of poverty' thinking found in the infamous Moynihan report following the American urban disorders of the 1960s. This focuses on what are seen as the personal defects and social development problems of rioters – their lack of 'resilience', inability to 'defer gratification', ill-discipline, absent fathers and lack of 'proper role models' – rather than attempting to address the sources of their grievances or structural factors in society. It is as though the Panel, in reaching its conclusion that it is necessary to give the rioters 'a stake in society', failed ever to consider what sort of society Britain has become. (Bridges 2012: 8)

Many of the parallels that Bridges draws here are significant to the discourses I analyse in this chapter. The two cases I consider reflect similar dichotomies that are projected through cultural, domestic and moral values in constructions of different social groups.

As Bridges also observed, 'Even when the Panel touches on more structural issues, it does so in ways that seem oblivious to the depth of the economic crisis and government austerity cuts, especially as they impact on the inner cities' (2012: 9). My previous analysis showed how initial responses in the right-wing press sought to suppress those voices on the 'cynical left' for 'making excuses' for riots by blaming austerity and social deprivation. By adopting Cameron's soundbite at the time, this was discursively projected as 'criminality, pure and simple' (Kelsey 2015b). Newspapers made explicit attempts to critically oppose voices that sought to provide 'sympathetic' explanations for the riots. This discursive mechanism also developed into instances of blame towards political correctness hindering police efforts to control the violence. These instances demonstrate how various interdiscursive mechanisms were cutting into the construction of blame and calls for harder policing and judicial responses.

This chapter does not try to explain why the riots happened or who was to blame. As Cavalcanti et al. (2012: 35) argue, fundamental problems faced in attempts to understand why these riots happened lie in reductionist discourses that constructed them as a product of one particular social, economic or political issue from either end of the political spectrum. So, whilst there was not one fixed explanation for the riots, these different responses discursively constructed the riots in political contexts. Even in instances when rioters supposedly lacked a political message or motivation, these events were still understood through mediatised and political (ideological) contexts and accounts from journalists, politicians and the public. Moral storytelling after the riots was significant since it was as restrictive to some voices as it was expressive for others through its mythological, metaphorical and ideological salience. Conceptual frameworks of mythology are fundamental to the discursive dynamics and cultural construction of moral storytelling. Hence I will briefly discuss the analytical framework adopted below.

The Discourse-Mythological Approach

Myths are psycho-discursive formations that are constructed and understood through language, signs, symbols, archetypes, stories and discourses that reflect particular ideals, values and morals in society (Kelsey 2015a, 2017, 2018; Lule 2001; Barthes 1993; Campbell 1949). As Jack Lule explains, 'Myth upholds some beliefs but degrades others. It celebrates but also excoriates. It affirms but it also denies' (2001: 119). Myth distorts meaning and often suppresses complexity. Kelsey (2015a, 2016) offers a discourse-mythological approach (DMA) that can be used to analyse mythology in news stories. A discourse-mythological analysis was beyond the scope of my previous research on the riots (Kelsey 2015b). However, this chapter revisits the concept of a sick society as a myth since this metaphor functioned ideologically to define particular social groups from a moral perspective and justify a political agenda against the welfare state. In part, a sick society metaphor relied upon forms of cultural mythology in British national identity to define who we are as a nation and who is responsible for the 'sickness' we need to 'cure'.

DMA adopts some of the tools and frameworks of critical discourse analysis in synergy with myth theory in order to analyse and understand how discourse constructs mythology and how mythology functions ideologically. Ideologies operate at multiple levels of society and communication whilst discourse and cultural mythologies also draw on the linguistic, semiotic and archetypal apparatus that we need in order to tell (and understand) stories. Therefore, the DMA framework has meticulously dealt with the overlapping albeit distinguishable terms of discourse, mythology and ideology and the interplays between these concepts: 'Discourse constructs the story (myth) that carries the ideology, whilst ideology also informs the construction of discourse' (Kelsey 2015a: 27). So it is not that we ever see a starting point between these three concepts through any form of communication; they have operated, negotiated and constructed semiotic phenomena endlessly over time and continue to function seamlessly through cultural forms of communication, such as storytelling. Metaphors are a discursive and conceptual mechanism that operate through thought and language.

Metaphors are an important component of mythological storytelling, which operates as a discursive and communicative vehicle for ideology. Much like mythology in its semiotic and archetypal forms, we cannot function conceptually without metaphors. Metaphors play a pervasive role in our everyday lives, 'not just in language but in thought and action' (Lakoff and Johnson 2003: 3). It is our conceptual structures that dictate 'what we perceive, how we get around in the world, and how we relate to other people. Our conceptual system thus plays a central role in defining our everyday realities' (Lakoff and Johnson 2003: 3). Hence, if we rely on mythological conventions and draw on metaphors as the creative and binding mechanisms of our conceptual thought processes, 'then the way we think, what we experience, and what we do every day is very much a matter of metaphor' (Lakoff and Johnson 2003: 3). As we see in the case studies of this chapter, metaphors of war and sickness both stimulate familiar ideological perspectives on the moral state of British society in the mythological storytelling of past and present contexts.

One particular phenomenon that my DMA research has already focused on is the myth of the Blitz. Those storytelling components that made this myth so symbolically persuasive in 1940 have preserved its cultural and discursive recurrence in a contemporary context. This myth has been examined by various scholars who have confirmed its role, but also challenged its validity, as a way of identifying the British public during the Second World War (Calder 1991, 1999; Connelly 2004; Manthorpe 2006; Heartfield 2005; Tulloch 2006; McLaine 1979; Ponting 1990, 1994; Panayi 1995; Thoms 1995). The popular mythology of British stoicism, defiance, resilience and unity during the Blitz is a simplified story of a time when morale was at breaking point, class divides and cultural tensions were high, looting was rife and crime rates increased dramatically. That is not to suggest people never pulled together. They did. But the simplification of this story in both its past and present contexts provides reason for further scrutiny. The myth of the

Blitz often suppresses particular complexities and less desirable social traits of wartime Britain when they do not suit the interests of popular memory and national narration for synchronic purposes.

The Myth of the Blitz: Destruction, Defiance and Unity

In the examples considered below I will reflect on the dialogical connections that operated between the riots and the Second World War, which became intertextually entrenched with other cultural mythology around the Blitz and British national identity. Discourses of defiance that subsequently appeared in response to the devastation caused by the riots were fundamental to the moral boundaries established between law-abiding citizens and the rioters. The familiar symbols of national narration and British identity that are so familiar in Blitz mythology (Kelsey 2015a; Calder 1991; Ponting 1990) contributed to the moral–immoral dichotomies necessary for other projections around social 'sickness' after the riots. Nostalgic processes of remembering – albeit selectively and inaccurately – are common discursive practices of national narration in constructing who we are and what we should aspire to be in terms of our social ideals and moral values. In this case, contextualising these ideals and values within familiar forms of popular memory and Blitz mythology fits them into a coherent and connected story about how the British respond in moments of crisis or devastation. As we have seen in previous cases (Tulloch 2006; Manthorpe 2006; Kelsey 2015a; Gilroy 2004), these narratives operate as ideological battlegrounds to either establish, reinforce or oppose political and moral agendas.

Worst Destruction since the Blitz

Newspaper headlines and images on the days following the riots provided graphic accounts of the destruction caused – especially through anarchistic symbols of burning cars, fires, flames from buildings, masked looters and acts of vandalism (Kelsey 2015b). This was understandably a discourse of civil disobedience that framed the extent of disorder. But in order to contextualise the extraordinary extent of this damage some stories drew on particular themes to accentuate the level of destruction caused. The images of buildings in London smothered in large flames of fires that completely destroyed them down to their bare frames was powerful in itself. Through their intertextual salience these images stimulated dialogical associations with the Blitz. These connections were not tenuous. However, as we often see when cultural mythology is invoked, the ways in which myths are recontextualised to explain current events becomes an ideological process.

Under the headline 'TORCHING OF TWO SUBURBS', a two-page spread focused on the destruction of cars and properties in Ealing and Croydon (Wilkes 2011: 6–7). The majority of this spread focused on Croydon with three photos of a large furniture store that had been owned and run by the Reeves family since the 1870s. One photo showed it burnt to the ground with just a shell remaining, another showed it up in flames during the riots and the other featured an old black and white photo of the business open back in its early days. The article made a number of references and analogies through the Blitz and Second World War. A large embedded quote taken from the article said: 'The furniture store was in the Reeves family for five generations. It survived the Depression and Hitler's bombs . . . but not the rampage of the arson bomb.' In a quote from the shop owner, he said:

> Children used to be well-behaved then but these days it doesn't seem to be the case. A lot of them leave school without the basic skills. And sometimes parents aren't doing their job. You see police going around town and they're too afraid to do anything. One policeman told me he is not actually allowed to do anything. We need Churchill to come down and sort it all out. (Wilkes 2011)

The interdiscursive mechanisms of this quote are interesting because the diachronic connections with the past stimulate a number of synchronic discourses in relation to education, parenting, policing and perhaps human rights, given the notion of police not being allowed to do anything. Churchillian mythology of the Second World War was then used as a nostalgic symbol to represent an idealised period when the country supposedly had a superior sense of social discipline and moral values, when schools and parenting were of a more respectable standard. The idea that strong moral values of family, schooling, and law and order have lost their way is fundamental to the concept of a sick society that reflects a deterioration of disciplined social order. Of course, as others point out, whilst these nostalgic qualities are not lies, they are certainly simplifications of Britain's past. There are numerous social, cultural and economic accounts from the past that are suppressed by the work of cultural mythology that constructs utopian stories of moral values and social cohesion behind the mask of nostalgia that hides other inconvenient nuances from the past.

After explaining how the Reeves family business had expanded throughout the First World War and Croydon became a significant branch during hard times in the 1930s, another reference to the Blitz occurred:

> During the Second World War, much of Croydon was destroyed in attacks by German V-1 flying bombs and V-2 rockets. But the Reeves store survived the blitz – Maurice remembers hiding in the cellar during air raids – and

there was a good trade in second hand furniture (all manufacturing during this time was devoted to the war effort). (Wilkes 2011)

These are affective qualities of the story since they project a sense of endurance and resilience that the business has displayed, in its domestic (family), economic and structural stoicism across so many historical periods. This is a genuinely devastating story. What is significant is the way in which its moral boundaries are distinguished through familiar traits of national narration and the nostalgic dynamics of diachronic storytelling. The interdiscursive layers of this account develop through the reflective, diachronic elements of the story and its perspective on a lack of current social values, which are more destructive for the Reeves family than any previous physical or financial threat they faced. This is one isolated example of the kind of story that – through its emotive sense of destruction, loss and injustice – constructed a discursive environment in which other moral stories, myths and metaphors could operate.

The *Daily Express* also provided a two-page spread that drew direct parallels between the riots and the Blitz and likened the threat of rioters with the threat once posed by Hitler. Under the headline 'Shock and outrage at worst scenes since Blitz', the article opened: 'Shell-shocked Britons woke yesterday to some of the worst scenes since the Blitz 70 years ago, with hundreds of shops ransacked and burnt-out businesses left blackened and smouldering' (Flanagan 2011: 4–5). After describing examples of the destruction caused it said: 'The Blitz spirit was seen elsewhere as businesses battened down in anticipation of further trouble in London suburbs and major cities across the country.' An eyewitness source said: 'The damage was worse than anything Hitler could do in the Blitz.' With all photos in black and white, dialogical connections were aroused through intertextual symbols of image and language. For example, this piece juxtaposed photos of a large building burning during the Blitz and a shell of the Croydon furniture store in 2011 with other photos above and below of firefighters tackling fires in other locations during the riots. The caption said:

> Still burning yesterday, the shells of once-proud businesses outraged Londoners. Once it was Hitler who caused the devastation, left. But it was local thugs who mindlessly burned out these shops in Croydon, above, the House of Reeves store, right, and the Sony Centre, Enfield, below. (Flanagan 2011)

The visual parallels in these photos are not tenuous. There is a morbid similarity, especially in black and white, between these scenes during the riots and the Blitz. For those members of the public who lost homes and livelihoods, this was as devastating as this article depicts. On the one hand, the devastation across London or any other city as a whole was nowhere near comparable to the Blitz. But on the other hand, the images of burning buildings, the personal stories and suffering, the affective insights and emotive sense of loss after historical endurance during previous threats and generational conflicts tell powerful stories. The stories stimulated further generalisations through other symbolic parallels with the Blitz, which continued to heighten perceptions of severity and scale during the riots. Through this symbolism and perception other intertextual parallels appeared in other moral tales of the public responding in their heroic 'front line' form.

The Myth of the Blitz Spirit

The myth of the Blitz continued to recur in stories about the general public after the riots. Whilst comparisons with the Blitz and Hitler were used to describe the scale of destruction and threat posed by rioters, the myth of the Blitz was also used to define the moral superiority of other citizens. Events like the riots become building blocks of national narration to suggest that consecutive generations adopt the hereditary spirit, stoicism, resilience and "British grit" of the past. However, as we have seen in the examples so far, nostalgic feelings of loss and moral decay – as if the nation is losing touch with its wartime spirit and values – also play a powerful role in these discourses. On the one hand, morally legitimate citizens are given familiar traits of national identity to confirm their British spirit. But at the same time, on the other hand, the idea that those British values of wartime mythology are disappearing, especially amongst the 'youth of today', provides another diachronic mechanism to pass moral judgement on the synchronic problems of contemporary society from an ideological perspective.

A common image across newspapers on 10 August featured a young woman with 'Looters are scum' written across her top as she turned out with other volunteers to help clean up the morning after the rioting the night before. Her image was often embedded next to other photos of volunteers holding brooms in the air as expressions of community solidarity. For example, the *Daily Express*'s front page on 10 August featured her photo next to the headline: 'SWEEP SCUM OFF OUR STREETS'. Under the headline '200 rioters caused this mayhem . . . 500 of us are here to clean it up', a *Daily Mail* article on the same day said:

> They came armed with brooms and the odd wheelbarrow. Where youths had roamed the streets with bricks and bats just hours earlier, a new army had appeared. Invoking London's famous 'Blitz spirit', volunteers

responded defiantly to the worst violence the city has witnessed in decades by rolling up their sleeves and helping in the clean-up. (McDermott and Jaffrey 2011: 12–13)

A source later on in the article said: 'There are more of us than them [rioters] and we are not going to let them claim our streets and neighbourhoods. I guess it's a Blitz spirit.' *The Sun* also ran a two-page spread under the banner 'BLITZ SPIRIT FOR CLAPHAM CLEAN-UP' with one article headlined 'LAVENDER HILL MOP' (Lazzeri et al. 2011: 8–9). The latter opened with the following description: 'A defiant army of Londoners fought back against the riot mobs yesterday – arming themselves with brushes to launch clean-up operations'. The language here continued to evoke military connotations that operate coherently through the myth of the Blitz and the popular memory of a people's army, consisting of citizens pulling together, improvising and fighting against the odds. Under the subheading 'Spirit', one source said: 'I just wanted to come here to show my solidarity with the local community.' The article later added: 'The clean-up campaign also took hold in Ealing, West London, where locals who gathered in their hundreds proudly spoke of the "Blitz spirit".' Another source added: 'This is about Londoners doing what Londoners do best. It's about the Blitz spirit coming out.' Somewhat ironically, the Blitz was a period when opportunist looting was a significant problem amongst general increases in crimes; looting became such a problem in London that the police had to set up an anti-looting squad in response (Ponting 1990). Second Lieutenant Arthur Bennie, of the 7th Battalion, King's Regiment refers to the occasions when they had to 'fix bayonets to prevent people entering bank vaults that were opened by the bombing' (quoted in Levine 2006: 411–12). Due to the social disruption caused by the war, juvenile crime also increased by 41 per cent in the year after the war started (Ponting 1990). Racism also increased dramatically during the war (Panayi 1995; Calder 1999; Kelsey 2015a). Panayi claims that 'some of the most systematic persecution of racial and ethnic minorities in recent history took place during the two world wars' (1995: 204).

As is typical of cultural mythology, nostalgia and discursive uses of the past, complexity is largely absent; contradictions are smoothed out since they would only compromise the moral clarity that the myth of the Blitz provides. The myth of the Blitz is such a salient story in popular memory and British national identity that it defines (for its believers) the pride of us as good versus them as evil. It was a moment in history that – despite particular complexities that are not suited to the popular story – can easily be mythologised through this dichotomy. But the riots were not that simple.

As we saw earlier, they could not be defined by one exclusive problem, motivation or social group. The psychology around rioting is also incredibly complex (Reicher and Stott 2011). But a discourse of war that invokes the symbolism and slogans of Britain's 'finest hour' reduces the complexity of the riots to a case where you are either with the good guys or part of the problem. And, as we have seen, when the government looked to cure a sick society of its perceived sickness and moral decay, it did so through a narrow paradigm that justified its ongoing ideological agenda against a specific social class.

Furthermore, there is a significant discursive implication to the moral and emotive affect that develops from this story when rioters are compared to Hitler. These moral discourses set the parameters for other perceptions and actions; they prohibit the salience of particular views and ideals whilst encouraging and often exacerbating others. Diachronic narration partially constructs synchronic perceptions of social groups, the threats they pose, the causes of conflict and the solutions we propose (or oppose) in resolving them. So the projected severity of the riots in comparison with the Blitz did not just function as way of defining the extent of the damage caused. It was also an ideological operation that invoked familiar traits of British national identity to define the moral spirit, values and ideals of the nation through the myth of the Blitz.

It is significant that the myth of the Blitz was not exclusive to news discourse. This was a distinct theme amongst many sources and members of the public. Hence, Blitz mythology and popular memory operate discursively through the shared social practice that we engage with culturally and generationally, which maintain the continual reproduction of popular myths albeit through synchronic forms of recontextualisation. Journalists and editors are wrapped up in this cultural mythology of national narration as much as anyone else. As I have previously argued, 'journalists, politicians and the public are caught up in complex fields of cultural rituals . . . and social practices . . . which influence and are influenced by popular memory' (Kelsey 2015a: 24). So, it is not the case that the media, politicians or public take any exclusive conspiratorial lead on these messages. They are culturally and discursively formed and recontextualised over time; it is the way in which they are expressed and articulated and the purpose they serve which then functions ideologically. In this instance it was the broader context of moral storytelling in response to the riots, which constructed a sense of moral decadence and sickness in British society that became deeply ideological in its juxtaposition with the moral superiority of communities expressing the Blitz spirit and embracing a mythologised construction of wartime (Churchillian) values.

The Myth of the Sick Society: A Case of Paradoxical Persuasion

Contentions between discourses of social class, morality, who the 'mob' consisted of (demographically), and what politicians mean when they refer to a 'sick society' mobilised a battlefield of ideological constructs. By considering these discursive nuances this analysis shows how, in the process of suppressing 'cynical excuses' for the riots, right-wing newspapers depoliticised the actions of rioters before redefining them as a political problem (a sick society) to justify legislative responses from the government. Here we see an example of 'paradoxical persuasion' (Kelsey 2015a, 2015b); when discursive mechanisms served an immediate (albeit contradictory) purpose that still maintained a broader, social and political agenda. In previous work I have considered how certain stories or discursive features might appear to contradict the ideological interests or political position of a particular source or newspaper (which we understand through the contextual and historical knowledge that we bring to our readings of texts). Despite the apparent contradictions that occur, a more nuanced contextual reading considers how different discursive mechanisms serve particular purposes in immediate and temporary environments. This reading can actually help to make sense of the ideological positions that are *maintained* through such 'contradictions' rather than compromising the broader interests that they serve. Particularly in the case of Laura Johnson, discussed below, a temporary purpose was served: Johnson was used as a discursive device to oppose suggestions that the riots were a product of social deprivation. But these stories actually complicate and contradict later developments in other stories when the government targeted housing benefits in order to punish some rioters in addition to their legal convictions. Despite the contradictions across these stories and events, the ideological consistency that these discourses serve operates beyond the contradictory foreground in a longitudinal context that functions beyond their immediate production and purpose. Hence the stories covered below, within the broader discursive landscape that I cover in this chapter, can be interpreted through this understanding of paradoxical persuasion. I argue that the sick society metaphor became an ideological tool to mythologise the riots and particular social groups who would subsequently need to be cured by Conservative social policy. The examples below show how 'ideological consistencies operating beyond the foreground and immediacy of individual texts can override the appearance of discursive contradiction across longitudinal contexts' (Kelsey 2015b: 243).

An Unlikely Mob and the Case of Laura Johnson

The *Daily Telegraph*'s front page on 11 August invoked Cameron's phrase in response to the riots, with the headline 'Our sick society', which was

accompanied by the following: 'As Cameron condemns riots, suspected looters in court include a boy of 11, a grammar school girl, and a teaching
assistant' (Gilligan 2011: 1). Another *Telegraph* headline on the same day,
said: 'GIRL WHO HAS IT ALL IS ACCUSED OF THEFT', and provided
a detailed account of Laura Johnson: 'Laura Johnson appears as far removed
as possible from the lawless "underclass" said to have been blighting Britain's
streets' (Whitehead and Watt 2011: 3). In Gilligan's article he also wrote,
'They were, some told us, the alienated poor, those without hope, lashing out
in rage and despair. But as the accused London rioters started appearing in
court they included university students, a rich businessman's daughter and
a boy of 11' (2011: 1–2). *The Sun*'s front page on 11 August also listed the
occupations of some of the accused: 'Lifeguard, postman, hairdresser, teacher,
millionaire's daughter, chef and schoolboy, 11' followed by a story across
pages 4 and 5, headlined 'MANSION GATES TO MAGISTRATES' (Nash
et al. 2011: 4–5). A heading across the top of the page also said: 'Riot courts
meet an unlikely mob'. Before covering the various identities of the accused
and their occupations the article focused on Laura Johnson:

> A teenage girl hauled into court for allegedly being part of a mob of 200
> looters is the privileged daughter of millionaire parents. Laura Johnson, 19 –
> one of dozens to appear in court yesterday – is said to have been arrested
> behind the wheel of a car filled with stolen electrical goods, cigarettes and
> alcohol worth over £6,000. . . . Privately-educated Johnson has two broth-
> ers. Neighbour David Turner said: 'They are a nice, respectable family.
> They never caused any problems.' (Nash et al. 2011: 4–5)

It is significant that this featured a background source expressing such surprise, describing the Johnsons as a 'nice, respectable family'. The concept of
feral teenagers or family background is implicitly excluded from the Johnson
family profile, unlike those of other rioters that fit the more predictable
stereotype of a 'sick society'. But this was a subtle exception to the rule with
most responses making an example of Johnson. For example, the front page
of the *Daily Mail* on 12 August featured a picture of Laura Johnson, next to
the main story and headline stating: 'YOU'RE A DISGRACE TO YOUR
COUNTRY' (Daily Mail 2011c: 1). Page 7 then featured a story about
Johnson: 'A STAR PUPIL FROM £1M HOME. HOW DID SHE END
UP IN THE DOCK?' (Bracchi 2011). This article was primarily focused
on the disbelief that someone from such a background had got involved in
looting:

> Whatever the reasons for Laura' ignominious predicament, they appear to
> have nothing to do with alienation or despair; not that this is any excuse

for the shameful events that have scarred the country this week. Indeed, it would be difficult to imagine a young woman with a brighter future; a future which has now been jeopardised; perhaps irrevocably so. (Bracchi 2011: 7)

As we can see, Johnson and the 'unlikely mob' were used to counter arguments blaming austerity and social deprivation. But as I will show, this contradicted other discourses in the same newspapers that blamed the welfare state for creating a sick society and 'something-for-nothing-culture'.

Punishing the Poor through Conservative Social Policy

The complexities and inconsistencies of discursive elements considered thus far should remain in mind when considering the legislative responses (and discursive support) that developed for Conservative measures on welfare and judicial punishments over the days concerned. The discourses considered in this section demonstrate the contradictory mechanisms that I mentioned earlier. Responses that sought to deal with (or punish) rioters and cure a sick society reverted from the discursive positions covered in the previous section; subsequently contradicting previous constructions of a moral underclass that transcended the social spectrum. The *Daily Mail*'s own opinion piece said: 'Indeed, if anything, it was Labour's nurturing of a benefits culture, in which youngsters believe there is no need to work to have a comfortable lifestyle, which sowed the seeds of the riots – not any "Coalition cuts"' (Daily Mail 2011a: 12). Whilst there is a distinct effort to suppress the blame aimed at austerity and deprivation, a comment like this brings political responsibility back into play; it argues that government policy is significant and that the riots could be linked to issues of social welfare, but only in support of a Conservative agenda. Similarly, the *Daily Mail*'s comment piece on 11 August praised Cameron's response and recognition of a 'sick society' whilst defining what this society consisted of:

> Meanwhile, the doling out of ever more benefits to the jobless has instilled a something-for-nothing entitlement culture which culminated in children as young as 11 this week looting shops. David Cameron, in a robust performance yesterday, finally indicated that he understands the crisis facing Britain, parts of which he correctly identified as being 'sick', rife with family breakdown and in need of urgent social repair. The bitter irony, after the mayhem of the past few days, is that if he were to boldly seize the opportunity to fix Britain's broken welfare state, law and order system, immigration controls and parlous family structures, he would find an electorate devastated by what it has witnessed fully behind him. (Daily Mail 2011b: 14)

Delivered within the context of unemployment and welfare, these references to a 'something-for-nothing entitlement culture' and 'family breakdown' demonstrate that cases like Laura Johnson were only mentioned as exceptions to the rule, or to serve a temporary purpose. Also, and in line with conventional Conservative ideals, the interdiscursive mechanisms above bound together right-wing perspectives on welfare, justice, immigration and family values. As the following examples show, the *depoliticised actions* of rioters were eventually redefined as a *politicised problem*; a problem responsible for a sick society, to be "cured" by Conservative policy.

Two articles in *The Sun* on 11 August – either side of the 'MANSION GATES TO MAGISTRATES' article earlier – featured a link between the riots and welfare culture through Cameron's response. Their positioning and layout is significant since they provide contradictions either side of an article that constructs a moral underclass transcending the social spectrum. Headlined 'PM vow: I will cure sick UK, one article said: 'In his emergency statement to the Commons today Mr Cameron will say we must restore discipline and end the something-for-nothing culture' (Wilson 2011: 4). Another article on the same two-page spread, headlined 'New law will evict riot thugs', said: 'Rioters and looters will be booted out of their council homes, the Government said yesterday. Housing minister Grant Shapps plans to extend powers to evict "neighbours from hell" to include riot yobs' (The Sun 2011a: 5). The issue of social welfare recurred in *The Sun*'s 12 August comment piece. Under the headline 'STOP BENEFITS', it projected a tenuous construction of public consensus on the issue of suspending benefits for rioters: 'MORE than 100,000 people last night demanded a Commons debate on axing benefits for convicted rioters. The No10 website crashed as angry Brits tried to sign an e-petition calling for tough sanctions' (The Sun 2011b: 9).

A *Telegraph* article on 11 August echoed Cameron's response on welfare policy, implying that he needed to convince the public that his response would be hard enough. Headlined 'WE WILL MAKE RIOTERS SUFFER, SAY MPs', it explained: 'David Cameron will announce a range of measures today aimed at convincing the public that rioters will face serious jail sentences and the loss of council homes and benefits' (Kirkup and Porter 2011: 4). To 'convince the public' that these measures would be carried out presupposed that there was a public consensus calling for them already. The discursive mechanisms that sought to condone a Conservative review of social welfare policy through legislative punishments relied on this juxtaposition of a moral public consensus against a dishonourable, immoral sick society. Despite the social complexities that I found across some vast, discursive ground in the full analysis (Kelsey 2015b), right-wing discourses still blamed

and punished those that, in other cases, it claimed were not centrally responsible for the riots. Despite these discursive contradictions, paradoxically persuasive mechanisms maintain an ideological consistency through support for
the socio-economic and 'moral' agenda of Conservative approaches to social
welfare and penal policy.

Conclusion

Tragic events, moral storytelling and recurring themes of cultural mythology
stimulate unpredictable discursive formations and developments. In the first
case we saw yet another example of how the myth of the Blitz can recur and
be comfortably recontextualised through the metaphorical dialogic of news
discourse. Images and language can intertextually trigger dialogical connections that are, much like the myth of the Blitz, shared collectively across
multiple generations of readers, journalists and politicians. They have become
increasingly engrained in culture, despite the cries of moral decay and a loss
of Churchillian values. During the riots, Blitz mythology became a stimulant
for moral storytelling that had other discursive implications beyond a simple
story of destruction and disorder. This became an event in which questions
around identity, values, morals, class, race and culture were raised – many of
which are beyond the scope of this analysis. The longing of nostalgia through
which we often mythologise and idealise previous generations relies on the
cultural perception and anxiety that we will lose our way if we do not hang
on to the traditions and values of the past. So many of us are caught up in
the discursive practices of national narration and the ritualistic habits that
occur through cultural mythologies. The connections we immediately draw
between synchronic events and diachronic points of reference demonstrate
our tendency to continue reusing and constructing the building blocks of
national narration through subtle recontextualisations and reinterpretations
of who we are as a society. National crises are often a time when such phenomena occur. But what is interesting about 'social sickness' as a metaphor is
that it does not attempt to naturalise a problem or mythologise a sick society
as an inevitably dangerous social group either. Much the opposite in fact.
For the right-wing press and Conservative rhetoric, social sickness is often
seen as a symptom of leftist ideology of which people can be cured. What is
constructed as an inevitability is the negative impact of leftist ideology that
supposedly encourages a culture of self-entitlement rather than a 'traditional'
ethos of hard work and respect. The "natural" characteristics and moral superiority of British identity and wartime spirit are regarded as the hereditary,
inbuilt cultural qualities of those who are not suffering from a sickness caused
by a welfare state that is constructed more as a sign of privilege than poverty.
As we have seen, discursive contradictions are not a problem for newspapers

with an agenda. The paradoxically persuasive nature of discourse means ideology is the binding mechanism of consistency, which can comfortably override inconsistencies in the visible foregrounds of moral storytelling.

Note

1. I do not make any quantitative claims about press coverage or argue that these articles are representative of any 'dominant discourse', but I do focus on significant discursive trends and traits that recurred throughout the press and other mainstream media coverage of the riots.

References

Angel, H. (2012), 'Governmental responses to the riots', *Criminal Justice Matters*, 87 (1), pp. 24–5.

Ball, R. and J. Drury (2012), 'Representing the riots: The (mis)use of statistics to sustain ideological explanation', *Radical Statistics*, 106, pp. 4–21.

Barthes, R. (1993), *Mythologies*, London: Vintage.

Benyon, J. (2012), 'England's urban disorder: The 2011 riots', *Political Insight*, 3 (1), pp. 12–20.

Bracchi, P. (2011), 'A star pupil from £1m home. How did she end up in the dock?', *Daily Mail*, 12 August, p. 7.

Bridges, L. (2012), 'Four days in August: The UK riots', *Race & Class*, 54 (1), pp. 1–12.

Calder, A. (1991), *The Myth of the Blitz*, London: Pimlico.

Calder, A. (1999), *The People's War*, London: Pimlico.

Campbell, J. (1949), *The Hero with a Thousand Faces*, New York: Pantheon Books.

Cavalcanti, R., C. Goldsmith, L. Measor and P. Squires (2012), 'Riotous connections?', *Criminal Justice Matters*, 87 (1), pp. 34–5.

Cavanagh, A. and A. Dennis (2012), 'Framing the riots', *Capital and Class*, 36, pp. 375–81.

Connelly, M. (2004), *We Can Take It!: Britain and the Memory of the Second World War*, London: Pearson Longman.

Daily Mail (2011a), 'Daily Mail comment: No excuses for this wanton criminality', *Daily Mail*, 9 August, p. 12.

Daily Mail (2011b), 'A broken society that needs a strong leader', *Daily Mail*, 11 August, p. 14.

Daily Mail (2011c), 'You're a disgrace to your country', *Daily Mail*, 12 August, p. 1.

Flanagan, P. (2011), 'Shock and outrage at worst scenes since Blitz', *Daily Express*, 10 August, pp. 4–5.

Fuchs, C. (2012), 'Social media, riots and revolutions', *Capital and Class*, 36, pp. 383–91.

Gilligan, A. (2011), 'Our sick society; as Cameron condemns riots, suspected looters in court include a boy of 11, a grammar school girl, and a teaching assistant: Swift justice for "sick society"', *Daily Telegraph*, 11 August, pp. 1–2.

Gilroy, P. (2004), *Postcolonial Melancholia*, New York: Columbia University Press.

Heartfield, J. (2005), 'Revisiting the Blitz Spirit: Myths about the Second World

War won't help us understand what is happening today', *Spiked*, 12 July, <http://www.spiked-online.com/index.php?/site/article/869/> (last accessed 1 May 2018).

Jefferson, T. (2012), 'Policing the riots: From Bristol and Brixton to Tottenham, via Toxteth, Handsworth, etc', *Criminal Justice Matters*, 87 (1), pp. 8–9.

Kelsey, D. (2015a), *Media, Myth and Terrorism: A Discourse-Mythological Analysis of the 'Blitz Spirit' in British Newspaper Responses to the July 7th Bombings*, Basingstoke: Palgrave Macmillan.

Kelsey, D. (2015b), 'Defining the sick society: Discourses of class and morality in British right-wing newspapers during the 2011 England riots', *Capital & Class*, 39 (2), pp. 243–64.

Kelsey, D. (2016), 'Hero mythology and right-wing populism: A discourse-mythological case study of Nigel Farage in the Mail Online', *Journalism Studies*, 17 (8), pp. 971–88.

Kelsey, D. (2017), *Media and Affective Mythologies: Discourse, Archetypes and Ideology in Contemporary Politics*, London: Palgrave.

Kelsey D. (2018*), Affective Mythology and 'The Notorious' Conor McGregor: Monomyth, Mysticism and Mixed Martial Arts, Martial Arts Studies*, (5), pp. 15–35.

Kirkup, J. and A. Porter (2011), 'We will make rioters suffer, say MPs; Emergency debate', *Daily Telegraph*, 11 August, p. 4.

Lagrange, H. (2012), 'Youth unrest and riots in France and the UK', *Criminal Justice Matters*, 87 (1), pp. 32–3.

Lakoff, G. and M. Johnson (2003), *Metaphors We Live By*, London: Chicago University Press.

Lazzeri, A., V. Soodin and A. Crick (2011), 'Lavendar Hill mop', *The Sun*, 10 August, pp. 8–9.

Lea, J. and S. Hallsworth (2012), 'Understanding the riots', *Criminal Justice Matters*, 87 (1), pp. 30–1.

Levine, J. (2006), *Forgotten Voices of the Blitz and the Battle of Britain*, London: Ebury.

Lule, J. (2001), *Daily News, Eternal Stories: The Mythological Role of Journalism*, New York and London: Guilford Press.

McDermott, N. and W. Jaffrey (2011), '200 rioters caused this mayhem . . . 500 of us are here to clean it up', *Daily Mail*, 10 August, pp. 12–13.

McLaine, I. (1979), *Ministry of Morale: Home Front Morale and the Ministry of Information in World War II*, London: George Allen & Unwin.

Manthorpe R. (2006), 'Spirit of the Brits', *The Guardian*, 1 July, <http://books.guardian.co.uk/departments/history/story/0,,1809895,00.html> (last accessed 1 May 2018).

Milburn, K. (2012), 'The August riots, shock and the prohibition of thought', *Capital and Class*, 36, pp. 401–9.

Nash, E., N. Parker, R. Sabey, A. Peake and N. Syson (2011), 'Lifeguard, postman, hairdresser, teacher, millionaire's daughter, chef and schoolboy, 11', *The Sun*, 11 August, pp. 4–5.

Palmer, S. (2012), '"Dutty Babylon": Policing Black communities and the politics of resistance', *Criminal Justice Matters*, 87 (1), pp. 26–7.

Panayi, P. (1995), 'Immigrants, refugees, the British state and public opinion during World War Two', in P. Kirkham and D. Thoms (eds), *War Culture: Social*

Change and Changing Experience in World War Two, London: Lawrence & Wishart, pp. 201–8.

Ponting, C. (1990), *1940: Myth and Reality*, Reading: Cox & Wyman.

Ponting, C. (1994), *Churchill*, London: Sinclair-Stevenson.

Reicher, S. and C. Stott (2011), 'Mad mobs and Englishmen? Myths and realities of the 2011 riots', *The Guardian*, 18 November, <http://www.guardian.co.uk/science/2011/nov/18/mad-mobs-englishmen-2011-riots> (last accessed 7 September 2012).

Taylor, P. (2012), 'The Just Do It riots: A critical interpretation of the media's violence', *Capital and Class*, 36, pp. 393–9.

The Sun (2011a), 'New law will evict riot thugs', *The Sun*, 11 August, p. 5.

The Sun (2011b), 'Stop benefits', *The Sun*, 12 August, p. 9.

Thoms, D. (1995), 'The Blitz, civilian morale and regionalism, 1940–1942', in P. Kirkham and D. Thoms (eds), *War Culture: Social Change and Changing Experience in World War Two*, London: Lawrence & Wishart, pp. 3–12.

Tulloch, J. (2006), *One Day in July: Experiencing 7/7*, London: Little, Brown.

Waddington, D. (2012), 'The law of moments: Understanding the flashpoint that ignited the riots', *Criminal Justice Matters*, 87 (1), pp. 6–7.

Waddington, P. A. J. (2012), 'Explaining the riots', *Criminal Justice Matters*, 87 (1), pp. 10–11.

Whitehead, T. and H. Watt (2011), 'Girl who has it all is accused of theft', *Daily Telegraph*, 11 August, p. 3.

Wilkes, D. (2011), 'Torching of two suburbs', *Daily Mail*, 10 August, pp. 6–7.

Wilson, G. (2011), 'PM vow: I will cure sick UK', *The Sun*, 11 August, p. 4.

Younge, G. (2011), 'These riots were political. They were looting, not shoplifting', *The Guardian*, 14 August, <http://www.guardian.co.uk/commentisfree/2011/aug/14/young-british-rioters-political-actions> (last accessed 9 September 2012).

3

Why Do They Protest?: The Discursive Construction of 'Motive' in Relation to the Chilean Student Movement in the National Alternative Press (2011–13)

Carolina Pérez-Arredondo

Introduction

It is impossible to ignore the role of student activism when we talk about discourses of social disorder. Protests such as the ones in May 1968 (France) or the iconic images from the Tiananmen Square protests in 1989 have left a mark in the countries in which they occurred in the shape of political, economic and social changes. It would be wrong to assume that this is a past phenomenon. Over the last few years, there have been several protests in which students are the common denominator, such as the 2010 protests in London against the rise of tuition fees, the protests led by Mexican students in 2012 against the then presidential candidate Enrique Peña Nieto (#YoSoy132), or the recent protests in South Africa against the increase in tuition fees. In this chapter, however, I want to focus on the Chilean student movement and the protests that sparked off in 2011, which resulted in a seven-month strike widely supported by civilians, the sacking of three Ministers of Education, and the later victory of four former student leaders (2011–12) in the parliamentary election held in 2013.

The Chilean student movement has always been a catalyst for social and political change in the country. In the early twentieth century, it played an essential role in the secularisation of education as well as in reforms to address social and class inequality. Most notably, its actions were crucial in the overthrow of both Carlos Ibáñez del Campo's (1931) and Augusto Pinochet's (1973–90) dictatorships. The movement's strong alliance with the Trade Union Movement as well as its influential role in the country have resulted in an antagonistic relationship with the media, in particular the mainstream press, which has been dominated by a politically and economically well-established duopoly ever since Pinochet's dictatorship (Monckeberg 2009).

The duopoly, namely the Edwards and Copesa groups, controls the main (four) newspapers in the country in terms of both readership and the acquisition of private and public funding (Monckeberg 2009; see also Sunkel and Geoffroy 2001). Their consolidation as the mainstream press was enhanced by the lack of implementation of policies that were intended to ensure fair competition and funding of the media once democracy returned, due to an assumption that the market would work as a fair regulator (Monckeberg 2009). This monopolisation of media outlets and the lack of private funding opportunities for circulation have forced newly emerging presses to retreat to digital platforms for survival, being referred to disparagingly as *alternative* media.

The common feature of these emerging media (in Chile and Latin America) is their sympathy towards groups that are systematically marginalised and criminalised by the political and economic powerholders (Lugo-Ocando 2008; Harlow and Harp 2013). It follows then that this kind of media plays a crucial role in the development and maintenance of social movements as it gives them access to the public sphere, resisting the dominant groups belonging to the status quo (Kenix 2011). Considering the current scenario in the country, which is far from being only applicable to the Chilean context, it is important to examine the alternative press more carefully, however small it is, in order to identify the kind of resistance to hegemonic discourse it offers. Within this resistance, representation of motive plays a central role: its inclusion and/ or exclusion can both help vilify a specific social movement as in the case of mainstream media as well as position and support it as a legitimate social cause.

Consequently, in this chapter I explore the different strategies used to construct and attribute motives[1] to the Chilean student movement demonstrators in the alternative press from 2011 to 2013. How motive is represented and distributed among the social actors involved is crucial in the identification of the distribution of power: whose actions are represented as appropriate (legitimate) or whose actions are presented as inappropriate (purposeless). As such, I additionally explore whether these attributions of motive serve as a strategy to legitimise the role of young students, as they tend to be excluded from hegemonic discourses (Cárdenas 2012) or criminalised in the established media (Pérez 2012, 2016).

Theoretical Background

A Grammar of Purpose

The conceptualisation of motive is discursively constructed in texts to explain human behaviour and social practices in action (van Leeuwen 2007, 2008).

In this regard, van Leeuwen's work on the representation of social actors led him towards the grammatical construction of purpose and legitimation. Van Leeuwen states that the analysis of purpose is fundamental in the identification of how power is distributed in 'concrete social practices' as well as in society (2008: 135). He identifies three main components in these constructions as seen below:

'A demonstrator said she was marching$^{PURPOSEFUL\ ACTION}$ for$^{PURPOSE\ LINK}$ her son's education^{PURPOSE} who is in high school.' (EC_2011_194_19Oct.txt)

The first element is the *purpose*, which explains the reasoning behind the *purposeful action* (action needed to achieve the *purpose*). These two elements must be linked through a *purpose link* that explains the relation between these two elements (van Leeuwen 2008: 126). This purpose link can be explicit or implicit and can be realised by the use of (explanatory) conjunctions, temporal adverbials, logical processes, finite and non-finite clauses or nominalisation, and can even be disguised as circumstances.

Van Leeuwen further distinguishes three general types of purpose constructions. The first is *goal-oriented constructions*, which focus on constructing the actor(s) as purposeful being(s), having particular intentions, motives, goals, and so on. A way of understanding this category is through the following formulaic structure: 'I do x in order to do (or be, or have) y' (van Leeuwen 2008: 127). I further develop this category when presenting the adapted framework proposed in this research for the analysis of news reports. *Means-oriented constructions*, on the other hand, objectify the action, constructing the purpose as in the action itself. The formula to understand this category can be summarised as 'I achieve doing (or being, or having) y by x-ing' or as 'x-ing serves to achieve being (or doing, or having) y', depending on whether agency is explicit or not (van Leeuwen 2008: 128). Finally, *effect-oriented purpose constructions* highlight the outcome(s) of action, rendering the agent as not fully purposeful. As a result, this category can be understood in terms of the results of the purposeful construction (as enabling actions) or its effects (as 'initiator of the purpose action') (van Leeuwen 2008: 130). Although all these categories can be further differentiated into different sub-categories, van Leeuwen uses the following examples to generally distinguish these categories:

[1] Mothers take their tots to the clinic to check their health [*goal-oriented*].
[2] Mothers check their babies' health by taking them to the clinic [*means-oriented*].
[3] Mothers take their babies to the clinic, so the doctors can check their health [*effect-oriented*]. (Van Leeuwen 2008: 130)

Van Leeuwen is conscious that these categories and realisations of purpose might change depending on the data and genre analysed. An exploratory analysis of my data confirmed the need to expand on how these categories are realised, mainly because of how actions are reported in the news genre.

The reporting of events, especially in news reports, includes more than actions and agents: it also includes information on how, when and where the event took place. The ways accounts have been acknowledged in the literature are widely varied and, needless to say, highly dependent on the area in which they are studied (cf. Buttny and Morris 2001 or Buttny 2008). For the purposes of this study, it is enough to clarify two main distinctions in the study of accountability, that is, accounts *for* actions and accounts *of* actions. While the first refers to the verbal response to an action which might have been regarded as (socially) problematic by others, or the agent itself (such as remedial responses or apologies), the second corresponds to an explanation focusing on the event and the influence that relationships, personal circumstances and so on might have had on the action being described (such as storytelling or narrative episodes (Buttny 2008)). Regardless of the approach to the study of accounts, these distinctions clearly have an explanatory component that cannot be overlooked: they supplement the *why* element of purpose constructions, adding an evaluative *how* element as well.

Throughout this research, accounts will be approached as narrative episodes, that is, accounts *of* actions. This decision is based on the nature of the genre of news reports, which revolves around the idea of replying to an implicit *why* question of the audience when accounting for the events being reported. The evaluative component of *how* this is reported is brought to the fore by the inclusion or exclusion of details, social actors, events, and so on that might conflict with the interests of the editorial board. This can shed some light on the way we interpret human interaction and attribute accountability in terms of motives, and how these are sometimes used to (de)legitimise particular social practices (Martin Rojo and van Dijk 1997).

Why a Corpus-Assisted Approach Was Used

The combination of corpus methods and critical discourse analysis approaches has been proven fruitful in different fields. The combination seems to address the most common criticisms made of critical discourse studies, namely, those of cherry-picking texts and cases to prove the author's beliefs and mistakenly claiming representativeness (Baker et al. 2008). In order to account for possible bias and explore larger amounts of data, I use some corpus methods, in particular concordance lines and keywords, to facilitate the identification of text patterns that construe motive.

A concordance line is 'a list of all the occurrences of a particular search term in a corpus, presented with the context that they occur in' (Baker 2006: 71), which usually means with some words to its right and left, the number of which can be set precisely. Its layout allows the researcher to sort the results at will while also identifying the most salient features associated with the term being analysed. While their analysis enhances the identification of underlying discourses and/or topoi used in legitimising representations, in this study these are only used to sample the corpus in order to examine the data more closely.

Simply put, keywords are words which are unusually frequent in a particular corpus when compared with another one. As such, their identification facilitates the comparison and contrast of two corpora (i.e. the corpus of Chilean alternative press articles and a similarly composed corpus from the established press) in relation to what the most salient topics are in them. In this study, these topics can shed light on the reasons why the student movement (still) protests. To facilitate the analysis of these topics, I categorised them semantically by using the USAS system (Archer et al. 2002) provided by the University Centre for Computer Corpus Research on Language (UCREL, Lancaster University) as a reference point.

Data and Methods

The data consists of 1,526 articles from three of the most popular digital alternative newspapers, *El Mostrador* (EMo), the *Clinic* (TC) and *El Ciudadano* (EC). These were collected online, based on a list of key words that emerged from a previous pilot study.[2] The results were downloaded to an Excel file for manual revision, to ensure the articles actually referred to the Chilean student movement, and finally saved in the form of UTF-8 text files. In all, the articles accounted for 872,743 words approximately.

The data was analysed qualitatively in its original language in the light of van Leeuwen's purpose framework. This was carried out by selecting a random sample of Spanish infinitives (verbs ending in *ar, *er and *ir) and gerunds (*ndo) as they were found to be the most prolific and consistent way of constructing motive according to the previous pilot study. This search generated 32,536 hits. I generated a much reduced sample by automatically selecting one hit in every 20, which amounted to 1,253 alphabetically sorted occurrences in total. Of these, only 387 consisted of infinitives and/or gerunds used to convey purpose.[3]

The analysis of this sample resulted in the identification of 10 main motives for the student movement to protest. In order to test its representativeness, I carried out a keyword analysis of the entire corpus so as to identify the most salient topics addressed and check whether there was a correlation between the results obtained qualitatively and the ones obtained in a slightly more quantitative analysis. The reference corpus used was a similarly built corpus comprising four of the most widely read established newspapers in Chile, which totalled 560,577 words approximately. From the results, I selected only the first 100 nouns (up to a p value of 0.0001) and categorised them semantically, following the criteria suggested by UCREL.

The examples in the next section correspond to the closest English translations of the original. Untranslatable words or terms are represented in **BOLD CAPITAL LETTERS** and explained in a glossary in the appendix at the end of the chapter. Similarly, the infinitives and gerunds analysed are included in **bold** while representations of motive are <u>thickly underlined</u>.

Why Do They Protest?

The qualitative analysis revealed that there were 238 instances that corresponded to references to the students' motives to protest. These were classified into 10 main motives described in Table 3.1.

The fight for *education* is clearly the main motivation attributed to the students' protests, comprising 44.1 per cent of all the instances. This fight,

Table 3.1 Classification of the students' motives to protest according to the alternative press

Motive	Freq	Example
For education	105	University students call to **march** this Thursday in <u>defence of public higher education</u>. (EC_2011_14_27April.txt)
To gather/ evidence popular support	28	Titelman [student leader] pointed out to reporters that the "bike-thon" is part of a group of ideas that university students want to bring in "in order to **attract** <u>everyone, the young and the old and families to protest joyfully with us</u>". (EC_2012_66_22August.txt)
For democratic rights	26	University and secondary students, along with various social organizations, participated this Saturday in a "pots-and-pans-banging" protest in Plaza Italia to **commemorate** <u>"Citizens' Awakening Day"</u>. (TC_2012_87_04August.txt)
Against neoliberalism	25	The main demand **is** still on the table, which is <u>the establishment of public, free and quality education through a reform</u> to the system imposed in 1981 by Augusto Pinochet's dictatorship, against which the young started to protest in 2011. (TC_2013_40_08May.txt)

Motive	Freq	Example
To reach consensus	23	On the other hand, **FEMES** spokesman announced that next Saturday they are holding a new national assembly, this time in Valparaiso, to decide the steps to **follow**. (2011_TC_31_19June.txt)
Against repression	15	The young woman who had been attacked called for all secondary students and all of those who have been hurt by the police force to **report** it "because this cannot keep happening, there are too many injustices taking place and they have not ceased". (EC_2013_77_21Nov.txt)
For social causes	6	This activity was framed within the initiatives of this left-wing student collective, which was set up in the middle of April, and regularly attracts around 70 students from San Ignacio del Bosque School who intend to **contribute** from their "sector" to the "social struggles" taking place nowadays. (EC_2011_228_17Nov.txt)
For benefits	5	A flashback to the beginning of 2011. That was what happened to the students who occupied the Junaeb facilities (Centre for School Help and Scholarships) in Santiago yesterday, **protesting** against for problems in the delivery of scholarships and loans two years and three weeks after. (TC_2013_41_08May.txt)
For transparency	3	"We don't want to get funding from private business nor from **APORTES RESERVADOS**, so that there is no room for doubt that there will be no conflict of interests in this campaign, that we are going to **act** independently, but [we are going to act] with determination for the trust the neighbours are entrusting us with" pointed out Jackson. (2013_EMo_113_16August.txt)
For justice	2	The plaintiffs asked the Chilean authorities to authorize a visit of **CIDH** to show the special situation of the children in the context of the demonstrations, to interview with NGO's and civil society, and to **provide** internal regulations to abide to the Latin-American Convention, among other aspects. (2011_EMo_103_28Oct.txt)

however, is specifically oriented to the achievement of definite features of education that are transversal to most of the other motives identified. The appeal to massive and transversal support from the Chilean people, their fight for justice, transparency and their democratic right to protest, as well as their fight for and against neoliberalism and repression are discursive triggers that frame their fight as righteous and, above all, justified.

In the following sections I will address only the motives that are more frequent (25≥), owing to space constraints. In these sections, the results of the (semantic) keyword analysis will be embedded and developed in the discussion of the students' motives in order to provide a more holistic description of the main findings.

For Education

Education is paramount when reporting on the student movement in the alternative press. It is not only the main motivation for students to protest, according to the corpus sample, but it also coincidentally positions itself as the 8th most frequent relevant keyword (see Table 3.2).

The table reveals two main features of this fight for education. First, it is directly linked to different educational institutions (e.g. *university*) and actors (e.g. *students, secondary* [students]) that pursue this goal. This is not as obvious as it might seem: as the protest paradigm suggests, social protest tends to be criminalised by the media (Shoemaker 1984). As such, the use of terms such as '(hooded) vandals', 'hoodies' or 'hooligans' is much more prolific in the mainstream press than identifying demonstrators as actual students as emerges here (Pérez 2016). This clear identification of social actors categorised in terms of their educational background seems to frame the narrative used to report on the students' actions. Second, education is qualified primarily as *free*. Along with '*No profit education*', '*free, quality* and *public*[4] *education*' became one of the most popular soundbites of the student movement and, as such, were reported on accordingly. Consider the following extracts taken from the sample:

(1) In Santiago's main square, students replicated the animated TV series Dragon Ball Z in which the character Goku asks to make a genkidama (a giant ball of energy) to **save** education, in a protest for an improvement of public education. (2011_TC_66_19July.txt)

Table 3.2 First 10 keywords of the alternative press

Rank	FQ	Keyness	Keyword	Rank	FQ	Keyness	Keyword
1	6119	445.621	students	6	760	104.203	social
2	2407	241.262	university	7	547	103.416	workers
3	2283	179.046	Chile	8	4543	100.372	education
4	288	165.972	**MAPUCHE**	9	455	98.034	free
5	217	133.137	dictatorship	10	1287	94.102	secondary [students]

(2) "I already participated in many demonstrations. I am here [protesting/marching] to **fight** for the rights of Chilean education and achieve the free and quality education we all need." [Christopher, Manuel Barros Borgoño High School]. (EC_2012_42_28June.txt)

(3) The [university student] leader [Camila Vallejo] pointed out that "the people clamour for the regulation of market education, we want to **end** the embezzlement in State universities and [education] for profit and to move forward towards free [education], because education is a right and not a commodity." (EC_2011_34_16June.txt)

These three extracts point to the qualities education must have according to the student movement: it must be public and thus not regulated by the market ((1)–(3)) as well as being free and of quality ((2)). In the first two extracts, *education* is constructed as a right that needs to be saved and, while the threatening actor is excluded, the *heroes* are clearly identified. The reporting of the students' motives tends to be framed in a narrative of moral values in which students are positively portrayed whereas the opponents to their cause (the protection of a basic constitutional right) are negatively represented. This negative other-representation is much clearer in (3), in which the current socio-political and economic system is targeted as being responsible for the current state of education. The student leader positions the movement as part of what *the people* want, that is, to regard education as a right. Two implications can be drawn from (3): educational institutions are not (properly) regulated and thus money is being embezzled; and the people demand a more active role from the State in the educational sector. These demands become all the more relevant when we consider that these protests erupted during the time of the first right-wing government to get back into power after the end of the dictatorship.

These extracts, as well as most of the examples in this category, represent students as purposeful actors, whose actions are rationalised through their determination to achieve a greater common good: the vindication of *free*, *quality* and *public education* as a constitutional right. The implications of this fight for education are numerous and, as briefly mentioned already, intimately related to the other motives to be discussed. *Education* is understood as an endangered social and constitutional right (left-wing ideology) that needs to be saved from its marketisation (right-wing ideology). Their ultimate purpose (*free*, *quality* and *public education*) is thus legitimised by appealing to moral values and left-wing discourses: from the students' point of view, the endangered state and marketisation of education are a product of the educational model imposed during the dictatorship and thus illegitimate (see 'To Gather/ Evidence Popular Support' and 'Against Neoliberalism (Status Quo)' below).

To Gather/Evidence Popular Support

The social emphasis on both the composition of the student movement and the scope of its demands cannot be missed. In this sense, the collectivisation of actors is used to highlight the different social areas involved in the students' fight for education rather than a backgrounding strategy. This collectivisation is also reflected in the keyword analysis (see Table 3.3).

Except for *dictatorship* (explored in 'Against Neoliberalism (Status Quo)' below) and *repression*, the remaining words enhance the social nature of the student movement and their motives. These motives are framed as affecting important parts of society: *workers, union, families, citizenry, (indigenous) people, communities* as well as different organisations (e.g. **FEMAE**; (Con) federation of students; **ACES**). Therefore it is within their best interests to convey the breadth of this transversal support to the authorities in order to effect changes in the educational system:

(4) Along the route [Heading: around 500 thousand <u>people reaffirm their commitment to education in the streets of Chile</u>], secondary students, university students and educational workers were seen, but also settlers, health workers, grandparents and children, chanting slogans and **showing** banners. (EC_2011_99_09August.txt)

(5) According to Geisho Jiménez, one of the (female) demonstrators [who yelled at the Chilean presidential committee in Australia] "We are all very aware of what is going on in Chile (. . .) We only want to **show** <u>support for the Chilean people</u>. Here we are not profit [Spanish: *no somos lucro*], we don't want to be in any political party, <u>we are for free [liberty] education in Chile, and for something else, because the Chilean police has acted violently towards the</u> **MAPUCHE**". (TC_2012_168_10Sept.txt)

The listing in (4) reflects the scope of support for reform to the educational system. The report emphasises that it is not only actors from the educational sector involved in the protests but also workers from the health sector as

Table 3.3 Semantic categorisation of keywords in relation to 'social actions, states and processes'

Social actions, states and processes	dictatorship; social; workers; free; right(s); organization(s); **FEMAE**; Assembly; repression; citizen; (Con)federation; society; fight(s); people(s); indigenous; settlers; **UDM**; movement; families; **ACES**; union; intercultural; humans; coordination; demand(s); sexual; events; teachers; citizenship

well as whole families (from grandparents to children). The more varied participation is, the more legitimate it is as different groups make up an alleged majority. In (5), on the other hand, there is a specific reference to a particular indigenous group (the **MAPUCHE**) and the kind of repression they are exposed to. The protest in Australia, originally to show solidarity with the students' cause, also aims at including the precarious situation of the **MAPUCHE** who are involved in an ongoing conflict with the government over the usurpation of their ancestral lands. As a result, there tends to be both invisibilisation and/or criminalisation in the mainstream media of this conflict (van Dijk 2005). Therefore, the inclusion of the **MAPUCHE**'s cause is not coincidental as it reflects a specific political stance from the alternative press as well as the student movement. Finally, these two extracts provide an excellent example of how motive constructions can work in the news genre. Deixis, in particular anaphoric references, are key features in identifying either the motive (4) or the purposeful action (5).

The reporting of the breadth of their support seems to achieve two main purposes in the alternative press. On the one hand, it contrasts with the crime narrative usually associated with social protests: grandparents and children are not the expected kind of actors associated with going on a demonstration. The tone of the report resembles that of a carnival, in which participants take to the streets to have fun. On the other hand, it includes other social causes such as the violence against the **MAPUCHE** so as to reflect the variety of social problems the student movement relates to. From the students' point of view, the more support they get from different sectors, the more pressure they can exercise on the authorities as representatives of a majority.

For Democratic Rights

Reports on the student movement in the alternative press position students as actors exercising their democratic rights, varying from their right to protest to their right to vote, and democracy itself (see Table 3.4).

Students are represented as politically empowered actors who know their way around the political vernacular. More importantly, they are represented

Table 3.4 Keywords from the 'social actions, states and processes' (S) semantic category

Rank	FQ	Keyness	Keyword	Rank	FQ	Keyness	Keyword
14	486	86.581	rights	16	1075	84.157	demands
73	273	27.798	democracy	84	591	24.002	right

as legitimate actors whose actions have forged a path towards a more democratic society:

> (6) Secondly, the learning and growth of the social movements in the last decade, steered by an active, critical and glowing [Spanish: *lozana*] youth, that is writing the path of the post-dictatorship by **raising** their voice for <u>the fight of the rights of the people</u>. (2011_TC_03_24 May.txt)

In this example, the students' actions are represented in terms of a metaphor. Metaphors can be briefly defined 'as thinking of one thing (A) as though it were another thing (B)' (Goatly 2007: 11). In (6), the purpose of the student movement's actions is represented in terms of a path towards change, as moving forward. Therefore, the metaphor can be represented as PURPOSE is DIRECTION (Goatly 2007). The metaphor pre-modifies the actual motive construction presented later. This in itself is a revealing finding in terms of how metaphors play an important role in both the news genre and the conveying of purpose. In this particular example, the effect of the metaphor is further highlighted by the adjectival phrase used to describe this collective youth (*glowing*, for instance, is usually associated with the narrative genre). Their agency is clear and glorified, thus positively legitimised.

The students' democratic rights also include the exercise of their rights such as the right to vote, either at a national level (7) or at a student level (8):

> (7) Vanesa Venegas, president of the Students Council of Carmela Carvajal High School, confirmed that today the high school withdrew their plan to occupy their facilities for the presidential and parliamentary elections and thus **continuing** <u>with a call for a conscious vote</u>. "Clearly in this decision is [the expectation people] mark Constituent Assembly"[5] specified Venegas. (EC_2013_72_13Nov.txt)
>
> (8) The objective of this meeting, according to Daniela López, president of the Students Federation of Universidad Central (Feucen), is <u>to discuss the democratization and funding; to form work teams; to **elect** spokespeople that can represent them, and to build the first organization to gather the specific needs of private universities in order to abide to national level requirements</u>. "This document goes in line with the one made by the CONFECH (Chilean Confederation of Students), but also it develops it. We are the ones most affected by the neoliberal model, indebting ourselves with loans" explained López. (EC_2011_207_02Nov.txt)

In (7), a secondary student leader is informing the press of the objectives of their actions in relation to the upcoming city hall elections. She represents the student collective as purpose-oriented towards a 'conscious vote' (i.e. subscribing to the campaign for a Constituent Assembly). Their actions are not only rationalised in this report but also related to bigger, more pressing social affairs the students identify themselves, such as the need for a new Constitution (see 'Against Neoliberalism (Status Quo)' below). Similarly, (8) reports the exercise of the students' right to hold elections in their educational institutions, highlighting their democratic drive. In this, a meeting is to be held in a particular university in order to achieve four main purposes, all of which involve debating ideas and reaching agreements democratically among the student community. The list of the objectives of the meeting shows both how organisation works within the student collective as well as how determined the students' motives are: these actions are oriented towards effecting change in the 'neoliberal model' that affects them deeply.

The exercise of their rights takes various forms in the reporting of the student movement. Regardless of its form, however, the students and their actions are always rationalised in terms of their purpose(s) and/or the effect(s) they try to make. More importantly, due to its many forms, they tend to co-occur with other motives such as the students' fight against neoliberalism, which is detailed below.

Against Neoliberalism (Status Quo)

So far, I have discussed three main motivations found in the qualitative analysis of the sample, which have also been supported by the analysis of keywords: students protest for (free, public and quality) education, to show transversal support, and for their democratic rights. What do they all have in common? All these motives point to an intrinsic problem with how things work in the country: education needs to be saved, the students need to show the breadth of their support in order to be heard by the authorities, and they need to demand their legitimate right to protest. From the perspective of the alternative press as well as the students' perspective, this problem stems from the still strong vestiges of Augusto Pinochet's dictatorship; see the keywords in Table 3.5, for example.

All the keywords in Table 3.5 make reference to the features students try to challenge and ultimately change: the eradication of the social reforms consolidated in the Constitution of 1981. The inclusion of Pinochet and his dictatorship ideologically frames the students' motives as righteous, democratic and thus legitimate: from their point of view, any so-called democratic society should abide by what the majority demands. The other keywords (*neoliberal, model, market* and *business*) do nothing but enhance this delegitimisation by pointing out the reasons why education and other areas of social welfare are in crisis. In this context, the implementation of a Constituent

Table 3.5 Keywords from the 'government and public' (G), 'money and commerce in industry' (I), and 'names and grammar' (Z) semantic categories

Rank	FQ	Keyness	Keyword	Rank	FQ	Keyness	Keyword
5	217	133.137	dictatorship (G)	49	127	39.21	Pinochet (Z)
19	329	71.852	model (I)	58	63	33.235	constituent (G)
29	107	60.167	neoliberal (G)	61	155	32.715	market (I)
44	168	43.063	constitution (G)	62	108	32.291	business (I)

Assembly resonates as a viable option to achieve these changes. However, it is the students who position themselves as (the only) actors capable of changing this situation:

(9) But at this point the control of civic order cannot contain the built-up anger. In the streets near Alameda the students improvise fire barricades and block the traffic and chant to the hit of the moment: "And it's gonna **fall**, and it's gonna fall, the education of Pinochet". (EC_2011_90_05August.txt)

The report uses anger to frame the students' protest. However, instead of attributing their actions to *social resentment*, the blocking of traffic and the setting up of fire barricades is explained in terms of their drive to eradicate Pinochet's educational system. The way in which motive is included is also worth noting: it is done through the inclusion of a protest chant. Students and demonstrators alike march to this chant every protest they organise: the core motive of their actions is realised through a song, represented here as direct speech. More importantly, students are once again represented as goal-oriented actors, determined to achieve their objective (eliminate Pinochet's educational system).

Another area that students are deeply concerned about is the electoral system, also imposed during the dictatorship. From the students' point of view, it is allegedly undemocratic (and thus invalid) as it is the people who should be empowered with the possibility of creating a new Constitution:

(10) The secondary student association will define their next actions in order to "**show the discontent towards the electoral system** and **demarcate** that the solution is in the organization and not in the ballot box". (2013_EMo_142_04Nov.txt)

(11) "I do not vote for this system": **ACES** starts a campaign [calling] not to **vote** in the next elections. (TC_2013_152_12August.txt)

There are two main implications that stem from these extracts. First, the negative other-representation of the government and the status quo in general is based on the grounds of its unrepresentativeness and lack of legitimacy. The fact that secondary students believe that social organisation is a better alternative to democratic elections (10) suggests the value they ascribe to *the people* as opposed to the authorities. Second, concrete actions such as boycotting the elections (11) are perfectly valid according to secondary students. For them, collective organisation to undertake other protest actions is not enough: boycotting elections unveils how truly unrepresentative the electoral system is. This boycott became a Twitter hashtag (#YoNoVotoPorEsteSistema) and was incredibly popular along with #YoNoVoto (*I don't vote*). Students are thus represented as goal-oriented actors, determined to achieve very specific goals (e.g. to eliminate profit in education and the criminalisation of the **MAPUCHE**, or to reform the electoral system, etc.). The overall motive of these actions is of course of an ideological nature: the resistance, and ultimate eradication, of the social welfare policies implemented during the dictatorship, in particular those affecting people's access to quality education.

Conclusion

Results suggest that the inclusion of motive is central to the legitimation of the students as well as of their actions. The sample consisted mostly of the students' voice as the protagonist of the reports, in which they explained their motives to the press and/or the authorities. In this, the editorial line of the alternative press perfectly aligned itself to the students' motives, enhancing their positive representation and consequently the negative representation of the status quo. Students are represented as determined, goal-driven actors and, as such, their agency in their actions is explicit and constructed as crucial. In addition, the constant references to an ideal social order served to legitimise their actions: the inclusion of Pinochet's dictatorship, the Constitution, an educational system regulated by the market, and the neoliberal political system (among others) frames the students' actions as legitimate through negatively evaluating the current (allegedly undemocratic) state of the educational and political arena in Chile.

The methodological approach to the data also served to identify how differently motive can be realised in the text. One of the most common ways was through the combination of indirect and direct speech. In this kind of press, direct speech can even refer to multimodal texts such as protest chants (see example (9)). Another important feature was deixis. There were instances in which motive was implicit and only made sense when other parts of the texts were considered (e.g. heading, previous paragraph). In addition, there were instances in which the reports on the students' actions drew from other genres to describe their motives. For example, the use of rhetorical language helped frame the report of the students' actions in a mythopoeic narrative.

Similarly, the use of metaphor both enhanced the students' motive for fighting for their democratic rights and legitimised such a purpose.

Last but not least, the methodological approach to the data (i.e. the combination of qualitative and quantitative methods) proved very fruitful in the identification of motive. It turns out that the motives identified in the qualitative analysis could also be identified in the analysis of keywords, and they proved to be essential in the legitimation of this particular social cause. This suggests that a similar methodological approach could be potentially useful to identify how the motives of other social movements are included (or excluded) and linguistically realised in the press. In this case, the analysis reveals that, in fact, the alternative press does provide a resistance to mainstream media, which has a tendency to abide by the protest paradigm (i.e. to criminalise social protests that challenge the status quo). Its analysis also implies that all the legitimising features of the social movement identified in the keyword analysis are particularly infrequent in the mainstream corpus, which leaves room for more investigation so as to identify how motive is included (if at all) in this kind of press.

Appendix: Glossary of Untranslatable Terms

ACES	Acronym for Asamblea Coordinadora de Estudiantes Secundarios (Coordinating Assembly of Secondary Students).
APORTES RESERVADOS	One of the three ways electoral campaigns are sponsored. The funding is only known by the benefactor and the electoral regulatory service and can amount to a maximum of 1,500UF (£38,751 approx.). Some believe that this reserved funding aims at hiding who sponsors campaigns from the public.
CIDH	Acronym for Centro de Integración y Desarrollo Humano (Center for Integration and Human Development).
CONFECH	Acronym for Confederación de Estudiantes de Chile (Confederation of Chilean Students). This is a student organisation comprising all the student federations from Chilean universities.
FEMAE	**MAPUCHE** Federation of Students.
FEMES	Acronym for Federación Metropolitana de Estudiantes Secundarios (Metropolitan Federation of Secondary Students).

MAPUCHE   The **MAPUCHE** people are an indigenous tribe located in the south of Chile.

UDM   Acronym for Universidad del Mar. This university became an emblematic case (and a symbolic win) for the student movement because, due to their requests for investigation, many administration irregularities (e.g. money laundering) were identified, proving the university was profiting from the students while not providing the minimum academic and quality standards. As a result, then Minister of Education Harold Beyer was impeached, the university is due to close down in 2018, and the university board is currently being prosecuted for fraud.

Notes

1. Motive, purpose, and intention(ality) are used interchangeably throughout this project, as seems to be the case in most of the literature reviewed (see 'Theoretical Background').
2. These key words were the Spanish equivalents of the following: student; protest(s); mobilisation(s); march(es); CONFECH; ACES; Cones; high school students; students; hooded vandals; barricade(s).
3. It is important to note that the sample contains more than 387 infinitives and/ or gerunds: each hit was considered in its immediate co-text, which inevitably results in more verbs in adjacent clauses/sentences.
4. While *public* comes 38th in the keyword ranking (Frequency: 822; Keyness: 46.457), *quality* comes 55th (Frequency: 63; Keyness: 34.188).
5. 'Marca AC' was a campaign started by a social movement which demands changes to the Constitution through a Constituent Assembly (AC).

References

Archer, D., A. Wilson and P. Rayson (2002), 'Introduction to the USAS category system', *Benedict Project Report*, <http://ucrel.lancs.ac.uk/usas/usas%20guide.pdf> (last accessed 17 May 2017).

Baker, P. (2006), *Using Corpora in Discourse Analysis*, London: Continuum.

Baker, P., C. Gabrielatos, M. KhosraviNik, M. Krzyzanowski, T. McEnery and R. Wodak (2008), 'A useful methodological synergy? Combining critical discourse analysis and corpus linguistics to examine discourses of refugees and asylum seekers in the UK press', *Discourse & Society*, 19 (3), pp. 273–305.

Buttny, R. (2008), 'Accounting research', in W. Donsbach (ed.), *The International Encyclopaedia of Communication*, Oxford: Blackwell, pp. 20–1.

Buttny, R. and G. H. Morris (2001), 'Accounting', in P. Robinson and H. Giles (eds), *The New Handbook of Language and Social Psychology*, Chichester: John Wiley & Sons, pp. 285–301.

Cárdenas, C. (2012), '¿Dónde debe emplazar su ojo la historia? (In)visibilización de las y los jóvenes en discursos disciplinares que recuperan el pasado reciente chileno (1970–1990)', *Discurso y Sociedad*, 6 (2), pp. 283–313.

Goatly, A. (2007), *Washing the Brain: Metaphor and Hidden Ideology*, Amsterdam: John Benjamins.

Harlow, S. and D. Harp (2013), 'Alternative media in a digital era: Comparing news and information use among activists in the United States and Latin America', *Communication & Society/Comunicación y Sociedad*, 26 (4), pp. 25–51.

Kenix, L. J. (2011), *Alternative and Mainstream Media: The Converging Spectrum*, London: Bloomsbury Academic.

Lugo-Ocando, J. (2008), *Media in Latin America*, Maidenhead: Open University Press.

Martin Rojo, L. and T. van Dijk (1997), '"There was a problem, and it was solved!": Legitimating the expulsion of "illegal" migrants in Spanish parliamentary discourse', *Discourse & Society*, 8 (4), pp. 523–66.

Monckeberg, M. O. (2009), *Los magnates de la prensa: Concentración de los medios de comunicación en Chile*, Santiago: Debate.

Pérez, C. (2012), 'The Chilean student movement and the media: A comparative analysis on the linguistic representation of the 04 August, 2011 manifestation in right-wing and left-wing newspapers', *Logos: Revista de Lingüística, Filosofía y Literatura*, 22 (2), pp. 4–26.

Pérez, C. (2016), 'La representación visual del movimiento estudiantil chileno en la prensa establecida y alternativa nacional: Un análisis multimodal', *Revista Austral de Ciencias Sociales*, 30 (1), pp. 5–26.

Shoemaker, P. J. (1984), 'Media treatment of deviant political groups', *Journalism & Mass Communication Quarterly*, 61, pp. 66–82.

Sunkel, G. and E. Geoffroy (2001), *Concentración económica de los medios de comunicación: Peculiaridades del caso chileno*, Santiago: LOM Ediciones.

van Dijk, T. (2005), *Racism and Discourse in Spain and Latin America*, Amsterdam: John Benjamins.

van Leeuwen, T. (2007), 'Legitimation in discourse and communication', *Discourse & Communication*, 1 (1), pp. 91–112.

van Leeuwen, T. (2008), *Discourse and Practice: New Tools for Critical Discourse Analysis*, Oxford: Oxford University Press.

4

Crying Children and Bleeding Pensioners against Rambo's Troop: Perspectivisation in German Newspaper Reports on Stuttgart 21 Protests

Gerrit Kotzur

Contextual Background: Development of the Stuttgart 21 Protests

Stuttgart 21 (henceforth S21) is a controversial urban development and railway project in the city of Stuttgart, county of Baden-Württemberg in Germany that inspired a wave of protests between 2009 and 2011. The protesters criticised a range of issues, including the project's costs and the station's supposedly minor performance increase, and raised environmental concerns about demolishing part of the castle park and gardens surrounding the station. Years of protest ensued which reached a violent climax in 2010 during the so-called Black Thursday demonstration. The protest developed into a civil movement with considerable support from the middle class and eventually required extensive mediation. It was provisionally resolved with a referendum on 27 November 2011 when 58 per cent voted for the project to be carried on as planned. The conflict about S21 was also seen as a symbol of a political crisis and as a symptom of the general public's alienation from the political establishment (*Süddeutsche Zeitung*, Neue Feindbilder, 2 October 2010).

The Black Thursday on 30 September 2010 turned out to be the most violent escalation of a protest against the project in particular, but also more generally in the region of Baden-Württemberg in over forty years. At least 130 demonstrators – some of them children – as well as six police officers were injured when police tried to shut off the area around the Stuttgart castle gardens in preparation for uprooting trees. Thirty people reported offences by police and twenty-nine protesters were arrested (*Tagesspiegel*, 1 October 2010). The event even received coverage on the BBC website on 1 October 2010: 'About 1,000 police were deployed to protect the site on Thursday, confronting several thousand demonstrators, German media reported. Several protesters were admitted to hospital, but their injuries were reported to be relatively light.'[1] It turned out that a protester would remain blind in one eye after being hit in the face by a water cannon. In 2015, the use of forceful measures by police such as water cannons was declared unlawful by the administrative court in Stuttgart.[2] In retrospect, it is interesting to see how the events were evaluated and perspectivised by opposing sides shortly after they took place when there was still room for interpretation, and when the local government was struggling to establish its view of them.

I will start by discussing the notion of news values in mass media reporting before moving on to clarify the concept of perspectivisation in cognition and discourse. Data and methodology are then explained. The remainder of the chapter discusses linguistic perspectivisation in nomination and predication strategies in the newspaper corpus.

News Values: The Logics of Mass Media Reporting

Media has the power to influence knowledge, beliefs, values, social relations and social identities (Fairclough 1995). As readers of news media, we often have no direct access to the events reported. Instead, we are presented with 'second-order observations', which, strictly speaking, cannot be neutral descriptions. Media, like any other complex system, operate by their own logic, which shapes how newsworkers[3] construct and mediate reality (Luhmann 2009). 'News reduces complex series of events . . . Making news is a heavily interpretive and constructive process, not simply a report of "the facts"' (Fairclough 2003: 84–5).

In addition to the role of informing and educating readers, news stories also fulfil entertainment functions. Mass media texts 'can be seen as instantiating the blurring of boundaries of various sorts: fact and fiction, news and entertainment, drama and documentary, and so forth' (Fairclough 2003: 33). This trend was also referred to as the mediatisation of politics, 'mediocracy' or 'politainment' (Meyer 2002). In crafting a story, journalists pay particular attention to news values. Aspects are selected, reduced in complexity and presented in a certain way. The most commonly attested news values are proximity, human interest or personalisation, conflict and unexpectedness, negativity and superlativeness (Bell 1991; Cotter 2010; Schulz 2011). Different text producers can, of course, place emphases on various factors: news values 'may be commonly held notions, but they are inevitably *interpreted* variably' (Cotter 2010: 84; original emphasis). The interpretations are partly a matter of perspective reflected in the use of evaluating and perspectivising strategies. Evaluation establishes significance, and a report that does not employ at least some form of perspectivisation and covertly expressed opinion is potentially less engaging or interesting (see also Conboy 2007: 87–8).

Drawing on Bucher's analysis of press reports on the anti-nuclear movement in Brokdorf, Germany, in the 1990s, we can distinguish three assessments of protests which could be relevant for this event (Bucher 1992: 266): (1) a protest-critical understanding when violent actions are seen as initiated by protesters (at the time supported by *Frankfurter Allgemeine Zeitung* and *Süddeutsche Zeitung*); (2) a government-critical understanding according to which police (unlawfully) interfere with protesters' right to carry out peaceful demonstrations (mainly supported by left-wing oriented papers); and (3) a more balanced view, which holds that the legitimate expression of the freedom of speech by protesters happened to be overshadowed by violent clashes between a few extreme protesters and police.

Other researchers have found that journalists overall favour the protest-critical understanding in (1) and engage grammatical structures that characterise protesters as violent deviants while authorities are depicted as defenders of civil order (Hart 2013, 2014, 2015; see also Montgomery 1986; van Dijk 1991). As I will show in my analysis, the S21 protest reporting presents a different and more complex picture. Most newsworkers either opt for a balanced (3) or even government-critical understanding (2).

Perspective and Perspectivisation in Cognition and Discourse

Humans filter and structure perceptual input, connecting it with already existing knowledge structures in long-term memory. This process is necessarily selective, for the most part unconscious and perspectively grounded (von Stutterheim and Carroll 2007: 36; see also Hartung 1997; Köller 2004). Due to its ubiquitous nature, it has been argued that perspectivity 'is not, and cannot easily be made into, a very precise notion. There is no single well-defined concept' (Linell 2002: 53). Challenges in operationalising perspectivity arise from the fact that it functions 'at the intersection of a psychological-cognitive and social-functional approach of discourse' (Ensink and Sauer 2003: 2). In this section, I will attempt to provide some clarifications to arrive at a framework for perspectivisation that can be applied in analysing news discourse.

Language users can construe the same situation in alternate ways (Langacker 2008: 43), but how exactly we describe an event and the actors involved in it is also shaped by the ideological positions we take. In cognitive linguistics, this aspect of conceptualisation is discussed under the umbrella term of 'construal operations'. Construal requires 'reference to a *subject's* perception, choice, or point of view' (Verhagen 2007: 58; original emphasis).[4] Rather than theorising perspectivisation as a specific construal operation amongst others (see Croft and Cruse 2004), though, it can be claimed to have a more general role in conceptualisation. Verhagen proposes that 'perspective is a central part of the entire range of possible construal relations, in fact a definitional aspect of prototypical instances of construal' (2007: 58). Drawing on Keim (1996), it is helpful to distinguish the more general, cognitively oriented notion of perspective from perspectivisation or perspectivising strategies as discursive phenomena.

Perspective is always already involved in discourse (Ensink and Sauer 2003: 2). No sentence 'in any discourse is free from a certain degree of perspectivization' (Sanders and Redeker 1996: 290). However, what is variable is the level of explicit marking of perspective through language and the means of achieving particular viewpoints. Perspectivisation can be used as a persuasive strategy to raise news value. It can be defined as a 'functional-communicative procedure which can be used to realise complex observations and different point-of-view relations' (Sauer 1996: 261); see also Schwarz: a 'perspectivised verbalisation focuses particular aspects of a referent through lexical and information structural means, that is, objects and events are coded from a particular point of view' (2008: 234; my translation).

In contrast to perspective as a primarily perceptual or ideological position, that is, a worldview, perspectivisation can be directly indexed via textual representations. By focusing on particular aspects of a situation, selecting which elements to encode and by what means, a text producer gives the readers an indication of their perspective. This point relates to what Langacker (2008: 260) calls subjective versus objective construal: an entity is maximally subjectively construed when it remains implicit in the offstage region of conception being fully immersed in the act of conceptualisation. This is a matter of degree. Perspective can be explicitly signalled through certain discourse or perspectivisation markers such as *to my mind, in my opinion, I think*, and so on (see Sandig 1996 for a more exhaustive list).

Another frequently discussed concept related to perspective is frame. Generally speaking, frames provide background knowledge. There are similarities between perspective and frame depending on one's research angle, but I will not discuss these further and instead refer readers to Ensink and Sauer (2003) who state that a 'frame is a *structure* of perception, a perspective is a *direction* of perception' (2003: 14–15; original emphasis).

Perspectivisation is often intricately bound to evaluation (Skirl 2012). The two concepts also have in common that both cut across a multitude of linguistic means of expression (Martin and White 2005). The similarities become apparent when evaluation is referred to as the expression of 'stance' or 'viewpoint'. Alba-Juez and Thompson define evaluation as 'a dynamic subsystem of language, permeating all linguistic levels and involving the expression of the speaker's or writer's attitude or stance towards, viewpoint on, or feelings about the entities or propositions that s/he is talking about' (2014: 13). Although the two concepts are interrelated, one of them can be more prominent than the other in a discourse unit (Skirl 2012: 335–6, 339).

In most cases, the writer may choose formulations that are more or less 'marked' (Mikame 1996), *demonstrators, protesters* and *police*, for instance, being fairly unmarked choices. Using another example from the corpus, referring to *children and pensioners* is not so much a matter of evaluation (there is nothing explicitly evaluative about this expression) but of perspectivisation. The writer directs the reader's focus of attention to these two groups of individuals, singling them out from a mass of different people from different social and economic backgrounds. While *children and pensioners* also take the role of *protesters* in this case, the two expressions profile different cognitive domains. We speak of profiling when 'two or more expressions evoke the same conceptual content yet differ in meaning by virtue of profiling different substructures within its common base' (Langacker 2008: 67). The expression *children and pensioners* might support a reading where these groups are seen as especially vulnerable and the police as ruthless and brutal for taking up forceful actions against them, which can serve to criticise or delegitimise police actions. The legitimisation function 'establishes the right to be obeyed, that is, "legitimacy". . . . Reasons for being obeyed have to be communicated linguistically, whether by overt statement or by implication' (Chilton and Schäffner 2011: 312).

However, we are not invariably fixed to a certain perspective. Language users can express multiple perspectives (Graumann 2002) and shift between different viewpoints (Sandig 1996). Empathy, for example, prompts us to mentally adopt another's perspective (see example (24) below), but the extent to which this can be done is certainly limited. The journalist may partly or predominantly express their assessment of things or that of the editorial board, but they may also adopt the view of one of the actors involved in the events. This shift in the deictic centre of the discourse is most evident in quotations and indirect speech (Ensink and Sauer 2003: 15). Since we have no way of determining a writer's intention through linguistic analysis alone, Molotch and Lester suggest 'not to look for reality, but for purposes, which underlie the strategies of creating one reality instead of another' (1981: 133–4). Thus, we are mostly concerned with rhetorical functions, coercion and the persuasive potential of discourse structures:

> Political actors will also often act coercively through discourse in setting agendas, selecting topics in conversation, positioning the self and others in specific relationships, making assumptions about realities that hearers are obliged to at least temporarily accept in order to process the text or talk. (Chilton and Schäffner 2011: 311)

According to Ensink and Sauer (2003: 10), linguistic structures that have been associated with perspectivisation are voice, quotation, lexical choice and deixis. Hart (2013, 2015) has demonstrated how point of view and event-construal influence the ordering of information and the patterning of grammatical structures to reflect ideological positions in news reporting on protest events. It is important to note that perspectivisation choices can also arise from purely stylistic requirements, that is, achieving a more varied style by employing alternating expressions with different profiles. In the following analysis, I will mainly focus on lexical choice in nominations and predications.

Referential or nomination strategies are used to construct and represent social actors through lexis. In a second step, the agents are linguistically characterised through predications describing their actions or actions inflicted upon them by others. Predicational strategies may be 'realized as evaluative attributions of negative and positive traits in the linguistic form of implicit or explicit predicates' (Wodak 2009: 320). Predicates include the use of adjectives, prepositional phrases and participial clauses, just to name a few (Reisigl and Wodak 2001: 54).

These two strategies are not always neatly distinguishable from one another in discourse. The 'referential identification very often already involves a denotatively as well as connotatively more or less deprecatory or appreciative labelling of the social actors' (Reisigl and Wodak 2001: 45).[5] For instance, the nominal *Rambo's troop* carries a (strong) negative evaluation, implicitly characterising police as brutal or ruthless. It is perspectivising insofar as it profiles the actors' violent behaviour at the expense of anything else. Readers arrive at the implied meaning via pragmatic inference, accessing the lexical entry for *Rambo*, which can be qualified as 'someone who uses, or threatens to use, strong and violent methods against their enemies' (*Cambridge Dictionaries Online*). Nevertheless, this example would be counted as a nomination strategy due to its linguistic form, namely a nominal group. Although the strategies are not always clearly separable from discourse-rhetorical functions, we can identify them as either nominal or predicational groups by virtue of their linguistic make-up. In the words of cognitive grammarian Langacker (2008: 124–5), a noun profiles a 'thing' in the widest sense (or a process reified as a thing, in the case of nominalisations), whereas a verb profiles a process.

The Newspaper Corpus

A newspaper corpus was sampled to find out how the project, the protest event and the social actors were portrayed and their actions evaluated and perspectivised on the days after the Black Thursday. The corpus consists of a total of sixty-eight articles in seven newspapers amounting to over 39,000 words. *Neues Deutschland* and *Handelsblatt* only contained three articles each, the other five papers between ten and fifteen. The articles were published online on the first and second day after the violent outburst (1 and 2 October 2010) and accessed via their respective web pages through the national library servers in Germany (Staatsbibliothek zu Berlin).[6]

Three of the papers are considered regional newspapers: *Stuttgarter Nachrichten, Stuttgarter Zeitung* and *Tagesspiegel* (for Berlin). The remaining four are national newspapers. *Süddeutsche Zeitung, Frankfurter Allgemeine Zeitung, Handelsblatt* and *Neues Deutschland* belong to the seven daily newspapers with the highest circulation in Germany. The newspapers have different political orientations, reaching from left-wing socialist (*Neues Deutschland*) to (left-)liberal (*Süddeutsche Zeitung* and *Handelsblatt*) and liberal-conservative (*Frankfurter Allgemeine Zeitung*).[7]

I manually coded the articles using the qualitative data analysis software NVivo 10. The subsections of 'Nomination Strategies' and 'Predication Strategies' below accurately reflect the structure of the coding categories. Word frequency queries available in NVivo allowed referencing the number of occurrences of frequent nomination strategies to give the reader an idea of how common or uncommon the expressions were.

Nomination Strategies

The Railway Project Stuttgart 21

The project itself is most commonly referred to simply as *railway project* (68 occurrences). We also find references such as *(transport) infrastructure project* (7 occurrences) that are more general in scope and emphasise the wider implications of the project for the region of Baden-Württemberg and beyond. Both labels can be considered neutral choices regarding evaluation. Supporters of the project and politicians involved in its execution also dubbed it a *centennial project* (*Stuttgarter Zeitung*, 2 October), a *project of the future* (*Tagesspiegel*, 2 October) or a *pan-European project* (*Frankfurter Allgemeine Zeitung*, 1 October), highlighting its significance for the development of the region and assigning more positive traits to it.

One of the opponents' arguments against the railway station reconstruction were the costs of over six billion euros. Journalists have taken up this nomination strategy even when not quoting demonstrators. We find the expression *multi-billion project* 8 times (*Süddeutsche Zeitung*, 2 October; *Neues Deutschland*, 1 October; *Handelsblatt*, 1 October), sometimes paired with the attribute *controversial. Grave of billions* (*Milliardengrab*) is used in columns rather than reports and is clearly more evaluative than the previous nominations. Of course, it would not make sense to deny that the project costs a lot of money, but for many opponents, the question remains whether the outcome justifies the investment.

Black Thursday: The Demonstration Event on 30 September 2010 as Violent Escalation

The event was often described by journalists of all political convictions as tumult, D-day (*Tag X*), outbreak of violence, exceptional state/state of emergency, scandal, riots (*Ausschreitungen*), conflict, serious clash, violent escalation/excess and, voicing both protesters and another major news magazine (*Der Spiegel*), even as resembling a civil war (*Tagesspiegel*, 1 October; see also a paragraph headline from *Stuttgarter Zeitung*, 2 October: 'castle garden has turned into a battlefield'). Although these labels have slightly different profiles, many serve to increase the urgency and importance of reporting the protests around Stuttgart 21 in the first place, thereby marking their newsworthiness. Significance is achieved through hyperbolic effects by drawing on topics with strong emotional and evaluative undertones such as riot, violence, excess and escalation. Most of these expressions do not work in favour of either side of the conflict but describe the whole incident as being violent.

More neutral equivalents can be found when referring to the series of protests as *civil protest* or *(gigantic) protest movement*. Some opponents of S21 call on supporters to exercise *civil disobedience* (*Stuttgarter Zeitung; Frankfurter Allgemeine*). To criticise and negatively evaluate police actions, terms such as *(massive) police operation* (58 occurrences), *eviction* and even *police assault* (*Neues Deutschland*, 2 October) are employed, combining perspectivisation with evaluation.

Police Forces and Politicians Supporting the Project

Besides obvious designations such as *police* (381 occurrences) and *police officer(s)* (20 occurrences), we also encounter expressions such as *Hundertschaften* (a group of hundreds) (19 occurrences), *task forces* (12 occurrences), *special operation forces* (5 occurrences) and *convoy* (3 occurrences). While these profile the professionalism and highly organised actions of police as well as their numbers, they also present the officers as the stronger force. In comparison with police in their suits and 'armour', protesters are seen as helpless and unprotected, as in the following examples:

(1)   They have no chance against the **wall of police**. (*Stuttgarter Zeitung*, 2 October)

(2)   **Police in protective uniforms** were guarding the clean-up . . . Children, young people and young adults ran for cover from **martially clad police** and water cannons. (*Frankfurter Allgemeine Zeitung*, 2 October)

(3)   Past a few hundred metres of fences, the demonstrators stood oppo-
      site **police in their armoured uniforms reminiscent of 'Star Wars'**.
      (*Neues Deutschland*, 2 October)

While *wall of police* is a case of dehumanisation, (2) and (3) might have been
used to convey protesters' fears (and possibly also evoke it in readers). Again,
these descriptions of police are in stark contrast to, for instance, *children
and young adults* in (2). It is worth noting that examples (1)–(3) were the
only instances of this kind in the corpus. They are not relevant in terms of
frequency, but they could still have an impact on readers, especially as they
stand out as quite drastic characterisations (see also Cotter 2010: 173).

Politicians of Stuttgart's local government such as Mayor Stefan Mappus
and his secretaries, are abstractly referred to as *the power of the state* and *state
authority*. Mappus is also labelled a *feared Rambo* and *law and order man*,
emphasising his relentlessness, or even ruthlessness. Cem Özdemir, president
of the Green Party, metaphorically referred to Mappus's political actions as
brutal bulldozer politics (*Stuttgarter Zeitung*, 1 October), which can also be
read as mindless and overly violent.

The Protesters: Ordinary Citizens or Left-Wing Extremists?

The unmarked choice for protesters is the German equivalent for *demonstrators* (312 occurrences). Profiling their role in the conflict, they are referred
to as *opponents of the project* (103 occurrences) or *critics* (11 occurrences).
Citizens (63 occurrences), sometimes combined with the attribute *average* or
ordinary, could serve to legitimise their activities as it is not only more general
in scope but also blanks out the act of protesting.

Furthermore, we find that certain social groups are focused on, such as
pupils (72 occurrences), *minors* (10 occurrences) and *pensioners* (19 occurrences). *The park protectors* (47 occurrences) are an initiative that formed when
the modernisation work of the railway station first had visible consequences
for the surrounding park. *The injured* (39 occurrences) focuses on the physical state of some of the protesters, implying harmful actions by the police (or
other protesters). *Activists* (25 occurrences) can be found across all newspapers
but is already a much less common choice. It profiles political action but
has perhaps gained a negative taint in the context of other protests whose
legitimacy was contested more vehemently in the past. Terms such as *crowd/
flock*, *masses* (8 occurrences) and *tens of thousands* or *ten thousand participants*
(20 occurrences) are employed to emphasise the sheer size of the movement.

Some labels can be considered more derogatory and carry negative connotations. However, in the reports I investigated, they are relatively rare and
never refer to the whole movement. It is made clear that we are talking about

the behaviour of a few 'deviants' that 'sneaked in' (see example (4)). If this were not made clear, it could call into question the legitimacy of the rest of the protesters. Examples are: *squatters/occupants* (3 occurrences; *Frankfurter Allgemeine Zeitung*), *disguised/hooded demonstrators* (*Vermummte*, 9 occurrences), *professional protesters* (*Berufsdemonstranten*, 6 occurrences), *old leftists* (6 occurrences; *Frankfurter Allgemeine Zeitung*; *Süddeutsche Zeitung*), *rioters* (2 occurrences; *Tagesspiegel*) and *left-wing extremists* (7 occurrences):

> (4) According to the Office for the Protection of the Constitution, **left-wing extremists** also sneaked in amongst the demonstrators in Stuttgart. (*Handelsblatt* and *Tagesspiegel*, 2 October)

Predication Strategies

Reciprocal Predication

In hindsight, we know that the police operation was not justified in the way it was carried out. However, this fact was established much later, so we should not be surprised to find reciprocal predications that put the blame for violent outbreaks on both police and protesters alike while sometimes omitting the actors – although these strategies are not too common altogether (see Hart 2013 for a more detailed cognitive account of reciprocal action schemas in reports on the London student protests):

> (5) **Call on both parties to be moderate** and at least **return to the negotiating table** as soon as possible. / Police and protesters **played a cat-and-mouse game**. (*Frankfurter Allgemeine Zeitung*, 2 October)
>
> (6) Everybody should have known that there **would be insults and hostility** at the direct line of contact between police and opponents. (*Handelsblatt*, 2 October)
>
> (7) **hard confrontations went on** for hours between police and Stuttgart 21 opponents. (*Stuttgarter Nachrichten*, 1 October)
>
> (8) **while shoulders collide, elbows are used** on both sides. / The skirmishes between police and demonstrators partly **turn into punch-ups**. (*Tagesspiegel*, 1 October)

These descriptions may also have been used to demonstrate neutrality or avoid taking sides. Journalists must often work with limited or conflicting information, especially shortly after an event such as this.

Rambo Wants to See Blood: Politicians Supporting the Project

The ruling conservative party CDU and the police department in Stuttgart defended their decisions while delegitimising protesters and their behaviour.

They accused the protesters of having used a demonstration by schoolchildren that simultaneously took place as a shield to protect themselves from police forces thereby risking the children being harmed (*Handelsblatt*, 1 October). Another CDU politician by the name of Guttenberg warned the protesters of 'overstepping the border to celebrated riots' (*Stuttgarter Zeitung*, 2 October).

Leaders of opposing political parties (Green Party, the Left and some social democrats) are quoted in all papers accusing Stuttgart's Mayor Stefan Mappus of *purposefully escalating/fuelling the situation*, perspectivising violence as an intended or at least accepted outcome on his part. He would further be *misusing the police, giving them leave to club older women and children, miming Rambo* and *employing methods used in Russia* while *conjuring up the violence on the side of the protesters*, ultimately *securing safety with draconic means*. Özdemir (Green Party) said Mappus *wanted to see blood*, an allegation he later revoked. We apparently witnessed the *nursing of a dangerous tank mentality* in Stuttgart city hall. Those expressions are clearly evaluative. Regarding perspectivisation, they draw on similar semantic fields related to violence, physical strength and military vocabulary. Mappus is portrayed as tough, resolved and vigorous but morally irresponsible with no regard for the consequences.

On the other hand, CDU politicians invest a lot of effort in defending the operation. They *call for prudence* and express *regret that such a course of action has become necessary* while *renewing their willingness to communicate* with protesters. As there is little room to argue about what happened, it seems that all that is left is to play down agency (calling actions *necessary* or *regrettable*) and to (re)assign blame to demonstrators.

Police Forces: Helpless or Ruthless?

In a similar vein, the police operation is many times justified by the head of police and the Mayor as *wholly proportionate, lawful, responsible, measured* and *de-escalating*. The blame is placed on the protesters; the police are said to have been forced to *react* to the violence they encountered (*were forced to use pepper spray*; *Stuttgarter Nachrichten*, 1 October). Their actions are seen as a kind of last resort after failed mediation:

(9) Even an anti-conflict team **was to no avail**. (*Stuttgarter Zeitung*, 2 October)

(10) Heribert Rech (CDU) defended the police's actions once more. He has 'no doubts' that the police '**acted lawfully**'. (*Handelsblatt*, 2 October)

(11) Heribert Rech (CDU) said demonstrators were solely responsible for the violence. 'At this moment, we **don't have any indication**

of misconduct by police.' (*Stuttgarter Nachrichten*, 1 October; *Süddeutsche Zeitung* and *Tagesspiegel*, 2 October)

(12) The police union **defended officers against reproaches**. From the beginning, police **were confronted with a high potential for aggression**, said police union chief Konrad Freiberg in Berlin. (*Stuttgarter Nachrichten* and *Tagesspiegel*, 1 October; *Süddeutsche Zeitung*, 2 October)

(13) First, it was said pupils attacked the police with stones. This was later denied. Officers **reacted using water cannons and pepper spray**. (*Süddeutsche Zeitung*, 1 October)

The protesters' actions allegedly included insults as well as physical attacks like throwing glass bottles, paving stones and fireworks at police. Investigations on the following days revealed that the weapons used were not bottles and cobblestones after all, but chestnuts. Interestingly, these justification strategies almost exclusively appear in quotations or indirect speech when citing CDU politicians and police forces rather than reporters using them on their own account. This clearly marks them as opinions, not necessarily bare facts, and possibly also achieves objectivity through multi-perspectivity. The case is somewhat different for the information that works in support of S21 opponents (see below).

Police actions mainly involve *clearing the park*, *taking action against* and *using pepper spray*. These predications are often combined with intensifying (and partly evaluative) attributes like *forcefully*, *disproportionately*, *unusually*, *brutally*, *violently*, *escalating*, *plentiful* and nominal hyperbole such as *fountains*:

(14) With water cannons, the group of hundreds **cleared the park**, and then they **fetched** squatters from the trees with lift trucks. (*Frankfurter Allgemeine Zeitung*, 2 October)

(15) To drive apart the masses, officers **spray fountains of pepper spray** in the group of people holding out (*die Ausharrenden*). (*Tagesspiegel*, 1 October)

(16) The police **had made plentiful use of pepper spray**. (*Frankfurter Allgemeine Zeitung*, 2 October)

(17) She [a pensioner] cannot believe that the police **took action against** pensioners and children **using water cannons**. (*Frankfurter Allgemeine Zeitung*, 2 October)

(18) But was it necessary that we see pictures from Stuttgart where police **brutally take action against** young people? (*Frankfurter Allgemeine Zeitung*, 2 October)

(19) 'Nobody understands it when special task forces **strike out at** young people and pensioners with batons,' said the Parliamentary Chairman

of the SPD in the Bundestag, Thomas Oppermann. (*Handelsblatt*, 1 October; *Süddeutsche Zeitung*, 2 October)

The strongest evaluations are found in the socialist-left newspaper *Neues Deutschland*: *ruthlessly* and *massively* – when referring to police actions – and explicit contrasts such as *police cleared away peaceful obstructionists* and *pupils were ambushed by police while making use of their right to demonstrate* (*Neues Deutschland*, 2 October); see also:

(20) Police **drove apart** an announced and peaceful demonstration while also **randomly harming** young people as well as older citizens. (*Neues Deutschland*, 2 October)

The Protesters: Peacefully Camping versus Throwing Paving Stones

There are four basic strategies for perspectivising demonstrators' actions: they are depicted as peaceful and impassive, injured victims of police actions, carrying out typical non-violent protest actions or initiating violent aggression:

(21) The atmosphere is getting more and more irritable. The demonstrators **remain peaceful**. (*Neues Deutschland*, 1 October)
(22) A repeated gathering of the 'Stuttgart 21' opponents on Friday with more than ten thousand participants **had remained peaceful**. (*Handelsblatt* and *Tagesspiegel*, 2 October)

Protesters are further described as involved in physical but non-harmful (protest) activities such as seeking shelter, impeding police/standing in the way of police/barring the way, sitting on/occupying trucks, camping, keeping watch, storming towards the castle gardens, chaining themselves to fences and putting up resistance. To speak of protesters being 'armed with whistles' (*Neues Deutschland*) reads like a sarcastic reply to other people's opinions of the protesters' supposed violent actions against the police:

(23) For Stumpf [head of police] it is already a form of aggression if a crowd of people **bars the way** and police get insulted or touched. (*Stuttgarter Zeitung*, 2 October)

While police were seen as either unnecessarily violent or fulfilling their professional role, we never get to adopt their point of view. However, newsworkers invest the effort to present demonstrators more up close and personal, showing their feelings or motivation, offering a chance to empathise with them. Some examples even bear resemblance to literary style:

(24) One demonstrator **sits beneath a tree** amongst a circle of memory lights, dismally supporting his head with his hands. He **stares at the**

ground. A 68- and a 40-year-old female protester **stand nearby**, tears in their eyes. (*Stuttgarter Nachrichten*, 1 October)

(25) Demonstrators **remain sitting, bobbing on the truck**, it looks as though they are **having fun**. (*Tagesspiegel*, 1 October)

(26) Here and there demonstrators **chat** with young police officers almost **cordially**. (*Süddeutsche Zeitung*, 1 October)

We are informed of demonstrators' injuries several times across all newspapers (*were injured, had to be admitted to hospital* and *suffered from eye irritation*). Finally, there are references to people's outright violent behaviour, although this is often achieved through perspective shifts and quotes and attributed to ruling politicians. Further, these assessments are often mitigated (*some, sporadic*) or limited to verbal insults. The descriptions do not reach the same level of intensity that we encountered when looking at police actions or the protest event in general. Predications include *throwing a few bottles, sporadic igniting of fireworks* (*Neues Deutschland; Stuttgarter Nachrichten*) and the following:

(27) It was always said that the so far peaceful protest – aside from minor exceptions – **could become militant** the day that workers would bring down the first trees. (*Frankfurter Allgemeine Zeitung*, 2 October)

(28) **flailing**, often older citizens that **are carried off** by police. (*Frankfurter Allgemeine Zeitung*, 2 October)

(29) that some of the demonstrators **threw missiles at** the officers. (*Handelsblatt*, 2 October)

(30) The general secretary of the CDU in Baden- Württemberg, Thomas Strobl . . . 'Because the **aggression came from** the demonstrators'. (*Handelsblatt*, 2 October)

(31) others **stand nearby** and **scream their anger at** the police, mixed with fear of what might be to come. (*Tagesspiegel*, 1 October)

To conclude this section, we get an overall quite balanced and varied picture of protesters' activities. Although there have been several attempts to construct them as initiating violence and as solely responsible for the escalation, this applies to an even greater extent to police actions and the politicians involved in planning the project – at least as far as the news reports are concerned. The protesters' language use on placards and demonstration posters, however, is far less innocent and often shows cases of violent metaphors and demonising hyperbole (see Kotzur forthcoming), which can in turn incite anger and indignation in politicians and police.

Conclusion

The protest against Stuttgart 21 may be a less prototypical instance of a demonstration event. Unlike other protests in recent years, S21 opponents received broad support from the middle class. Children and pensioners are not what we typically associate with protesters. This could be one reason why the news media, rather than demonising the group, aim for more balanced or at times even legitimising characterisations. Nevertheless, it is striking that the delegitimisation attempts employed at length by the CDU, the Mayor and the police department did not find more support among newsworkers at the time. Concerning the papers' political orientation, there seems to be no clear pattern of favouritism – apart from the more drastic, negatively evaluating depictions of police used by the left-wing socialist *Neues Deutschland*.

In the absence of explicit evaluations, perspectivisation can function as a means to single out particular character traits and behaviours of social actors, ultimately raising a story's news value. By focusing on the violent actions of one group and contrasting those with the peaceful behaviour or futile resistance of another, we recognise binary patterns of good–evil, powerful–powerless and just–unjust (Chilton 2004: 199), necessities for drama and conflict and a popular design of most stories worth telling.

Notes

1. 'Germany digs up park after clash in Stuttgart', *BBC News*, 1 October 2010, available at <http://www.bbc.co.uk/news/world-europe-11451563> (last accessed 4 May 2018).
2. 'Polizeigewalt gegen Stuttgart-21-Demonstranten war rechtswidrig', *Spiegel Online*, 11 November 2015, available at <http://www.spiegel.de/politik/deutschland/stuttgart-21-polizeigewalt-gegen-demonstranten-war-rechtswidrig-a-1063391.html> (last accessed 22 May 2017).
3. Texts in mass media are often produced by more than one identifiable author. Several people are involved in their production, including news agencies, reporters, journalists and editors. Their contribution to the final text is not always clear. This needs to be kept in mind when I speak of the language use of journalists or text producers. Bell (1991) proposes the term 'newsworkers' to describe all those who are regularly involved in overseeing, writing or editing news.
4. In conceptual metaphor theory, perspectivisation is implied in the notions of highlighting and hiding (Lakoff and Johnson 1980).
5. See Hart (2014) for a similar upshot concerning the interdependence of construal operations in cognitive linguistics.
6. Due to lack of space, I only provide the German wording when there are considerable semantic differences between the original and the range of available English translations.

7. The political classifications of newspapers are to a degree variable as well as partly subjective. Tabloid papers were not included due to issues of accessibility (Germany lacks a freely accessible central press archive).

References

Alba-Juez, L. and G. Thompson (2014), 'The many faces and phases of evaluation', in G. Thompson and L. Alba-Juez (eds), *Evaluation in Context*, Amsterdam: John Benjamins, pp. 3–26.

Bell, A. (1991), *The Language of News Media*, Oxford: Blackwell.

Bucher, H.-J. (1992), 'Informationspolitik in der Presseberichterstattung: Kommunikationsstrategien bei der Darstellung gesellschaftlicher Konflikte', in E. W. B. Hess-Lüttich (ed.), *Medienkultur – Kulturkonflikt. Massenmedien in der interkulturellen und internationalen Kommunikation*, Opladen: Verlag für Sozialwissenschaften, pp. 259–89.

Cambridge Dictionaries Online (2018), Includes full text of the *Cambridge Advanced Learner's Dictionary and Thesaurus*, 3rd edn (2008), <https://dictionary. cambridge.org> (last accessed 12 May 2018).

Chilton, P. (2004), *Analysing Political Discourse: Theory and Practice*, London: Routledge.

Chilton, P. and C. Schäffner (2011), 'Discourse and politics', in T. A. van Dijk (ed.), *Discourse Studies: A Multidisciplinary Introduction*, London: Sage, pp. 303–30.

Conboy, M. (2007), *The Language of the News*, London: Routledge.

Cotter, C. (2010), *News Talk: Investigating the Language of Journalism*, Cambridge: Cambridge University Press.

Croft, W. and D. A. Cruse (2004), *Cognitive Linguistics*, Cambridge: Cambridge University Press.

Ensink, T. and C. Sauer (2003), 'Social-functional and cognitive approaches to discourse interpretation: The role of frame and perspective', in T. Ensink and C. Sauer (eds), *Framing and Perspectivising in Discourse*, Amsterdam: John Benjamins, pp. 1–22.

Fairclough, N. (1995), *Critical Discourse Analysis: The Critical Study of Language*, London: Longman.

Fairclough, N. (2003), *Analysing Discourse: Textual Analysis for Social Research*, London: Routledge.

Graumann, C. F. (2002), 'Explicit and implicit perspectivity', in C. F. Graumann and W. Kallmeyer (eds), *Perspective and Perspectivation in Discourse*, Amsterdam: John Benjamins, pp. 25–39.

Hart, C. (2013), 'Event-construal in press reports of violence in political protests: A cognitive linguistic approach to CDA', *Journal of Language and Politics*, 12 (3), pp. 400–23.

Hart, C. (2014), 'Cognitive models and conceptualisation in the context of political protests', in J. Flowerdew (ed.), *Discourse in Context: Contemporary Applied Linguistics 3*, London: Bloomsbury, pp. 159–84.

Hart, C. (2015), 'Viewpoint in linguistic discourse: Space and evaluation in news reports of political protests', *Critical Discourse Studies*, 12 (3), pp. 238–60.

Hartung, W. (1997), 'Text und Perspektive. Elemente einer konstruktivistischen Textauffassung', in G. Antos and H. Tietz (eds), *Die Zukunft der*

Textlinguistik: Traditionen, Transformationen, Trends, Tübingen: de Gruyter, pp. 13–25.

Keim, I. (1996), 'Verfahren der Perspektivenabschottung und ihre Auswirkung auf die Dynamik des Argumentierens', in W. Kallmeyer (ed.), *Gesprächsrhetorik. Rhetorische Verfahren im Gesprächsprozess*, Tübingen: Narr, pp. 191–278.

Köller, W. (2004), *Perspektivität und Sprache. Zur Struktur von Objektivierungsformen in Bildern, im Denken und in der Sprache*, Berlin and New York: de Gruyter.

Kotzur, G. (forthcoming), 'Metaphors for protest: The persuasive power of cross-domain mappings on demonstration posters against Stuttgart 21', in M. Huang (ed.), *The Language of Crisis: How Metaphor, Metonymy and Frames Construct Crisis Discourse*, Amsterdam: John Benjamins.

Lakoff, G. and M. Johnson (1980), *Metaphors We Live By*, Chicago: University of Chicago Press.

Langacker, R. W. (2008), *Cognitive Grammar: A Basic Introduction*, New York: Oxford University Press.

Linell, P. (2002), 'Perspectives, implicitness and recontextualization', in C. F. Graumann and W. Kallmeyer (eds), *Perspective and Perspectivation in Discourse*, Amsterdam: John Benjamins, pp. 41–57.

Luhmann, N. (2009), *Die Realität der Massenmedien*, Wiesbaden: Verlag für Sozialwissenschaften.

Martin, J. R. and P. R. White (2003), *The Language of Evaluation*, Basingstoke: Palgrave Macmillan.

Meyer, T. (2002), *Media Democracy: How the Media Colonize Politics*, Cambridge: Polity Press.

Mikame, H. (1996), 'Markierte Perspektive, perspektivische Annäherung des Sprechers an das Objekt und direkte Wahrnehmung. Zur Signalisierung der psychisch-kognitiven Nähe des Sprechers zum Objekt', *Sprachwissenschaft*, 21, pp. 367–420.

Molotch, H. and M. Lester (1981), 'News as purposive behaviour: On the strategic use of routine events, accidents and scandals', in S. Cohen and J. Young (eds), *The Manufacture of News: Social Problems, Deviance and the Mass Media*, London: Sage, pp. 118–37.

Montgomery, M. (1986), *An Introduction to Language and Society*, London: Routledge.

Reisigl, M. and R. Wodak (2001), *Discourse and Discrimination: Rhetorics of Racism and Antisemitism*, London: Routledge.

Sanders, J. and G. Redeker (1996), 'Perspective and the representation of speech and thought in narrative discourse', in G. Fauconnier and E. Sweetser (eds), *Spaces, Worlds and Grammar*, Chicago: University of Chicago Press, pp. 290–317.

Sandig, B. (1996), 'Sprachliche Perspektivierung und perspektivierende Stile', *LiLi. Zeitschrift für Literaturwissenschaft und Linguistik*, 26 (102), pp. 36–63.

Sauer, C. (1996), 'Echoes from abroad – speeches for the domestic audience: Queen Beatrix' address to the Israeli parliament', *Current Issues in Language and Society*, 3 (3), pp. 233–67.

Schulz, W. (2011), *Politische Kommunikation. Theoretische Ansätze und Ergebnisse empirischer Forschung. 3., überarbeitete Auflage*, Wiesbaden: Verlag für Sozialwissenschaften.

Schwarz, M. (2008), *Einführung in die Kognitive Linguistik. 3., vollständig überarbeitete und erweiterte Auflage*, Tübingen: Francke.

Skirl, H. (2012), 'Zum Emotionspotenzial perspektivierender Darstellung', in I. Pohl and H. Eberhardt (eds), *Sprache und Emotion in öffentlicher Kommunikation*, Frankfurt am Main: Lang, pp. 335–59.

van Dijk, T. A. (1991), *Racism and the Press*, London: Routledge.

Verhagen, A. (2007), 'Construal and perspectivization', in D. Geeraerts and H. Cuyckens (eds), *The Oxford Handbook of Cognitive Linguistics*, New York: Oxford University Press, pp. 48–81.

von Stutterheim, C. and M. Carroll (2007), 'Durch die Grammatik fokussiert', *LiLi. Zeitschrift für Literaturwissenschaft und Linguistik*, 37 (145), pp. 35–60.

Wodak, R. (2009), 'The semiotics of racism. A critical discourse-historical analysis', in J. Renkema (ed.), *Discourse, of Course: An Overview of Research in Discourse Studies*, Amsterdam: John Benjamins, pp. 311–26.

5

Taking a Stance through the Voice of 'Others': Attribution in News Coverage of a Public Sector Workers' Strike in Two Botswana Newspapers

Boitshwarelo Rantsudu

Introduction

Public disorder in the form of industrial strikes and its representation in the media has been studied in varying contexts with much focus on confrontation and picket violence (Waddington 1992), and its framing in terms of war between the state and workers' unions (Hart 2014). It is therefore common to find that in reporting industrial strikes, the use of language alongside pictorial representations in the media can project these negative themes and create a situation in which news audiences are led to take sides with either of the social actors involved in the industrial dispute. This is mainly because in such instances as reporting industrial disputes, the news media is characterised in its role of 'watchdog' (Berkowitz 2009), thus purporting to represent factual details of events. In this chapter I examine the media representation of the 2011 nationwide public sector workers' strike in Botswana, paying specific attention to how the use of quotations that are attributed to external voices sets the tone of framing of the strike. While the events of the strike did not result in far-reaching picket violence, one of the ideas that I discuss in this chapter is how the views expressed by external news sources project a sense of looming disorder. In addition, and more significantly, I examine how, despite the use of quotations that are attributed to external voices, news writers take on particular stances in their coverage of the strike. Before looking at some scholarly views on the feature of attribution in the news, let us briefly look at the context of the public sector workers' strike in Botswana.

The Public Sector Workers' Strike in Botswana

Before the strike began, the public sector union representatives had lobbied for a 16 per cent salary increase and entered into negotiations with the representative committee of the employer, the government. However, the negotiations collapsed, leading to the negotiation of strike rules between the government and the public sector workers' unions. The strike itself lasted for approximately eight weeks, starting on 18 April and ending on 6 June 2011. One of the central arguments advanced by the government during the negotiation process was that the economic status of the country could not allow for an increment in salaries for the public sector, due to the global economic recession from which the country was still recovering. With the rules of the strike negotiated, the commencement of the strike attracted wide media coverage and the events of the strike remained a topical issue for many media outlets. As the events of the strike unfolded nationwide, it became clear that the importance of the media could not be overlooked, and the media constructed much of their coverage on the basis of statements given by external news sources. Furthermore, as an instance of an industrial dispute, the strike was somewhat set from the perspective of relations between the government and the workers' unions. This chapter is therefore based on the observation that since much of the news content was explicitly sourced from external voices, the media were successful in keeping their audiences interested in what the concerned social actors would say about the events of the strike.

It is perhaps important to mention at this point how the representation of public disorder (in the form of a workers' strike) is an interesting site for a linguistic analysis. The advocacy for neutral reporting is a highly esteemed ideal in the Botswana press. However, some media researchers in Botswana, particularly Tutwane (2011) and Rooney (2012), have argued that state-controlled media selectively present the voice of the government, and that during the strike there was bias in the government media. While these contentions about media practice can be studied in various ways, central to media reports is the use of language. So questions of who is given voice in the news, how media reports are crafted such that differing views of social actors are accounted for, and how certain meaningful effects are achieved can be successfully investigated by considering the linguistic features involved. As indicated in the introduction, attribution, particularly its use in news texts, is one feature of language worth exploring. In the next section, I provide an overview of the feature of attribution as a means by which journalists craft news stories that appeal to their readers.

Attribution in the News

The representation of the speech, viewpoints and opinions of external voices is one of the fundamental characteristics of news discourse, and as a practice, it has received some vast scholarly attention. For Caldas-Coulthard (1994: 296), including the speech of another in the form of a quotation within written texts involves introducing one text into another, resulting in the merging of two texts. In a similar way, Piazza (2009: 171) takes this view further by stating that news content that is attributed to external sources presents an echo of other voices to the news audiences. This is carried out by foregrounding some voices and downplaying others. Another important notion that Piazza (2009) raises is that of co-construction of discourse, a notion that accords the news writer control of the text while acknowledging the voice of external sources. The recognition of the ability of the news writer to merge texts and echo a variety of other voices underlines the multifaceted nature of news reporting and the success of news writers in crafting news stories that depict an aura of factuality (Berkowitz 2009: 107). Furthermore, when considered alongside the professional demands of news reporting, it can be argued that typical use of attribution, particularly in hard news, is possibly the most common means through which journalists distance themselves from viewpoints and attitudinal assessments expressed in hard news stories. Through this distancing, journalists achieve a news narrative interwoven with varying external voices. In this way, news writers are able to claim a neutral and objective slant of the news stories. However, as is discussed later in the chapter, attributing news content to external sources is a strategic element of hard news through which news writers succeed in taking a backgrounded position. However, this backgrounded position does not necessarily prevent the news writers from expressing their own opinions and viewpoints. With the explicit expression of subjective opinions and viewpoints, or attitudinal standpoints confined to the utterances sourced from external news sources, the news writer has the role of constructing the news text such that it gives the reader a sense of comprehension about the reported events.

Considering the vast attention that has been directed towards the study of attribution in the news, it can be argued that attribution is without doubt an important feature to explore linguistically. Various questions that are addressed in the existing literature on attribution in the news attest to this importance. Such questions relate to, for example, the choice of which news sources to quote, the different forms of voicing and the type of reporting verbs used to frame the quotations (Caldas-Coulthard 1993; Piazza 2009), and how news reporters' use of 'unnamed' sources 'opens a wealth of rhetorical possibilities that undermine alleged factuality' (Stenvall 2008: 229). In an earlier work, Hunston (1995: 134) established that attribution is a resource that provides space for implicit evaluation because of the layers of interpretation involved in representing the words of others. In Hunston's view, what is presented to the audience as the words of a speaker, constituting a reported clause, often projects meaning rather than wording. If the reported clause projects meaning, the reporting clause therefore presents a comment on the reported clause. This differentiation between meaning and comment is one perspective that forms the basis of my main argument in this chapter that it is important to examine the dynamic strategies involved in attribution.

Sharing the view of Thomson et al. that a typical hard news report 'involves a strategic avoidance of certain key evaluative meanings and, it backgrounds and potentially conceals the subjective role of the journalist author' (2008: 224), I highlight in this chapter that the complex nature of hard news texts points to a possible range of linguistic devices available to the news writer. For the interests of this chapter, I examine how the idealised notion of neutrality, through attribution, and strategic stance-taking play out in the news coverage of the public sector workers' strike. Considering that attribution in the news involves two types of clauses, the reporting and the reported clause, it is not surprising that the analysis of reporting verbs is also central to the study of attribution. As pointed out by Piazza (2009), reporting verbs can convey a significant cue for the identification of a neutral, positive or negative attitudes.

Having covered briefly some of the linguistic ideas in relation to the complex nature of attribution, I now outline the methodological approach I have taken to examine the interplay between attribution and stance-taking in the news coverage of the workers' strike in Botswana. I describe the data and the analytical approach, and outline the features I focus on in my analysis.

Methodology

Data

The news excerpts analysed in this chapter are randomly selected from four complete news articles which were collected from the online editions of two Botswana dailies, the *Daily News* and *Mmegi*. The four news articles comprise two pairs of parallel texts that were collected as part of my PhD study with the aim of gaining a comparative perspective of how different newspapers covered the workers' strike. In addition, the four news excerpts represent an important time-line of the strike coverage, including the pre-strike period, which consisted of a build-up of opinions and attitudes about the strike, the public sector workers, and the government. The two events reported in the news articles are:

1. The parliamentary question time during which solutions and measures taken by the government to address the strike were debated by MPs. This is covered in Texts A and B.
2. The opposition party leaders' press conference, stating their support for the public sector workers (or the strike). This is covered in Texts C and D.

Analytical Approach

In 'Analysis and Results' below, I carry out an analysis of the news excerpts described above. Appraisal theory (Martin and White 2005) is central to my analysis, with reference to the system of Attitude. The analysis presented explores how some targets of evaluation (outlined below) are evaluated in each pair of news texts reporting the same event. In analysing Attitude, the language of the news texts is explored to establish how the resources of Judgement and Appreciation are used to evaluate various targets identified. The category of Judgement deals with the assessment of human behaviour. According to Coffin and O'Halloran (2006: 82), the assessment of human behaviour is often done by referring to some valued norms which govern how people should and should not behave. In my analysis, the sub-categories of Judgement utilised are *Propriety*, *Veracity* and *Capacity*. The second category of Attitude, Appreciation, deals with the evaluation of events and states of affairs, and the analysis focuses on the sub-category of *Valuation*. Both categories of Attitude can be realised in either positive or negative terms, and as indicated in the analytical key, positive Attitude is shown by a [+ve] annotation whereas negative Attitude is shown by a [-ve] annotation. Realisations of Appraisal analysis categories are indicated in the body of the news texts and enclosed in square brackets. The analytical key is as follows:

> [+ve Prop.] = Positive Propriety
> [-ve Prop.] = Negative Propriety
> [+ve Cap.] = Positive Capacity
> [-ve Ver.] = Negative Veracity
> [+ve Val.] = Positive Valuation
> [-ve Val.] = Negative Valuation

Also considered within the news texts are the reporting verbs used in the reporting clauses. Following Lauerbach (2006), Van and Thomson (2008) and Piazza (2009), the reporting verbs are marked for their function as either neutral or argumentative. Neutral reporting verbs are marked as acknowl-edgements [ack.] and this applies mostly to forms of the verb *say*. Verbs that are marked as endorsing [end.] are those that connote meanings that are indicative of the news writer's warranting of the viewpoint expressed. Highlighting is used in the news examples for analytical focus. As indicated within the texts, the entities targeted by each of the evaluations in the events reported are also enclosed within the square brackets, and the targets are:

- opposition politicians
- the government (as a collective entity and in some cases as represented by various officials)
- the strike as an event
- the economy
- the process of salary bargaining between the government and the unions.

While I treat these as individual central targets, I also note that Appraisal resources can overlap to some degree in the news data. For instance, in using negative Appreciation to talk about the economy in Text (D) (analysed in 'Analysis and Results' below), opposition party leaders make a simultaneous negative Judgement of the government. In some cases, simultaneous evaluations can function where one of the entities is a proxy target. However, the overlapping of Appraisal systems and targets evaluated is beyond the scope of the present discussion.

Features Analysed

In the preceding sections, I have noted and discussed some of the main notions associated with attribution as a resource for constructing texts, and have outlined the analytical approach I use to analyse the appearance of attribution in the news coverage of the workers' strike. In this section I outline the features that I focus on in my analysis. The analysis focuses on how the concepts of attribution and stance are played out in the representation of the workers' strike. At the centre of this representation is the subtle threat of looming disorder. Within the news coverage of the strike, the reports seem to highlight that there are three key social actors involved in the industrial dispute. These are the government, the workers' unions and the opposition party leaders. In order to attend to the interplay of attribution and stance in news discourse, I focus on the following:

1. How the news texts display an integration of the voices (Caldas-Coulthard 1993) of the journalists and the external voices. This feature

is considered particularly in the structural construction of the headlines and lead sentences.

2. Reference to unspecified news sources.
3. The choice of reporting expressions that are used to frame the attributed statements.

More generally, these features are discussed in relation to how they function to express legitimations (Hart 2014), and validation and pronouncement of facticity (Marín Arrese 2015). In addition, I touch on competing discourses surrounding the social actors to show the lines of contention displayed through the news texts.

Analysis and Results

As established in the introduction, this chapter examines the use of attribution in the news, specifically news covering the 2011 nationwide public sector workers' strike in Botswana, and how the expression of the writer's stance is managed through various attributed statements. This management of the expression of the writer's stance forms the basis of the analysis carried out in this section. Premised on the idea that citation involves 'managing the words of others to convey and serve the purpose of the writer, and giving a slant to what is said' (Calsamiglia and López Ferrero 2003: 149), and that news reporting involves the co-construction of discourse (Piazza 2009), the analysis shows that there is a notable difference between the two newspapers. On one hand, the quotations expressly mitigate the possibility of disorder and project peaceful relations between the government and the workers. On the other hand, some quotations expressly propagate views about an imminent escalation of disorder. On one level, these contrastive views reflect the viewpoints and stances of the quoted news sources. On another level, and more significantly, the news writer's voice interplays with these external voices to create his or her stance or validate the stance taken by the news source.

In order to place the analysis in a broader context, let us consider the first pair of news texts – Texts (A) and (B) – reporting on the first event, the parliamentary question time during which solutions and measures taken by the government to address the strike were debated by MPs. Text (A) is taken from the *Daily News* and Text (B) from *Mmegi*, the two newspapers used for the present study. These news excerpts are sampled from the pre-strike coverage and both are the openings of the news articles, constituting the headlines and the lead sentences. At the point at which the parliamentary debate that is reported took place, the workers' strike was planned to start within three days. My analysis of these two excerpts is focused on the integration of voices of the news writer and the external sources, and the choice of reporting verbs.

These are then discussed in relation to legitimation and the validation and pronouncement of facticity:

Daily News, 18 April 2011 (Text (A))

(1) Govt protects [Government: +Prop.] workers' rights

GABORONE: Government will ensure protection of workers' rights [Government: +Prop.] during industrial action, presidential affairs and public administration minister assured [end.] Parliament on Friday.

Mmegi, 18 April 2011 (Text (B))

(2) Masisi 'raps'[+Cap.] opposition MPs over strike

Only an irresponsible government [Opposition parties: -Prop.] like the one the opposition wishes to form would promise on public service salary increments when they do not have the money, the Minister for Presidential Affairs and Public Administration, Mokgweetsi Masisi said [ack.] in Parliament on Friday.

What is of interest in Text (A) is the validation of the positive propriety for the government, first expressed by the news writer in the headline, and followed by an attributed statement in the lead sentence. In the headline, the news writer uses a non-modalised assertion or pronouncement to foreground the moral and legal duty of the government to *protect the rights of the workers* during the strike. Structuring the headline as a pronouncement is a feature of news texts that conveys a 'common ground' (Haarman 2009: 130) with the quoted viewpoint of the government representative introduced in the lead sentence. Notice also that the activity verb *protects* is in the present tense, a construction that plays an important role in putting the events described in a continual formulation. While the news writer introduces an attributed statement in the lead sentence, the headline is indicative of an established evaluative orientation (White 2004) in which a positive stance about the government is expressed, validated and conveyed as a fact. In according the government positive Judgement at the beginning of the news text, the modal of prediction *will* stands out in the lead sentence. According to Haarman (2009: 126), the predictive use of modals often creates a forward-looking Attitude that expresses certainty. In addition to expressing certainty, modals of prediction also express the degree of desirability for a state of affairs (Van linden and Verstraete 2011). Accordingly, the positive Judgement of the government overlaps with an overall positive evaluation in relation to how the government plans to handle the industrial

action. Overall, the viewpoint of the news source, a government representative, in the lead sentence is integrated into the headline, a strategy that, I
argue, affords the news writer the space to take a positive stance towards the
government. Another feature worth paying attention to in Text (A) is the
reporting expression *assured*, a choice of verb that validates the position of
the government and reinforces the positive view towards the government.
This reporting verb is clearly selected by the news writer to convey a sense
of certainty of what the news source said, and also covertly applaud the
government for its positive actions.

Turning now to Text (B), the news opening shifts attention to a
confrontational debate between the government representative and the
opposition party MPs. While Text (A) puts emphasis on the protection of
workers' rights, thereby the positive propriety of the government, Text (B)
deals first with the incapacity of the opposition MPs to withstand the robust
debate coming from the government representative, a strategy that is set on
a continuum of 'praising and disparaging' (White 2008: 567). The lead sentence then attributes the statement about the impropriety of the opposition
to the government minister. Evidently, the headline expresses the negative
evaluation in explicit terms, but more interesting is the attributed statement
about the 'irresponsibility' of the opposition. Though attributed, it is also
important to notice the integration of the two voices here. Within the lead
sentence the separation of the voice of the author and the voice of the news
source is fuzzy. With the use of praise alongside a disparaging construction,
the news writer draws a line of contention between the government and
opposition MPs. As illustrated in these two brief examples, the voice of the
news writer is strategically interwoven into the attributed statements in two
ways, namely, voice integration and a reporting expression that endorses
the view and position of the government. In (A) this integration of voices
functions to validate the position of the government, which is evaluated
positively, while in (B) the integration of voices functions to delegitimise the
potential government formed by the opposition parties.

Similar to the analysis of Texts (A) and (B), Texts (C) and (D) are analysed with attention to the integration of voices and the choice of reporting
verbs. In addition, especially for Text (D) the analysis brings out another
feature, the reference to unspecified news sources. These news articles are
framed mainly in terms of imminent disorder. One of the themes prominent
in (C) is the potential instigation and escalation of disorder predicted by
the opposition party leaders. An overall gleaning of the news article seems
to indicate that the theme of a potential escalation of disorder dictates the
choice of reporting expressions used by the news writer. Furthermore, the

framing of coverage focuses on the inevitability of a crisis and potential political disintegration:

Mmegi, 18 April 2011 (Text (C))

Opposition backs civil servants' strike

(1) . . . This he said was clear from government's refusal [Government: -Prop.] to accept workers' demands for a pay hike, under the pretext [Government: -Ver.] that the economy has not yet recovered from the recession.

(2) He dismissed the excuse saying [ack.] the same government continues to fund questionable projects and departments [Government: -Prop.] such as the Directorate of Intelligence and Security (DIS), yet it claims there is no money for workers. . . .

(3) He warned government that it would not be easy to control the direction of events once the strike gains momentum [Strike: +Val. evoked]'

(4) Not in as many words, Boko said [ack.] that by turning a deaf ear to workers' cry [Government: -Prop.]' government could inevitably bring about its own collapse, even before the 2014 general election, considering the current protest mood and calls for reform in the continent.

(5) He said [ack.] that if matters reach boiling point [Potential political situation: -Val.]' it will be difficult to wait for 2014 for the electoral process and no one wants this.

The authorial formulation in line (2) *he dismissed the excuse* precedes a 'neutral' verb of reporting *saying*. Despite the use of this verb, this pre-quotation sequence referred to by the author as an act of dismissing the excuse given by the government gives us a cue of the news writer's critical stance towards the government. Following on from the attributed statement in line (1) the writer interprets the government's point of view, referred to as a 'refusal' and a 'pretext' by the opposition, as the excuse. A close reading of lines (1) and (2) displays an integration of voices. It is clear that in line (1) the opposition party leader is quoted to have made reference to the impropriety of the government to refuse the accept workers' demands. This negative Judgement is further reinforced by the implication of lack of truth on the part of the government. The news writer then takes on the negative view and interprets the actions of the government as an example of making excuses, thus integrating his or her voice with that of the news source. Arguably, the news writer makes a value-laden Judgement of the government but achieves this through the strategic management of the words of external voices (Calsamiglia and López Ferrero 2003), in this case the opposition party leaders.

The strategic management of the words of external voices not only functions to cast social actors in particular evaluations but also projects the news writer's interpretation of quoted speakers' behaviour. According to Thompson and Yiyun (1991), when the writer gives reported information through behaviour interpretation, the writer provides an exposition of the quoted speaker's attitude or purpose. The reporting expression *warned* in line (3) is a case in point. It introduces the viewpoint of an imminent escalation of disorder in which the speaker paints a picture of the difficulty of controlling the direction of events. It can also be noted that the potential of escalation of disorder is expressed in indeterminate terms. For example, it is not explicitly stated what 'events' are likely to take place, hence the statement leaves the reader with vague details, hinting at increasing disorder and possibly creating a sense of fear. In contrast, there is seeming validation of the workers' strike indicated through the expression *gains momentum*. The strike is accorded qualities of rapid motion. Alongside this rapid motion the events will not be controlled easily, hence the justification of predicting disorderly events. This is emphasised in line (4) by the expression *not in as many words*. This expression is an authorial formulation that frames the attributed news content through indirect reference. The emphasis is placed on the responsibility of the government for the negative turn of events. The phrase *if matters reach boiling point* in line (5) is an interesting metaphorical reference to an escalation of disorder. This is expressed in hypothetical terms, allowing the speaker, through the text, to assume the power of prediction. With an emphasis on the difficulty of controlling the direction of events stated in lines (3) indicated by the clause *it would not be easy* and (5) indicated by the clause *it will be difficult*, the arduous nature of the social and political state gives justification to political dissent and the blame accorded the government. This again foregrounds the line of contention between the parties involved.

In the final news excerpt, Text (D), it can be observed that the news article is framed in emotionally charged and expressive terms such as *sympathy* in line (3):

Daily News, 18 April 2011 (Text (D))

Opposition supports workers

(1) . . . He noted that the cost of living in the country was high [Economy: -Val.], while government had worsened the situation [Government: -Prop.] by increasing value added tax (VAT).

(2) The BCP leader criticised government for allegedly not showing any commitment to avert the salary increment crisis [Government: -Prop.; Bargaining process: -Val.]'

(3) He therefore urged government to show sympathy towards the work-
     force [Government: -Prop.]˙

In line (1) the impropriety of the government is emphasised in relation to the
economic status of the workers. Following on from line (1) the news writer
frames the next quoted statement as a criticism in line (2). Three items are
of interest here: the verb *criticised,* the adverb *allegedly* and the noun *crisis.*
While there is no overt integration of the voice of the news writer and that of
the news source, the verb *criticise* gives the reader a sense of how the quoted
words were spoken, and interpreted by the news writer. Different to the verb
warned discussed earlier, the verb *criticised* indicates a clear disparaging of the
government by the opposition leaders and conveys the writer's interpretation
of the opposition party leader's behaviour when expressing his delegitimation
of the government's actions. Here again we see a formulation in which the
authorial voice takes a backgrounded position and explicit evaluations are
confined to the voice of external voices. In line (2), both the government
and the bargaining process are evaluated negatively. On one hand, the government's lack of commitment is cast in terms of impropriety, and on the
other, the bargaining process is given a negative evaluation as a result of the
government's actions.

The adverb *allegedly* stands out in the news text as it connotes an
aura of secrecy about the specific news sources who made the allegation about the government's lack of commitment. While it appears
to be attributed to the external voice, I will argue that this adverb functions to frame a contentious proposition. Reference to some unspecified
news sources can be viewed as one strategy through which news writers
express their stance without any explicit terms. Considering the idea of
'mythical groups of reference', through which newspapers refer to 'undefined anonymous groups' (Menz 1989: 236), it can be suggested that the
adverb aids the news writer to mitigate a contentious claim. With such
undefined 'sources', contentious claims are expressed in concealed quotations and these, Stenvall (2008) argues, are rhetorical constructs. The contentious proposition that is framed through concealed citation accords the
news writer the success in achieving a faceless stance. The proposition that
government did not show any commitment to avert the salary increment crisis
is a contentious claim and by framing it in concealed quotation, the news
writer averts a pronounced assertion. Interestingly, the authorial formulation of using the adverb *allegedly* implicitly accords the unspecified news
'sources' the identity of analysts, as those who have analysed the process
of negotiation between the government and the public sector workers'
unions. Similar to the function of the adverb *allegedly,* the news article ends

with a sentence in which the adverb *therefore* plays a key role in connecting the earlier and the latter parts of the news text. When considered alongside the reporting expression *urged*, the opposition party leader is framed as a social actor who holds a dialogue with the government, speaking on behalf of public sector workers.

General Discussion

In the preceding analysis, news coverage of the public sector workers' strike has been considered as an interesting site to observe how news sources can be given voice to express their viewpoints about who they blame for disorderly events, how they frame potential events, and how they use their viewpoints to draw lines of contention. With an array of voices in their reach, news writers construct news stories to keep audiences informed about current events. As noted in the analysis, news writers not only act in their role as information givers but they also express value-laden judgements about social actors and about the events they report. This has been observed in instances where news writers integrate their voice with those of the news sources in news leads. Hunston observes that 'an attributed statement may not be a report of something that was actually said' (1995: 135). With this in mind, it can be argued that in order to integrate their voice with those of news sources, news writers engage in selective constructions of statements not necessarily to reproduce what was said but rather to capture an overall spirit of what was said. The choice of reporting verbs and making reference to unspecified sources are important in the framing of attributed news content. By using verbs of endorsement as in the case of the verb *assured*, as shown in the analysis, the news writer covertly indicates an evaluative stance. According to Van and Thomson, when a writer uses verbs of endorsement 'the framing is such as to indicate that the writer holds the material to be true or valid' (2008: 55). In a sense, such verbs are indicative of the reporter's belief that what the news source said was true (Hunston 1995: 134), and that the writer's descriptions of what a speaker said can shape readers' perceptions of the events reported (Machin and Mayr 2012).

Expressions of (de)legitimation have also been observed as an interesting finding in the news coverage of the strike. This has been clear in the expression of political dissent and blame rhetoric. Similar to Waddington's (1992) findings about the role of the media during times of riots and protests, the news texts construct an inter-party debate to frame the industrial dispute as more of a contest of political views than involving the unions on their own. This inter-party debate portrays the opposition MPs on the side of the workers and playing the role of the advocate.

Conclusion

In this chapter, I set out to investigate the phenomenon of attribution within the context of hard news reporting, and focused on how attributed statements can function to give the news writer his or her own voice in expressing some viewpoints or opinions about the events reported and the social actors involved. The analysis has predominantly paid attention to the linguistic strategies that news writers use in order to manage their stance-taking. Based on the parallel news excerpts analysed, it can be observed that reporting about the workers' strike highlights in some way the discourse of inter-party debates between the government and opposition political parties. This comes into play especially where opposition politicians express their opinions by according blame to the government. Framed from the perspective of imminent escalation of disorder during the workers' strike, inter-party debate and political dissent are very pronounced. With regard to the comparative perspective taken about the news texts, there are some notable differences in the foregrounding of news content. As noted in 'Analysis and Results' above, Text (A) foregrounds and validates the positive propriety of the government, whereas the confrontational debate depicted in Text (B) delegitimises the potential government that opposition parties aspire to form. Similarly in the second pair of news excerpts, Text (C) particularly foregrounds the instigation and escalation of disorder, whereas Text (D) leans more towards the emotionally charged details of the opinions of the news sources.

While the conclusions advanced in this chapter are limited to four news excerpts, it can be proposed that when studied within the context of hard news reporting, the use of attribution and acts of stance-taking are not mutually exclusive, but that the variety of linguistic resources employed in news texts affords the journalists success in expressing some evaluations while maintaining the neutrality ideal. Specifically, in the representation of forms of disorder, such linguistic resources allow for the coexistence of evaluations expressed by news sources and the embedded evaluations by the news writers. The variety of reporting expressions used in the news data is not a surprising finding because the inclusion of external voices is a feature mainly pointing towards the 'neutral' style of hard news reporting. However, as has been shown in the investigation of the news articles presented, other factors are at play and as such there is an array of evaluations expressed in the news.

When reporting the events of an industrial strike, taking a stance through the words of external sources is a strategic representation of events and the participants in them. There is a significant level of interpretation of quoted news content because the news writers retain control of what goes into the news article (Scollon 1998). As stated by Hunston (1995), attribution involves layers of covert interpretation, and the nature of this interpretation is one of the interesting factors that make attribution such an important resource for making (subjective) judgements in ostensibly objective writing.

References

Berkowitz, D. A. (2009), 'Reporters and their sources', in K. Wahl-Jorgensen and T. Hanitzsch (eds), *The Handbook of Journalism Studies*, New York: Routledge, pp. 102–15.

Caldas-Coulthard, C. R. (1993), 'From Discourse Analysis to Critical Discourse Analysis: The differential representation of women and men speaking in written news', in J. M. Sinclair, M. Hoey and G. Fox (eds), *Techniques of Description: Spoken and Written Discourse*, London: Routledge, pp. 196–208.

Caldas-Coulthard, C. R. (1994), 'On reporting reporting: The representation of speech in factual and fictional narratives', in M. Coulthard (ed.), *Advances in Written Text Analysis*, London: Routledge, pp. 295–320.

Calsamiglia, H. and C. López Ferrero (2003), 'Role and position of scientific voices: Reported speech in the media', *Discourse Studies*, 5 (2), pp. 147–73.

Coffin, C. and K. O'Halloran (2006), 'The role of appraisal and corpora in detecting covert evaluation', *Functions of Language*, 13 (1), pp. 77–110.

Haarman, L. (2009), 'Decoding codas: Evaluation in reporter and correspondent news talk', in L. Haarman and L. Lombardo (eds), *Evaluation and Stance in War News: A Linguistic Analysis of American, British and Italian Television News Reporting of the 2003 Iraqi War*, London: Continuum, pp. 116–39.

Hart, C. (2014), *Discourse, Grammar and Ideology: Functional and Cognitive Perspectives*, London: Bloomsbury.

Hunston, S. (1995), 'A corpus study of some English verbs of attribution', *Functions of Language*, 2 (2), pp. 133–58.

Lauerbach, G. (2006), 'Discourse representation in political interviews: The construction of identities and relations through voicing and ventriloquizing', *Journal of Pragmatics*, 38, pp. 196–215.

Machin, D. and A. Mayr (2012), *How to Do Critical Discourse Analysis*, London: Sage.

Marín Arrese, J. I. (2015), 'Epistemicity and stance: A cross-linguistic study of epistemic stance strategies in journalistic discourse in English and Spanish', *Discourse Studies*, 17 (2), pp. 210–25.

Martin, J. R. and P. R. R. White (2005), *The Language of Evaluation: Appraisal in English*, Basingstoke: Palgrave Macmillan.

Menz, F. (1989), 'Manipulation strategies in newspapers: A program for critical linguistics', in R. Wodak (ed.), *Language, Power and Ideology: Studies in Political Discourse*, Amsterdam: John Benjamins, pp. 227–49.

Piazza, R. (2009), 'News is reporting what was said: Techniques and patterns of attribution', in L. Haarman and L. Lombardo (eds), *Evaluation and Stance in War News: A Linguistic Analysis of American, British and Italian Television News Reporting of the 2003 Iraqi War*, London: Continuum, pp. 170–94.

Rooney, R. (2012), 'Characteristics of the Botswana press', *Global Media Journal: African Edition*, 6 (1), pp. 1–22.

Scollon, R. (1998), *Mediated Discourse as Social Interaction: A Study of News Discourse*, London: Longman.

Stenvall, M. (2008), 'Unnamed sources as rhetorical constructs in news agency reports', *Journalism Studies*, 9 (2), pp. 229–43.

Thompson, G. and Y. Yiyun (1991), 'Evaluation in the reporting verbs used in academic papers', *Applied Linguistics*, 12 (4), pp. 365–82.

Thomson, E. A., P. R. R. White and P. Kitley (2008), '"Objectivity" and "hard news" reporting across cultures: Comparing the news report in English, French, Japanese and Indonesian journalism', *Journalism Studies*, 9 (2), pp. 212–28.

Tutwane, L. (2011), 'The myth of press freedom in Botswana: From Sir Seretse Khama to Ian Khama', *Journal of African Media Studies*, 3 (1), pp. 43–55.

Van, T. T. H. and E. Thomson (2008), 'The nature of "reporter voice" in a Vietnamese hard news story', in E. Thomson and P. R. R. White (eds), *Communicating Conflict: Multilingual Case Studies of the News Media*, London: Continuum, pp. 51–63.

Van linden, A. and J. Verstraete (2011), 'Revisiting deontic modality and related categories: A conceptual map based on the study of English modal adjectives', *Journal of Pragmatics*, 43, pp. 150–63.

Waddington, D. (1992), *Contemporary Issues in Public Disorder: A Comparative and Historical Approach*, London: Routledge.

White, P. R. R. (2004), 'Subjectivity, evaluation and point of view in media discourse', in C. Coffin, A. Hewings and K. O'Halloran (eds), *Applying English Grammar: Functional and Corpus Approaches*, London: Arnold, pp. 229–46.

White, P. R. R. (2008), 'Praising and blaming, applauding, and disparaging – solidarity, audience positioning, and the linguistics of evaluative disposition', in G. Antos, E. Ventola and T. Weber (eds), *Handbook of Interpersonal Communication*, New York: Mouton de Gruyter, pp. 567–94.

6

Media 'Militant' Tendencies: How Strike Action in the News Press Is Discursively Constructed as Inherently Violent

Matt Davies and Rotsukhon Nophakhun

Introduction: Militarised News Discourse and the Labour Movement

The contribution of 'militarised discourse' to the systematic negative representation of UK Labour Party leader Jeremy Corbyn in the UK news media is the subject of a study by Freedman and Schlosberg (2016). They review three pieces of substantial empirical research which they claim demonstrate 'the comprehensive denigration of Jeremy Corbyn together with the disproportionate amount of attention paid to his critics' (Freedman and Schlosberg 2016: n.p.). One of these studies (Schlosberg 2016), conducted on behalf of the Media Reform Coalition in association with Birkbeck, University of London, notes that 'one of the most striking patterns that emerged was the repeated use of language that invoked militarism and violence' with, for instance, BBC correspondents tending to 'ascribe militancy and aggression exclusively to Jeremy Corbyn and his supporters' and not to those Labour MPs who publicly opposed Corbyn's stance and position as leader (Schlosberg 2016: 13). It is likely to be no coincidence, therefore, that the morning after a suspected ISIS-supporting suicide bomber killed twenty-two people and injured many more at the end of a concert in the Manchester Arena on 22 May 2017, one edition of *The Sun* newspaper juxtaposed on its front page a report of the atrocity with another report claiming to link Jeremy Corbyn with support for terrorist activities by the IRA in the 1980s. With just over two weeks left before polling day in a parliamentary general election scheduled for 8 June 2017, Britain's highest-circulation print newspaper – openly promoting Conservative leader Theresa May as its preferred candidate for prime minister – reported on 23 May 2017 that '[a]n ex-IRA killer says Jeremy Corbyn has blood on his hands – because without his support, the terrorist murders would have ended much earlier' (with the headline 'IRA BRUTE RAPS CORB'; Newton Dunn 2017: 1).

The reliance on what Freedman and Schlosberg (2016) describe as 'militarised discourse' to systematically and habitually demonise individuals and groups who challenge dominant ideological norms and values accords with our research on the (mis)representation of trade union endorsed strike action in the UK news press. Our view is that a key technique in the habitual stigmatisation of strikes is to misleadingly associate them with violence and aggression by routinely employing lexis from a semantic domain that has variants of the word 'militant' at its heart.

There is of course a more than coincidental relationship between overly critical reports of trade union forms of protest and the election (and re-election) of the more socialist-orientated Corbyn as Labour Party leader. At the time of writing, Corbyn and his shadow chancellor, John McDonnell, have been seeking to reposition the Labour Party back towards its trade unionist roots. As a key role of trade unions is to prevent their members being exploited by unscrupulous employers, unions are often perceived and represented as a threat to the dominant neoliberal modus operandi. According to Monbiot, for instance, '[n]eoliberalism sees competition as the defining characteristic of human relations' whereby 'the organisation of labour and collective bargaining by trade unions are portrayed as market distortions that impede the formation of a natural hierarchy of winners and losers' (2016: n.p.). The bulk of the mainstream news media, as global businesses themselves, are central in perpetuating discourse which naturalises these relations.

A Media Reform Coalition (2015) report entitled *Who Owns the UK Media?* draws attention to the fact that the UK's 'TV channels, news outlets, radio stations, search engines and social media platforms are owned by a handful of giant corporations' (2015: 3). They pose the rhetorical question: '[w]hat does it mean to have "independent media" when many of our most influential media organisations are controlled by individuals and Boards that are [very] closely connected with vested interests?' (2015: 3). The report shows that 60 per cent of UK national newspaper circulation is controlled by just two companies – Rupert Murdoch's News Corp UK, which publishes *The Sun, The Sun on Sunday, The Times* and *The Sunday Times*, and Lord Rothermere's Daily Mail Group (*Daily Mail* and *Mail on Sunday*) (2015: 7). *The Sun* and *Daily Mail* between them account for roughly 50 per cent of the total daily share of UK newspaper circulation (approximately 3.5 million per day) (2015: 4).

It is unsurprising therefore that *The Sun* and *Daily Mail* have taken a consistently antagonistic stance towards attitudes and values which challenge the neoliberal orthodoxy, including offering consistent support for the Conservative Party in general election campaigns (apart from *The Sun*'s temporary support for Tony Blair's Labour government between 1997 and 2007) and support for increased suppression of trade union activism, including the Trade Union Act 2016 (see Keir 2016; Emplaw Online 2016) which aims to further obstruct the ability of trade unions to conduct legal strike action. These newspapers reacted to Corbyn's September 2015 victory in the Labour Party leadership contest and his unambiguous support for trade union rights with typically apocalyptic headlines such as that on the front page of the *Daily Mail* on 14 September 2015 – 'CORBYN UNION PALS PLEDGE STRIKE CHAOS (As Labour plunges into bitter civil war)' (Groves and Martin 2015: 1). What would purport to be a 'straight' news report implies a conspiracy between Corbyn and the trade unions to overthrow the government whereby intimidation is a key tactic. The introductory sentence sets the tone – 'Jeremy Corbyn's union allies last night threatened strikes and civil unrest to topple the Government and install him in Downing Street' (Groves and Martin 2015: 1). Unmistakeably negative discourse such as 'threatened' is sustained in the article with lexis applied to Corbyn and the unions such as 'break the law', 'sinister threat', 'extreme foreign policy positions', 'thuggish elements', 'reckless and damaging strikes', 'civil unrest' and 'threat to national security'. Central to maintaining a cohesive semantic field containing aggressive and violent discourse is the consistent employment of forms of 'militant' to label the referents and their actions in the reports. The *Daily Mail* article cited above (Groves and Martin 2015), for instance, refers to elected trade union leaders as 'militant chiefs' and later on as '[m]ilitant union leaders'. Our study demonstrates that the sense of 'militant(s)' and 'militancy' has taken on an increasingly negative 'semantic prosody' by being used uncritically in news that reports incidences of terrorism which often involve acts of extreme violence, typically leading to civilian deaths. As 'militant' is rarely used in any contexts other than to refer to terrorist activities and reports of trade union action, it is therefore significantly tarnished by the lexical company it keeps in reports of terrorism. Our corpus of news reports containing variant forms of 'militant' from 2000 to 2015 provides convincing evidence of the word's overwhelmingly negative associations and confirms a study by Davies (2014) which shows how reports of strike action are peppered with the discourse of 'violence' and that 'militant' is central to this strategy. We draw on the concept of 'semantic prosody' (see, for example, Louw 1993; Partington 1998; Baker 2006; Xia and McEnery 2006; Stewart 2010; McEnery and Hardie 2012; Begagić 2013) as a way of explaining how a specific lexical item and its variants can contribute towards the transference of negative connotations from one news topic to another. We also propose that the negative press on trade unions is unrepresentative of 'public opinion', suggesting that there is another agenda at work. For instance, in a 2014 MORI opinion poll 'around three in four (77%) Britons agree that trade unions are essential to protect workers' interests while [only] 14% disagree' (Ipsos MORI 2014: n.p.). MORI claim that this is a consistent trend since 1975 when they first started asking the question. According to Gideon Skinner, Head of Political Research at Ipsos MORI, 'trade unions are seen as vital for the workers they represent, and there is much less concern about them wielding too much power than in the past' (Ipsos MORI 2014: n.p.).

An examination of the reporting of a strike by junior doctors in England can illustrate the disparagement of industrial action in the UK news media which uses implications of intimidation as part of a strategy of vilification.

'Militant Medics' and Media Manipulation

On 12 January 2016 up to 45,000 junior doctors in England took part in a 24-hour nationwide strike – providing only emergency cover – in a dispute with the Conservative-led government over contractual issues relating to overtime payments and weekend working. Of the 76 per cent of the membership of the medical trade union, the British Medical Association (BMA), who participated in the ballot, an overwhelming 98 per cent voted in favour of strike action, the first industrial action by junior doctors in the UK since November 1975 (see Campbell 2016a). Further strikes in February and March 2016 failed to achieve the desired concessions from the government. This led to the first ever all-out doctors' strike on 26 April 2016, whereby junior doctors withheld not only routine but also emergency care for that day (Triggle 2016).

An Ipsos MORI poll for *BBC Newsnight* and the *Health Service Journal* published on 11 January 2016 found that 66 per cent of the public in England supported the first strike (as long as emergency cover was provided) with only 16 per cent opposed to the strike (Ipsos MORI 2016b).

A similar poll published on 25 April 2016, after several more strikes and the day before emergency cover was also withdrawn, still found majority support (57 per cent) from the public, with 26 per cent in opposition to the walkouts (Ipsos MORI 2016a). Typically, support for this strike and strike action in general was not mirrored in the pages of the mainstream national UK press. The two highest-circulation print newspapers, *The Sun* and the *Daily Mail*, were less than magnanimous towards striking doctors when they would not accept an unsatisfactory revised contract on 5 July 2016. For instance, a *Daily Mail* report (6 July 2016) with the headline 'JUNIOR DOCTORS REJECT PAY DEAL, RAISING FEAR OF SUMMER STRIKES', characteristically emphasised the negative impact of the strike on patients rather than the working conditions of the doctors. The tone of the headline matches the opening few sentences of the article:

> Junior doctors yesterday threw out a contract offered by the Government, prompting fears of summer strike action. They voted to reject the revised deal even though it promised higher rates of weekend pay and extra support to make working lives easier. (Borland 2016: 12)

The subtle undermining of the junior doctors' case is partially achieved by classifying their latest decision through negative verb processes such as 'threw out' and 'reject' whereas the government 'offered' a 'deal'. The junior doctors are portrayed therefore as selfish and inflexible whilst the government is depicted as generously bending over backwards to accommodate the doctors, a stance which is confirmed in the second sentence. Here, the contrast – emphasised by the conjunction 'even though' – between what appears to be substantial beneficial modifications to the contract associated with the government (e.g. through the adjectives 'higher', 'extra' and 'easier') and its rejection, contributes towards making the doctors appear unreasonable.[1]

Nestling within this rather unspectacular example is an example of a darker trend: the association of strike action with sinister forces, including threatening behaviour and violence. News discourse reporting strike action is littered with lexis from these semantic fields, regardless of any evidence within the reports that such activities have taken place. For instance, in the *Daily Mail* example cited above (Borland 2016), the choice of nominalised 'fear' in the headline and opening sentence, as opposed to a form of the verb 'to fear' (e.g. '*x* feared *y*') gives news reports the capacity to encourage apprehension amongst the readership, whilst providing no evidence of who has expressed this trepidation. The ubiquity of 'militant' in these reports assists in generating a tone of menace in relation to strike action.

So the *Daily Mail* article continues its report with the news of the resignation of the chairman of the BMA's Junior Doctor Committee, Dr Johann Malawana, who had encouraged acceptance of the deal, 'prompting fears he will be replaced by a more *militant* colleague', described later in the article as 'the hardline Yannis Gourtsoyannis' (Borland 2016: 12; our emphasis). A profile of Dr Gourtsoyannis which constitutes a separate article in the same edition has the headline 'MILITANT WHO WANTS TO BRING DOWN THE TORIES') (Daily Mail 2016: 12). The following day, *The Sun* newspaper describes the interim chair of the BMA's junior doctors committee, Dr Ellen McCourt, as a 'militant medic', choosing the headline 'LEFTIE WILL LEAD DOC STRIKE CALL' (Wooller 2016: 2). *The Express* newspaper (6 July 2016) also describes those who voted to reject the contract as 'militant medics' (Maddox 2016b), a decision the *Daily Telegraph* represents in its leader column on the same day as 'militant intransigence' (Daily Telegraph 2016).

To give some idea of the negative associations, or 'semantic prosody', of the word 'militant' (and its variants) encouraged by these news outlets, the 6 July 2016 online edition of *The Express* carries the disturbing headline 'ISIS *MILITANTS* BOILED ALIVE AS PUNISHMENT FOR FLEEING BATTLEFIELD' (Bayliss 2016). The opening sentence of the report – '[d]epraved Islamic State militants boiled seven of their own fighters to death for fleeing the battlefield in their latest warped method of execution' – indicates that the 'militants' referred to in the atrocity denote both the ISIS deserters and their executioners in the same organisation. The use of 'militant' in the same edition of a national newspaper, referring simultaneously to trade union activists and those who carry out acts of extreme violence, is not an unfortunate coincidence. We can demonstrate this initially in a simple way by summarising the results generated when searching for all instances of variants of 'militant' used in UK national news reports on 6 July 2016. Inputting the search term 'militan*'[2] in the LexisNexis news database and using the 'UK national newspapers' filter generates 24 articles which use the singular or plural form of 'militant' at least once.[3] This breaks down as follows: *Independent* – 7, *Daily Telegraph* – 4, *Daily Mail* – 3, *The Express* – 3, *The Times* – 3, *Daily Mirror* – 2, *The Guardian* – 2. Of these, 18 articles had as their main subject matter terrorist activities, mostly involving so-called Islamic State (ISIS), and these constitute a total of 42 out of 48 aggregate uses of 'militan*' in these articles.

Three of these are included in headlines giving some indication of the violent nature of the subject matter:

(1) ISIS MILITANTS BOILED ALIVE AS PUNISHMENT FOR FLEEING BATTLEFIELD (*The Express*)

(2) ESCAPED ISIS MILITANT REVEALS REALITY OF THE JIHADIST GROUP'S BRUTALITY: 'THEY ABUSED AND MUTILATED DEAD BODIES' (*Independent*)

(3) SICKENING FOOTAGE FROM DEAD TERRORIST'S PHONE SHOWS ISIS MILITANTS LAUGHING WHILE WOMAN IS RAPED (*Daily Mirror*)

Other examples within the main text include:

(4) In Yemen, where suicide bombers and other militants carried out at least seven simultaneous attacks in the southern port city of Mukalla against security targets on 27 June, 43 people were killed. (*Independent*)

(5) In January, an Isis militant was accused of publicly executing his own mother in the Syrian city of Raqqa after accusing her of apostasy. (*Independent*)

(6) Paul, 65, lost his civil engineer brother Ken to Islamic militants, who took him hostage in Baghdad in 2004 before beheading him on video 22 days later. (*Daily Mirror*)

(7) In Bangladesh on Friday Isis militants murdered 20 restaurant guests and injured 30 in a siege that shocked the country with its brutality. (*The Times*)

(8) No group has claimed responsibility but Islamic State militants have carried out similar bombings in the US-allied, Sunni Muslim-ruled kingdom in the past year, targeting minority Shi'ites and Saudi security forces. (*Daily Telegraph*)

It is significant therefore that five of the six other articles use 'militan*' in relation to trade union activity. Three of these (from the *Daily Mail, The Express* and *Daily Telegraph*) are cited above. They also include a reference to 'militant medics [who] voted 58 to 42 per cent against the deal agreed by the British Medical Association and the Government' (*The Express*), and a story about inter-party conflict in Australia which references 'industrial law breaches by the militant construction union' (*The Guardian*). The only mildly positive example occurs in a *Guardian* opinion piece by former Stop the War Coalition and Socialist Worker's Party member Lindsey German who relates the 'militant response' of anti-war protestors to the announcement of the conclusions of the Chilcot inquiry into the UK's involvement in the bombing of Iraq in 2003. German's use of the adjective here is more in line with the way 'militant' is used by political campaigners to refer to vigorous campaigning, and is rarely used in this sense in the mainstream news media.

'Militant' Meanings and Leanings

So what are the varying senses of 'militant' and how have they shifted diachronically towards the extremely pejorative senses they undoubtedly hold today in the UK news media?

'Militant' is clearly polysemic in that although its etymological roots are clear, related but divergent senses have evolved. The *Oxford English Dictionary* (OED Online 2018) provides a useful snapshot of the varying senses of 'militant' across several hundred years, with its first recorded citation as an adjective dating back to circa 1425, and defined as '[e]ngaged in warfare, warring. Also: disposed towards war; warlike' and frequently 'metaphorically of the

Church'. The other key sense claimed by the *OED* is one which conflates the concept of protest in general with possessing an aggressive demeanour.

The first definition provided by the *OED* – '[c]ombative; aggressively persistent; strongly espousing a cause; entrenched, adamant' – cites texts from as far back as 1603 ('[h]e would maintain by militant reasons') to an entry from *The New York Times* in 1992 ('[i]f my mother had one rule, it was militant ecumenism in all matters of food and experience'). It is worth pointing out that a citation in 1961 refers to 'an arrogance among certain militant pacifists which . . . prevented them from respecting the views of those who thought freedom worth fighting for', indicating that in this example at least 'militant' has a sense which logically means the opposite of 'military' otherwise it would be an oxymoron.

A second definition provided by the *OED*, of the *non*-military sense of 'militant', gives an indication of how the UK press can take advantage of its semantic prosody to imply that more exuberant trade union and other protest activity necessarily involves some kind of threatening behaviour. This is defined in the *OED* as '[a]ggressively pursuing a political or social cause, and often favouring extreme, violent, or confrontational methods'. This more modern sense has as its first citation a quote from the *International Journal of Ethics* (1893) which asserts that '[t]he unionist . . . subordinates himself to a body which aims at securing a desired end for all its members. A trade union is necessarily militant.' This is followed by a claim in the *Journal of Political Economy* (1896) that '[t]he aggressive or "militant" side of the activity of trade unions was emphasized during 1893'. Note that the sense in the 1893 example implies that militancy merely involves loyalty to its members, whereas in the second example it is treated as synonymous with aggressiveness, indicating a tension between different senses. Further citations include an extract from Emily Pankhurst's 1914 autobiography *My Own Story* in which she refers to 'our militant suffrage organisation, the Women's Social and Political Union' and a reference in the *Daily Express* (1930) to the leader of the UK's Independent Labour Party, James Maxton – a trade unionist and pacifist conscientious objector – who 'leads a group of I.L.P. members who have brought a militant policy with them'.

If the *OED* is a reliable gauge of semantic shift, then the use of 'militant' to refer to acts of isolated and targeted aggression is a phenomenon born of the latter half of the twentieth century. In this sense its first *OED* citation as an adjective is from 1971 in a book called *Days of Martin Luther King* which refers to a bombing incident which 'was the work of . . . a militant black who wanted to incite his people to riot'. The latest entry here is from a 1992 edition of *The New York Times* which describes a shootout between 'militant Muslims' against the police. This shift in emphasis seems to be confirmed when looking at similar citations for the noun 'militant' where there are references to suffragette 'militants' in 1909, trade union militancy in 1968 ('ultra-left militants in the Electrical Trades Union') and 1983 ('our dealings with the [union] militants'), after which the latest entry in 1997 from *The Economist* relates how 'Assamese militants blew up three oil pipelines in November to assert their supremacy'. An important recent addition to the *OED*, which was given its own entry in 1979, is 'Militant tendency', referring to a group of socialist campaigners based around the *Militant* newspaper (which changed its name to *The Socialist* in 1997). Although a few of the several citations included in the *OED* use inflammatory language to describe the activities of its supporters (e.g. 'sectarian hardliners' in the *New Statesman* 1979), there is no indication that the word has military connotations and indeed supporters of the group used it in the traditional labour movement sense of protesting and organising against capitalist injustice and exploitation (see Taaffe and Mulhearn 1988; Taaffe 1995).

Our assertion then is that the tensions between the sense of 'militant' as referring to actions of peaceful protest – often anti-establishment – and terrorist violence are exploited by the press in the reports of the former.

Semantic Prosody and the Staining of 'Militant'

The concept of 'semantic prosody' perhaps best encapsulates the way that word forms such as 'militant' take on negative (and in rarer cases, positive) connotations because of the company they keep, that is, the discourse with which they commonly collocate. For instance, in the 6 July 2016 articles, words and phrases which occurred in the same sentence as 'militant(s)' include 'boiled alive', 'death', 'execution', 'depraved', 'killed', 'spectacular violence', 'war', 'shot', 'suicide bombers', 'deadliest ever terror attack', 'one of the worst war crimes', 'beheading', 'raped', 'murdered' and 'brutality'.

The term 'semantic prosody' was originally coined by Sinclair (1987) and developed by Louw who described it as the 'consistent aura of meaning with which a form is imbued by its collocates' (1993: 157).

According to Partington, semantic prosody occurs 'where an item shows a preference to co-occur with items that can be described as bad, unfavourable or unpleasant, or as good, favourable or pleasant' (2004: 149). When the item is not co-occurring with any of its common collocates, it is still possible to colour the meaning of a specific discourse in ways dictated by its collocates in other texts. Stewart admits difficulties in pinning down a precise definition of semantic prosody but claims that it can be 'instantiated when a word such as *CAUSE* co-occurs regularly with words that share a given meaning or meanings, and then acquires some of the meaning(s) of those words as a result. This acquired meaning is known as semantic prosody' (2010: 1). In the corpus discussed in this chapter, for instance, a concordance list for 51 instances of 'cause' produces examples such as the following:

knew or should have known was likely to	**cause**	distress, alarm or offence to others in a
Janner said he feared that Mr Farrakhan could	**cause**	racial tensions if he repeated his previous
He called upon fellow animal rights activists to	**cause**	"maximum destruction". In January 2003 Mr
The trauma such demonstrations can	**cause**	to children, Dr Best argued, was
of 'ill-informed, conservative doctors' were a	**cause**	of 'great concern' to moderate Muslims. Some
disease, which lay waste to human life and	**cause**	untold misery and suffering. It is on
thousands. But the foreign suicide volunteers	**cause**	the greatest carnage, and the supply of
the way, to stop him using people to	**cause**	mayhem." The militant group led by Yusuf, a

Here, the words and phrases placed as the grammatical object of the verb 'cause' include 'distress, alarm or offence', 'racial tensions', 'maximum destruction', 'untold misery and suffering', 'the greatest carnage' and 'mayhem' and others in its immediate vicinity include 'trauma', 'disease', 'lay waste to human life' and 'suicide volunteers'. It is possible therefore that a consistent use of 'cause' in a stretch of discourse may be indicative of and/or trigger the expectations of troubling subject matter.

Although clearly only a miniscule snapshot from a corpus whose content is largely based on stories of human suffering (evidence that the term 'militant' also has such associations), the point about semantic prosody is that continual use in such contexts is likely to instil or 'colour', 'infect', 'rub off on' (see Stewart 2010: 42–3) words, providing them with senses which may have been weaker or non-existent in earlier usages, hence taking a diachronic approach is often essential in such studies. Writing about 'cause', Bublitz discusses how 'constant association (through collocation) of CAUSE with clearly unpleasant, negative words could, at some point, result in the word itself acquiring unpleasant, negative connotations' (1996: 11–12). Partington aptly sums up this relationship by citing a Chinese proverb that claims 'he who stays near vermilion gets stained red, and he who stays near ink gets stained black' (1998: 67).

Crucially, a word saturated with a specific semantic prosody tends to express the attitude of the speaker/writer towards their subject matter and this is clearly the case in many news reports on strikes and in our corpus. So the sense of 'militan*' in the reporting of strike action could easily be stained by embracing the semantic fields of violence quoted in the examples above. Also, semantic prosodies 'may not be accessible from our conscious knowledge' (McEnery and Hardie 2012: 136) and therefore much of their ideological impact stems from their engagement at a subconscious level. It is only since the advent of computer-assisted corpus analysis that researcher intuition can be confirmed by empirical study, often of millions of words, by generating, for instance, concordance lines to study collocation, keywords and significant semantic fields using programs such as WordSmith and Wmatrix. The examples of 'militan*' based on one day of news reporting do not provide anywhere near enough evidence towards demonstrating its negative semantic prosody, nor therefore a general tendency towards demonisation of strike action in the UK national news media.

So to give some credence to the claim that 'militant' – in the news press at least – is imbued with connotations of violence in the twenty-first century, using the LexisNexis news database we built a corpus based on news articles from the national UK press from 2000 to 2015 that contained the key word 'militant' and its variants. To make the sample manageable, we assembled articles published on the dates 1 March and 1 August for each year to ensure a random but even spread diachronically over the 15-year period and searched for articles on these dates which contained 'militant(s)' or 'militancy' (using the search term 'militan*'). The search generated 274,122 words in 357 articles, producing 686 examples of the search term.

As our aim was to gauge the subject matter and significant semantic domains in news stories using 'militan*', we used the corpus analysis and comparison tool, Wmatrix, an online service hosted by Lancaster University (see Rayson 2008). Wmatrix tags each of the words in a corpus and assigns it to one of 21 major semantic domains, such as EDUCATION, WORLD AND THE ENVIRONMENT and SCIENCE AND TECHNOLOGY.[4] These are broken down further into 232 semantic sub-categories, so GEOGRAPHICAL TERMS, WEATHER and GREEN ISSUES fall under the more general heading of WORLD AND THE ENVIRONMENT. The software not only generates lists of the most frequent semantic categories which occur in any dataset, it is also capable of providing some insight into the 'keyness' of semantic categories which seem to be dominant in the corpus. It does this by comparing it with one of several reference corpora, in our case a one million word sample of written data from the British National Corpus (BNC), available as part of the Wmatrix service. This is important because in itself frequency of semantic category produces mundane results. It is unsurprising, for instance, that top of the frequency list is the category GRAMMATICAL BIN, which in our corpus comprises 88,170 words, constituting 32.16 per cent of the entire dataset. This consists, for example, of 18,081 instances of 'the' (6.6 per cent of the whole corpus), followed by 'of' (7,714 tokens), 'to' (7,023), 'a' (6,524), and so on. The second most frequent category is that of PRONOUNS (17,574 or 6.41 per cent), followed by GEOGRAPHICAL NAMES (3.65 per cent), UNMATCHED – that is, words unrecognised by the software's dictionary – (2.33 per cent), and EXISTING – dominated by forms of the verb 'to be' – (2.17 per cent).

But when we generate a list of key concepts compared with the BNC written sample, a much more interesting pattern emerges, one which concords with our initial suspicions regarding the semantic prosody of 'militan*'. Table 6.1 is an edited version of the results.

Table 6.1 Key semantic categories generated by Wmatrix for news data containing 'militan*'

No.	News	%1	BNC	%2	LL	Semantic category
1	10,002	3.65	14,502	1.5	4,321.97	GEOGRAPHICAL NAMES
2	4,011	1.46	3,152	0.33	3,867.71	WARFARE, DEFENCE AND THE ARMY; WEAPONS
3	2,914	1.06	1,647	0.17	3,662.26	VIOLENT/ANGRY
4	3,256	1.19	3,542	0.37	2,194.98	GOVERNMENT
5	1,726	0.63	1,585	0.16	1,422.94	DEAD
6	1,038	0.38	570	0.06	1,330.51	CRIME
7	2,271	0.83	3,016	0.31	1,143.62	RELIGION AND THE SUPERNATURAL
8	1,715	0.63	2,418	0.25	779.62	LAW AND ORDER
9	3,524	1.29	7,024	0.73	714.03	SPEECH: COMMUNICATIVE
10	292	0.11	48	0.00	629.66	ANTI-WAR
11	785	0.29	885	0.09	504.72	HINDERING
12	730	0.27	815	0.08	475.56	DAMAGING AND DESTROYING
13	2,386	0.87	4,809	0.50	466.90	OTHER PROPER NAMES
14	399	0.15	296	0.03	405.37	UNEMPLOYED
15	1,999	0.73	4,064	0.42	380.51	POLITICS
16	116	0.04	0	0.00	350.60	DEGREE
17	2,596	0.95	5,888	0.61	0.64	PLACES
18	204	0.07	93	0.01	293.72	ALIVE
19	2,446	0.89	5,811	0.60	255.50	BELONGING TO A GROUP
24	443	0.16	727	0.08	149.06	NO CONSTRAINT
27	448	0.16	757	0.08	141.11	FEAR/SHOCK
32	81	0.03	54	0.01	90.03	EVALUATION: BAD
33	587	0.21	1,275	0.13	88.90	DISEASE
35	286	0.10	516	0.05	76.76	UNETHICAL

They are listed in order of significance, with the most significant at the top, and include statistics for both the researcher corpus and the reference corpus. So row 1 indicates that the most significant category is GEOGRAPHI-CAL NAMES (the third most frequent category), consisting of 10,002 words which constitute 3.65 per cent of the 274,122 words in the corpus. The BNC corpus, on the other hand, consists of just 1.5 per cent of its one million words (14,502) in the same semantic domain, which produces a log-likelihood (LL) of 4,321.97, a figure which represents the likelihood of that category being significant through coincidence alone. The higher the figure, the less likely that this is just a chance occurrence (see Baker 2006: 125–7).

The prevalence of geographical names is perhaps not surprising given that news stories rely on specifying the location of the events being reported. Its importance for our hypothesis, however, is twofold. First, it demonstrates the robustness of Wmatrix's ability to appropriately identify the most prevalent semantic domains in the news data and therefore allows the user to hazard a reliable guess as to the nature of the inputted material without even having read any of the articles. Second, a glance at the screenshot of the most frequent words in this category (see Table 6.2) shows that the geographical focus of the news content is predominantly the Middle East, with the Israeli–Palestinian conflict and countries associated with Islamic military groups (Iraq, Afghanistan, Syria) foregrounded.

It is clear from Table 6.1 that other highly significant categories confirm the notion that 'militant' correlates with semantic domains primarily associated with subversive and/or aggressive and violent behaviour – WARFARE, DEFENCE AND THE ARMY (2nd), VIOLENT/ANGRY (3rd), DEAD (5th), CRIME (6th), LAW AND ORDER (8th), DAMAGING AND DESTROYING (12th), FEAR/SHOCK (27th), DISEASE (33rd), UNETHICAL (35th). We can see from some

Table 6.2 A Wmatrix screenshot of the most frequent words in the category
GEOGRAPHICAL NAMES

Word	Semtag	Frequency	Relative Frequency		Summary information:		
Israel	Z2	527	0.19	Concordance	Number of types shown: 1119		
israeli	Z2	508	0.19	Concordance	Total frequency of types shown: 10002 (3.65%)		
british	Z2	373	0.14	Concordance	Total frequency overall: 274122		
London	Z2	361	0.13	Concordance			
Gaza	Z2	318	0.12	Concordance	Number of items shown with a given frequency:		
Pakistan	Z2	303	0.11	Concordance			
Britain	Z2	263	0.10	Concordance	Frequency	Types	Tokens
palestinian	Z2	261	0.10	Concordance	1	606 (54.16%)	606 (6.06%)
Iraq	Z2	253	0.09	Concordance	2	154 (13.76%)	308 (3.08%)
Afghanistan	Z2	217	0.08	Concordance	3	72 (6.43%)	216 (2.16%)
palestinians	Z2	179	0.07	Concordance	4	38 (3.40%)	152 (1.52%)
taliban	Z2	178	0.06	Concordance	5	37 (3.31%)	185 (1.85%)
Syria	Z2	170	0.06	Concordance	6	25 (2.23%)	150 (1.50%)
american	Z2	145	0.05	Concordance	7	26 (2.32%)	182 (1.82%)
UK	Z2	124	0.05	Concordance	8	12 (1.07%)	96 (0.96%)
pakistani	Z2	111	0.04	Concordance	9	11 (0.98%)	99 (0.99%)
India	Z2	106	0.04	Concordance	10	9 (0.80%)	90 (0.90%)
Egypt	Z2	103	0.04	Concordance	> 10	129 (11.53%)	7918 (79.16%)
iraqi	Z2	96	0.04	Concordance			

of the other categories high on the list – GOVERNMENT, RELIGION AND THE SUPERNATURAL, OTHER PROPER NAMES, BELONGING TO A GROUP, and so on – that they are reliable indicators of the subject matter of stories we predicted would appear when searching for 'militant'.

The most frequent word in the second most significant category is 'military' (344 – 0.13 per cent) followed by 'bomb(s)/bombing' (249 – 0.09 per cent) and 'war' (245 – 0.09 per cent). This is unsurprising given the blatant etymological roots of the search word (although this is allocated to a different category – see below). Indeed, one criticism that could be levelled at our hypothesis is that building a corpus comprising only texts containing instances of 'militant' is bound to generate content in which stories of military conflict dominate. It is worth a reminder therefore that if the *OED* is a reliable indicator, in some contexts the sense of 'militant' clearly has very tenuous semantic links with military-related activity, such as those referring to instances of peaceful protest or simply active participation in a trade union, and should in no way entail the dominance of military discourse in a corpus search for 'militant'.

The modern canonical association of militancy with aggressiveness is presumably why its word forms appear in the VIOLENT/ANGRY category in Wmatrix and partially account for that semantic domain's high level of significance in the statistics. Of the 232 different word forms ('types') represented in that category, 'militants' (374), 'militant' (291) and 'militancy' (16) constitute 681 (23 per cent) of the 2,914 words ('tokens') occurring in this category. Anticipating accusations that it is stating the obvious that texts sourced using a specific search term are bound to generate a high frequency of that very word, our next step then is to consider the contexts in which these words appear and the 77 per cent of other words in the VIOLENT/ANGRY category which sit in close proximity to our search term. A small sample of a concordance list gives an indication of some of the typically frenzied contexts in which 'militants' appears in the news data:

He said: "As a movement it has more trained	**militants**	with expertise that can be used in terrorist operation
troops and a minibus carrying suspected Islamist	**militants.**	Local people insist they were innocent civilians.
recent assassination attempts on him by Islamist	**militants.**	The New York Times quoted a US official overseeing
which they say will boost the cause of Muslim	**militants**	who argue that parts of the Government suffer from"
workers, who were kidnapped by Palestinian	**militants**	on Friday night , were sheltering yesterday in the

alarmed at the extremist tactics **militants** in the animal-rights movement, it
displayed by unveiled a package

what happens (at general elections) **Militants** linked to al-Qaeda ally Abu
in January. Musab al-Zarqawi claimed

They are due here in September to **militants** at a training camp in Tonbridge,
lecture 300 Kent, about direct

and continued behind-the-scenes **militants** and diplomats alike to alter the
plotting by landscape. If the

execution deadline by 24 hours to **militants,** who call themselves the Black
last night. The Banners brigade of the

yesterday 's attack underlined the **militants** to strike. As in previous blasts,
ability of the they targeted

the peace process, after a suicide **militants** in Tel Aviv on Friday was con-
bombing by demned as the work of

of people in the West. Politicians **militants** as "al Qaeda" helps the public
think labelling understand the threat

Table 6.3 shows the most frequent of the 232 word forms in the VIOLENT/ANGRY category. Other words include 'persecution', 'brutal(ity)', 'mayhem', 'thug(s)', 'abuse', 'barbaric', 'bloodbath' and 'sadistic', providing a stark indication of the company kept by the search term.[5]

This is confirmed when we study the high-frequency words appearing in some of the other significant categories. So 0.63 per cent of all the words in the corpus (1,726 tokens) fall in the DEAD category. Table 6.4 shows them in order of frequency and makes explicit that the deaths reported are inflicted on people in violent ways with 723 (42 per cent) of these being forms of 'kill', and also near the top of the frequency list are forms of 'suicide',

Table 6.3 The most frequent word forms in the VIOLENT/ANGRY category

militant(s)/militancy	681	clashes	28
attack(s)(ed)	650	wounding	23
violence/violent	230	Holocaust	22
threat(s)/threaten(s)(ed)(ing)	224	bloodshed	20
fighter(s)	105	outrage	17
force	92	riots	16
hit	69	torture	16
anger/angry	58	unrest	15
assault(s)	51	aggressive	14
revenge	36	fierce	13

Table 6.4 The most frequent word forms in the DEAD category

kill(er)(s)(ed)(ing)	723	funerals	5
die(d)/dead(ly)(liest)/death(s)	496	lethal	5
suicide	145	fatalities	5
murder(er)(s)(ing)	87	decapitated	3
assassination(s)(ed)(ing)	79	corpses	3
massacre(s)	27	lifeless	3
execution(er)(s)(ing)	26	mortuary	3
behead(ed)(ing)(s)	20	morgue	3
slaughter(ed)	8	perished	3
genocide	7	cremated	3

'murder', 'assassination', 'massacre', 'execution', 'behead', 'slaughter', 'genocide', and so on.

Items closely semantically related to 'dead' also appear in the CRIME category (6th most significant) and confirm the association of 'militant' with brutal events. Criminality in itself does not necessarily entail violence, but here the 358 instances of 'terrorist(s)(ism)' constitute 34 per cent of the 1,038 words in the category, which also includes forms of 'kidnap', 'gunmen', 'paedophile' and 'rape' in the 20 most frequently occurring words (see Table 6.5).

Other significant semantic categories likely to imply violence include: DAMAGING AND DESTROYING (12th most significant) with 'victim(s)', 'destroy(ed)', 'destruction', broke(n)', 'damage(s)(ed)' and 'collapse(s)(ed)' at the top of the list; FEAR/SHOCK (27th), which is dominated by 'terror', followed by 'fear(s)(ed)(ing)', 'shock(s)(ed)' and 'horror(s)'; and the category DISEASE, which consists mainly of casualty-related words with 'injure(s)(ing)(ed)' the most frequent followed by 'wound(s)(ed)' and 'casualties'.

Table 6.5 The most frequent word forms in the CRIME category

terrorist(s)/terrorism	358	revolt	16
kidnap(p)(er)(s)(ing)(ed)	97	lawless	11
crim(e)(inal)(s)	63	insurgent	9
illegal(ly)	49	arson	8
plot(s)(ting)	48	offence	7
suspect(s)	43	rape	7
gunmen	34	smuggled	7
guilty	24	conspiracy	7
paedophile	24	injustice	7
violation(s)	17	theft	6

That 'militant' is strongly allied in the UK press with specific world-views which are often represented in the UK media as antagonistic to western values also comes as no surprise, with the 7th most significant category RELIGION AND THE SUPERNATURAL constituting nearly 1 per cent (2,271) of all the words in the corpus. The list of 244 separate word forms is dominated by 'Islam(ic)(ist)(s)' (453), 'Hamas' (326), 'Muslim(s)' (280), 'mosque' (78) and 'sunni' (57); and 'ISIS' is by far the most frequent item (161 instances) to appear in the 13th most significant category OTHER PROPER NAMES.

The data presented here substantiates the conclusions of Davies (2014), who used similar analytical techniques to study the representation in the UK news press of a series of one-day strikes taken by British Airways cabin crew staff in March and April 2010 and a one-day public sector strike of teachers, lecturers and civil servants on 30 June 2011. Using Wmatrix to identify key semantic domains, Davies found that the VIOLENT/ANGRY category was prominent in both the 138,000 word corpus of news reports on the BA strike (8th most significant) and the 64,000 word public sector strike corpus (10th most significant). In each case, forms of 'militant' again dominated (largely in the *Daily Mail*, *The Times* and *The Sun*), topping the frequency list in the case of the BA strike, alongside variants of 'threat' and 'bully'. Significantly, unlike the data analysed above in which reports of tangible violence, often resulting in multiple deaths, are clearly apparent, very few of the keywords in these categories are replicated in any data reporting on trade union strike action, for the obvious reason that no evidence could be provided for it. The news reports rely largely on the use of unsubstantiated, subjective and evaluative lexis such as 'threat' and the semantic prosody of 'militant' in attempting to undermine support for industrial action. Our prediction is that any substantial corpus of reports on industrial action in the UK news press, in the past or at least for the foreseeable future, will over-represent 'militan*' in its discourse and contribute to continuing the tendency to stigmatise strike action.

Conclusion

For a closing reconfirmation of the way that depictions of strike action are tarnished with the unsubstantiated illusions of intimidation and violence, it is useful to juxtapose press reports and opinion which employ at least one instance of 'militant' in discourse relating to the 26 April 2016 all-out junior doctors' strike, with other reports which employ the word in the same edition of the paper.

The 27 April edition of the *Daily Telegraph* includes a letter from a retired doctor complaining that the BMA 'has become as militant as the miners were during the Seventies' (headline: 'Frustrated patients will have little sympathy for disruptive strike action') (Berkeley 2016: 17), whilst in the same edition it relates a story about how '[m]ilitant Islamist fighters take part in a military parade along the streets of northern Raqqa' (Agence France-Presse 2016). *The Express* reports that 'Labour Party leader Jeremy Corbyn and shadow chancellor John McDonnell joined militant doctors at a protest' (Maddox 2016a), and simultaneously includes 'militant' in several stories on terrorism, in one referring to '[b]arbaric Islamic State militants' (Reynolds 2016). And whilst the more liberal *Guardian* uses the concept of militancy in a less evaluative fashion, referring to the 'militant mood among many [BMA] committee members' (Campbell 2016b), it still runs a story about the killing of a Canadian hostage who 'was killed by Abu Sayyaf militants' (Kassam 2016) and therefore arguably also contributes to the negative semantic prosody discussed earlier.

To conclude, we relate the results of another Ipsos MORI poll conducted in 2013, which asked interviewees to respond to the statement '[m]ost trade unions are controlled by extremists and militants' (Ipsos MORI 2013). There is an assumption here of a shared understanding of the sense of 'extremists' which presumably matches that of the semantic prosody of 'militant'. Interestingly, however, only 23 per cent of respondents agreed with the statement and 60 per cent disagreed. So despite the maintenance of discursive strategies obviously designed to alienate news readers from trade union activism, they clearly do not uncritically assimilate the ideologies of the major news corporations. To quote again the Head of Political Research at Ipsos MORI, Gideon Skinner:

> At a time when unemployment is in the top 3 concerns of Britons, support for the need for trade unions to protect workers' interests remains high. There has also been a steady decline in those who think they are controlled by extremists. (Ipsos MORI 2013: n.p.)

The media's 'militant' tendencies still proliferate, but the discourses of disorder they perpetuate are not going unchallenged.

Notes

1. The *Daily Telegraph*'s editorial column published on the same day took a similar stance with its headline 'SELFISH TRADE UNIONS' (Daily Telegraph 2016).
2. The insertion of an asterisk at the end of a string of unspaced letters will generate any words containing any combination of unspaced letters after the asterisk, hence 'militan*' will generate 'militants', 'militancy', and so on, if they appear in the text(s) in the search parameters.
3. This result is after duplicate articles are removed, initially 34.

4. We are using the typographical convention of small capitals to signify the lexical representation of concepts.
5. Variant word forms of similar or the same lexemes have been aggregated.

References

Agence France-Presse (2016), 'Coalition squeezing Islamic State's funds in economic warfare campaign', *Daily Telegraph*, 27 April.

Baker, P. (2006), *Using Corpora in Discourse Analysis*, London and New York: Bloomsbury.

Bayliss, C. (2016), 'Isis militants boiled alive as punishment for fleeing battlefield', *The Express*, 6 July, <http://www.express.co.uk/news/world/686677/ISIS-boiled-execution-killed-militants> (last accessed 28 May 2017).

Begagić, M. (2013), 'Semantic preference and semantic prosody of the collocation make sense', *Jezikoslovlje*, 14 (2–3), pp. 403–16.

Berkeley, G. (2016), 'Frustrated patients will have little sympathy for disruptive strike action' [Letters], *Daily Telegraph*, 27 April, p. 17.

Borland, S. (2016), 'Junior doctors reject pay deal, raising fear of summer strikes', *Daily Mail*, 6 July, p. 12.

Bublitz, W. (1996), 'Semantic prosody and cohesive company: Somewhat predictable', *Leuvense Bijdragen: Tijdschrift voor Germaanse Filologie*, 85 (1–2), pp. 1–32.

Campbell, D. (2016a), 'Junior doctors in England to strike next week after talks break down', *The Guardian*, 4 January, <https://www.theguardian.com/society/2016/jan/04/junior-doctors-to-strike-next-tuesday-after-talks-with-government-break-down> (last accessed 28 May 2017).

Campbell, D. (2016b), 'Junior doctors' strike has become the mother of all deadlocks', *The Guardian*, 27 April, <https://www.theguardian.com/society/2016/apr/27/junior-doctors-strike-has-become-the-mother-of-all-deadlocks-jeremy-hunt> (last accessed 28 May 2017).

Daily Mail (2016), 'Militant who wants to bring down the Tories' [Editorial], *Daily Mail*, 6 July, p. 12.

Daily Telegraph (2016), 'Selfish trade unions' [Editorial], *Daily Telegraph*, 6 July, p. 19.

Davies, M. (2014), 'Militancy or manipulation', *Babel*, 6, pp. 19–24.

Emplaw Online (2016), 'Trade Union Act 2016', *Emplaw Online*, 6 May, <https://www.emplaw.co.uk/article/trade-union-act-2016> (last accessed 28 May 2017).

Freedman, D. and J. Schlosberg (2016), 'Jeremy Corbyn, impartiality and media misrepresentation', *OpenDemocracyUK*, 29 July, <https://opendemocracy.net/uk/des-freedman-justin-schlosberg/jeremy-corbyn-impartiality-and-media-misrepresentation> (last accessed 28 May 2017).

Groves, D. and D. Martin (2015), 'Corbyn union pals pledge strike chaos', *Daily Mail*, 14 September, pp. 1–2.

Ipsos MORI (2013), 'Trade unions poll', *Ipsos MORI*, 19 July, <https://www.ipsos.com/ipsos-mori/en-uk/trade-unions-poll> (last accessed 28 May 2017).

Ipsos MORI (2014), 'Trade unions seen as essential, though not as powerful as in the 1970s and 80s', *Ipsos MORI*, 5 February, <https://www.ipsos.com/ipsos-mori/en-uk/trade-unions-seen-essential-though-not-powerful-1970s-and-80s> (last accessed 28 May 2017).

Ipsos MORI (2016a), 'Majority support junior doctors ahead of first full walkout', *Ipsos MORI*, 25 April, <https://www.ipsos.com/ipsos-mori/en-uk/majority-support-junior-doctors-ahead-first-full-walkout> (last accessed 28 May 2017).

Ipsos MORI (2016b), 'Widespread public support for junior doctors' strike', *Ipsos MORI*, 11 January, <https://www.ipsos.com/ipsos-mori/en-uk/widespread-public-support-junior-doctors-strike> (last accessed 28 May 2017).

Kassam, A. (2016), 'Britain and Canada to urge other nations halt ransom payments to terrorists', *The Guardian*, 27 April, <https://www.theguardian.com/world/2016/apr/26/britain-canada-halt-ransom-payments-terrorists-john-ridsdel-killing> (last accessed 28 May 2017).

Keir, J. (2016), 'The Trade Union Act 2016: What is changing?', *Brodies LLP*, 9 May, <http://www.brodies.com/blog/employment/trade-union-act-2016-changing> (last accessed 28 May 2017).

Louw, W. E. (1993), 'Irony in the text or insincerity in the writer? The diagnostic potential of semantic prosodies', in M. Baker, G. Francis and E. Tognini-Bonelli (eds), *Text and Technology: In Honour of John Sinclair*, Amsterdam: John Benjamins, pp. 157–76.

McEnery, T. and A. Hardie (2012), *Corpus Linguistics: Method, Theory and Practice*, Cambridge: Cambridge University Press.

Maddox, D. (2016a), '"Sad day" for the NHS as junior doctors go on first all-out strike', *The Express*, 27 April, p. 2.

Maddox, D. (2016b), 'Junior doctors vote to reject 7-day deal', *The Express*, 6 July, p. 2.

Media Reform Coalition (2015), *Who Owns the UK Media?*, Media Reform Coalition, <http://www.mediareform.org.uk/wp-content/uploads/2015/10/Who_owns_the_UK_media-report_plus_appendix1.pdf> (last accessed 28 May 2017).

Monbiot, G. (2016), 'Neoliberalism – the ideology at the root of all our problems', *The Guardian*, 15 April, <https://www.theguardian.com/books/2016/apr/15/neoliberalism-ideology-problem-george-monbiot> (last accessed 28 May 2017).

Newton Dunn, T. (2017), 'IRA brute raps Corb', *The Sun*, 23 May, pp. 1–2.

OED Online (2018), 'militant, adj. and n.', March 2018, Oxford University Press, <http://www.oed.com/view/Entry/118418> (last accessed 18 May 2018).

Partington, A. (1998), *Patterns and Meanings: Using Corpora for English Language Research and Teaching*, Amsterdam and Philadelphia: John Benjamins.

Partington, A. (2004), '"Utterly content in each other's company": Semantic prosody and semantic preference', *International Journal of Corpus Linguistics*, 9, pp. 131–56.

Rayson, P. (2008), 'From key words to key semantic domains', *International Journal of Corpus Linguistics*, 13 (4), pp. 519–49.

Reynolds, L. (2016), 'Annihilation of Christianity: ISIS blows up church as horror onslaught against Christians continues', *The Express*, 27 April, <http://www.express.co.uk/news/world/664713/ISIS-blows-up-historic-church-as-onslaught-against-Christians-continues> (last accessed 28 May 2017).

Schlosberg, J. (2016), *Should He Stay or Should He Go? Television and Online News Coverage of the Labour Party in Crisis*, Media Reform Coalition in association with Birkbeck, University of London, <http://www.mediareform.org.uk/wp-content/uploads/2016/07/Corbynresearch.pdf> (last accessed 28 May 2017).

Sinclair, J. (1987), *Looking Up*, London and Glasgow: Collins.

Stewart, D. (2010), *Semantic Prosody: A Critical Evaluation*, Abingdon: Routledge.

Taaffe, P. (1995), *The Rise of Militant*, London: Militant Publications.

Taaffe, P. and T. Mulhearn (1988), *Liverpool: A City that Dared to Fight*, London: Fortress Books.

Triggle, N. (2016), 'Junior doctors' strike: All-out stoppage "a bleak day"', *BBC News*, 26 April, <http://www.bbc.co.uk/news/health-36134103> (last accessed 28 May 2017).

Wooller, S. (2016), 'Leftie will lead doc strike call', *The Sun*, 7 July, p. 2.

Xiao, R. and T. McEnery (2006), 'Collocation, semantic prosody, and near synonymy: A cross-linguistic perspective', *Applied Linguistics*, 27 (1), pp. 103–29.

PART II

MULTIMODALITY

7

Metaphor and the (1984–5) Miners' Strike: A Multimodal Analysis

Christopher Hart

Introduction

Recent research in cognitive linguistics and cognitive linguistic critical discourse studies (CL-CDS) has shown that metaphor plays a significant role in structuring our understanding of social identities, actions and events. This research also demonstrates that metaphorical modes of understanding are not restricted in their articulation to language but find expression too in visual and multimodal genres of communication. In this chapter, I show how one metaphorical framing – STRIKE IS WAR – featured in multimodal media representations of the 1984–5 British Miners' Strike. I analyse this metaphorical framing from a critical semiotic standpoint to argue that the conceptualisations invoked by these framing efforts served to 'otherise' the miners while simultaneously legitimating the actions during the strike of the government and the police. I begin with a brief introduction to the British Miners' Strike. I then introduce in more detail cognitive metaphor theory and the notion of multimodal metaphor. Next, I briefly introduce the data to be analysed. Subsequently, I show how the STRIKE IS WAR metaphor featured in the language of news reports as well as in two multimodal genres – press photographs and editorial cartoons – and consider the potential (de) legitimating effects of this framing. Finally, I offer some conclusions.

The Media and 1984–5 British Miners' Strike

The 1984–5 British Miners' Strike represents one of the most pivotal and controversial periods in British industrial relations history. The action began on 6 March 1984 in response to the closure of several coal pits and the belief that the government planned further closures which would ultimately bring the UK coal industry to an end. The strike lasted a year until the miners returned to work on 4 March 1985. The year-long strike witnessed bitter disputes between Margaret Thatcher, the then prime minister, and the National Union of Mineworkers led by Arthur Scargill. Throughout the strike, there were also several flashes of violence between police and miners on the picket line, most notoriously at the Orgreave coking plant. This often involved so-called flying pickets, miners who would travel to picket still operational mines, and Metropolitan Police officers who had been redeployed in key areas of Yorkshire and Nottinghamshire.

Media coverage of the strike remains a much contested issue with miners, journalists and other commentators claiming the mainstream media pursued a consistently anti-trade union agenda, systematically demonising the striking miners while justifying government policy and aggressive police tactics (Williams 2009, 2014). As one example of controversial media practice, in May 1984, *The Sun* planned to publish a front page with a picture taken of Arthur Scargill at a rally in Mansfield with his arm outstretched in a pose reminiscent of Adolf Hitler. The picture was to be accompanied by the headline 'MINE FUHRER'. However, the printers refused to put this copy into production and on 15 May the paper appeared instead with the following statement printed on plain background: 'Members of all The Sun production chapels refused to handle the Arthur Scargill picture and major headline on our lead story. The Sun has decided, reluctantly, to print the paper without either' (see Figure 7.1).

(a) Planned page   (b) Published page

Figure 7.1 *The Sun*, 15 May 1984. © News UK & Ireland Ltd

The picture, in conjunction with the reference to Hitler in the headline, serves to frame the strike as a war by connecting with background knowledge relating to World War II. In spite of the controversy surrounding this particular edition of *The Sun*, this metaphorical framing was in fact a persistent feature of media discourses throughout the strike.

Despite the significance of the strike itself and the media's stance towards it, surprisingly little discourse-analytical work has been carried out to investigate, systematically and empirically, the semiotic resources used in reporting the strike and their potential ideological effects. One well-known exception is Montgomery (1995: 241–5). Coverage of industrial disputes tends to focus on the disruptive consequences of the action rather than on the causes behind it (Glasgow Media Group 1976, 1980, 1982). This held true for coverage of the miners' strike where violence on the picket line was considered one of the most newsworthy dimensions of the action. However, Montgomery's analysis reveals a further, more subtle, pattern in the different participant roles assigned to actors in the violence reported. He found that the police were typically assigned the grammatical role of 'patient' while miners were assigned the role of 'agent' in the actions described. This grammatical patterning is not natural or inevitable but is a particular representation which not only reflects an underlying ideological position but which, when systematically repeated in privileged communication channels such as daily newspapers, serves to discursively construct a certain way of seeing and thinking about the events depicted that is difficult to recognise as anything other than natural. In this context, such a grammatical patterning contributes to constructing a discourse in which the police are seen as victims of violence acted out by the miners.

Montgomery's analysis is primarily a transitivity analysis. He does note, however, in the sphere of vocabulary, a tendency to use words associated with military campaigning, whereby pickets 'stage an ambush' and 'bombard the police' who in turn 'send in the mounted brigade on two flanks' and 'charge dramatically'. Such expressions, when they occur systematically inside a given discourse, are not independent lexical choices but, rather, are reflective of and constitutive of underlying conceptual metaphors which serve to structure our understanding of complex social situations. In this chapter, it is shown that militarising metaphors were a persistent feature in media framings of the miners' strike, in both language and image. We turn to cognitive and multimodal metaphor theory in the next section.

Metaphor in Language and Image

In cognitive linguistics, metaphor is regarded not primarily as a linguistic device but as a cognitive process of frame projection which is reflected in and effected through metaphorical expressions in discourse (Lakoff and Johnson 1999, 2003; Fauconnier and Turner 2002). From this perspective, metaphor is a matter of construal in which one *frame* is selected to provide a means of understanding a situation or event belonging to another frame. Through repeated patterns of metaphorical projection, an entire frame may come to be structured in terms of another inside a system of conceptual metaphors that makes up a worldview.

Frames are open-ended, encyclopaedic knowledge structures, conceptual in nature, representing particular areas of knowledge and experience (Fillmore 1982, 1985). They exist at different levels of abstraction such that one frame may be said to elaborate and entail a more general frame. Frames are made up of *elements*: 'core' elements are those which are essential to the meaning of a general frame while 'non-core' elements characterise more specific instantiations of the general frame (Ruppenhofer et al. 2010). In discourse, frames are accessed or activated by references to the frame itself or to its elements. Any element therefore provides an entry point to the rest of the frame, which is then available to contribute to meaning construction and affect. Metaphorical construals arise when the text, through various types of textual relation, establishes a correspondence between elements belonging to two different frames, one of which functions as the *source* and the other as the *target*. Conceptual correspondences between other frame elements, not made explicit in the text, are established as a consequence of the metaphorical projection invoked.

In metaphors, embodied or culturally salient frames get selected to provide structure to otherwise unfamiliar or underspecified frames, including frames for complex social and political situations. In doing so, metaphors reduce complex situations to more tangible scenarios, accentuating certain aspects of reality while simultaneously obfuscating others.

In CL-CDS, metaphor is therefore seen as an important ideological framing device. Metaphors define how social situations are to be understood but also how they are to be reasoned about, reacted to emotionally, and responded to materially (Beer and De Landtsheer 2004; Charteris-Black 2004; Chilton 1996; Dirven et al. 2003, 2007; Hart 2010; Koller 2004; Musolff 2004, 2006, 2016; Semino 2008; Stockwell 1999; Wolf and Polzenhagen 2003). Metaphors problematise situations in specific ways, promote particular solutions to those 'problems', and pave the way for actions which accord with the metaphor. For example, as Fridolfsson observes, conceptualising political demonstrations as war not only serves to demonise the protesters but, as it translates into action, the metaphor 'establishes the plausibility for military intervention when dealing with political protest' (2008: 138). Metaphorical expressions in texts are, thus, an important focal point in studying the discursive construction of ideology, as it is encoded in conceptual metaphors, and the legitimation of social action.

An important development in cognitive metaphor theory has been to show that conceptual metaphors are not restricted in their articulation to language but find expression also in visual and multimodal texts (Bounegru and Forceville 2011; Forceville 1996, 2002, 2006, 2008; Forceville and Urios-Aparisi 2009). This is to be expected since, as Lakoff and Johnson state, metaphor is 'primarily a matter of thought and action and only derivatively a matter of language' (1980: 153). Visual (or pictorial) metaphors arise when the source and target frame are each referenced in the image. This often involves intertextuality whereby the image itself or a particular feature of it invokes another image belonging to the source frame. This may be a specific image such as a famous painting or an iconic, mythologised image in collective cultural memory (Werner 2004). Multimodal metaphors arise when the target frame is determined in one modality (typically the visual) while the source frame is supplied in another (typically the linguistic, which may also involve intertextuality). In many cases, however, the boundary between visual and multimodal metaphor is blurred. The image alone may be enough to invoke a metaphorical reading but the source frame is nevertheless supplied in linguistic co-text. In such cases, following Barthes (1977), the linguistic co-text is said to provide an 'anchor' which functions, in case of any ambiguity, to reinforce the metaphorical reading.

One frame which has been found to play a fundamental structuring role in a range of discourses, from media discourses of migration to business discourses around mergers and acquisitions, is a WAR frame (Hart 2010; Koller 2002). The WAR frame features in visual and multimodal as well as verbal articulations of these discourses (El Refaie 2003; Koller 2005). The WAR frame has also been found to feature in both verbal and visual discourses of political protest (Fridolfsson 2008; Hart 2014a, 2014b). I describe the WAR frame below and in the following section show how it featured in linguistic, visual and multimodal representations in media discourses of the miners' strike.

The WAR Frame

The WAR frame, as Semino observes, is particularly wide in scope, at least in Anglo-American English, where it may be metaphorically applied to 'any domain of experience that involves difficulties, danger, effort and uncertain outcomes' (2008: 100). In the domain of politics, the WAR frame is conventionally used 'in relation to conflict between individuals, groups, parties and governments and oppositions' (Semino 2008: 100). The WAR frame is made up of a number of structural elements as shown in Table 7.1. Core elements

Table 7.1 The WAR frame

Entails frames	VIOLENT ENCOUNTER	
	OPPOSITION	
Elaborated in frames	WWI	
	WWII	
	COLD WAR	
Core frame elements	Participants	*Army, soldiers*
	Processes	*Invade, attack, launch, peace talks*
	Purpose/Issue	*Fight for freedom*
Non-core frame elements	Time	*War of 1914–1918*
	Place	*Battle of Trafalgar*
	Manner	*Bloody war*
	Instrument/Means	*Tanks, guns, horses*
	Duration	*30 years war*
Associated concepts/ scripts	Danger	
	Justice/Injustice	
	Responsibility	

include PARTICIPANTS (*army, soldiers*, etc.) and PROCESSES (*invade, attack, peace talks*, etc.). Other elements include the PLACE where war occurs and the INSTRUMENT/MEANS with which it is carried out. References in text to any of these elements are likely to trigger a war framing.

The WAR frame entails, that is, has as an inherent component of its meaning, more general frames or schemas for VIOLENT ENCOUNTER and OPPOSITION. Scenes and events construed in terms of the WAR frame inherit these structural properties as 'metaphorical entailments'. Metaphorical applications of the WAR frame in the domain politics therefore serve to 'dramatize the opposition between different participants in politics (who are constructed as enemies), and to emphasize the aggressiveness and seriousness of political debates, conflicts or elections' (Semino 2008: 100). The frame necessarily involves perspective and construes one opposing participant as the aggressor and the other as the victim.

The generic WAR frame has instantiations in frames for specific, culturally salient, wars which are also available for metaphorical projection. For British citizens, this is most likely to include frames for World War I and World War II, which are most widely taught in schools and referenced in popular television, film and literature. A war framing may therefore be realised through references or allusions to the particular people, processes, places, instruments, and so on involved in a specific war. Thus, a WORLD WAR II frame, for example, is likely to be invoked by references to Churchill, Hitler, Normandy or the

Battle of Britain. When a specific war frame is selected for projection, not only does the target scene inherit the structural properties associated with the generic WAR frame, which is entailed by the more specific frame, but collective memories and emotions associated with those specific historical moments are also conjured. Media *framing efforts* depicting the miners' strike as a war, then, are likely to have had a number of specific *framing effects* in shaping public understandings of, and attitudes towards, the strike.

Data

The data analysed was collected from the Newsroom archives of the British Library. Six major events in the year-long period were identified and the data oriented to these. The data centred on instances of violence between police and picketing miners. The six major events were:

- 12 March 1984 – Beginning of strike
- 15 March 1984 – Death of miner David Jones
- 18 March 1984 – Mass mobilisation of police forces
- 29 May 1984 – First use of police riot gear at Orgreave coking plant, Sheffield
- 18 June 1984 – 'Battle of Orgreave'
- 4 March 1985 – Strike ends, miners return to work

Seven national newspapers were included in the sample: the *Daily Mail*, the *Daily Mirror*, the *Daily Express*, *The Sun*, *The Times*, the *Telegraph* and *The Guardian*. For each newspaper, all pages covering the events were selected from first editions published the following day or two days later in cases where the story continued to run. Cartoon data was supplemented using the British Cartoon Archive held electronically at the University of Kent (https://www.cartoons.ac.uk/).

Analysis: STRIKE IS WAR

Language

Headlines and lead paragraphs framed the strike metaphorically in terms of a generic WAR frame. In headlines, this was often by means of reference to the frame itself as in the following examples:

(1) PIT WAR: Violence erupts on the picket line as miner fights miner (*The Sun*, 13 March 1984)
(2) Crushed to death in Scargill's picket war (*Daily Express*, 16 March 1984)
(3) 8,000 cops on alert to foil pits war (*The Sun*, 19 March 1984)

Headlines are especially important in providing a frame for understanding the subsequent text. Not only are they visually salient, often appearing in large and bold print, but as van Dijk (1988) observes, they serve to express the semantic macro-structure of the text. In other words, headlines perform a *frame setting* function, providing a reference point around which the remainder of the text is oriented and interpreted.

While these headlines evoke the WAR frame via the lexical item *war*, in the lead paragraphs that follow, the war framing is further expounded by reference to frame elements, including PARTICIPANTS ('mum's army of miners' wives', 'armies of pickets', 'an army of 8,000 police'), PROCESSES ('battle', 'rampage', 'besiege') and MANNER ('bloody pit war'):

> (4) A <u>mum's army of miners' wives</u> <u>did battle</u> with 200 of Arthur Scargill's flying pickets yesterday . . . and won. The angry housewives squared up to <u>massed ranks</u> of spitting, snarling pickets and cheered their men safely into work. (*The Sun*, 13 March 1984)
>
> (5) Despite the tragedy, Yorkshire miners' leaders have refused to call off their <u>rampaging armies of pickets</u> – in defiance of a High Court ban. Six hundred of them were out in force the night Mr Jones died at the <u>besieged</u> Nottinghamshire pit. (*Daily Express*, 16 March 1984)
>
> (6) An <u>army of 8,000 police</u> were at <u>battle stations</u> last night – ready for the final bust up with Arthur Scargill's flying pickets in the <u>bloody pit war</u>. (*The Sun*, 19 March 1984)

With WAR providing a structuring frame from early on in the strike, subsequent events become conceptualised as processes associated with war. For example, violence at Thorseby pit, near Ollerton, was referred to by *The Sun* as the 'Battle of Thorseby Colliery' (16 March 1984). This was a strategy that persisted throughout the strike, most notoriously in the so-called battle of Orgreave. Negotiations between government, the Coal Board and the National Union of Mineworkers were construed as 'peace talks'. And the miners eventually returning to work was seen as an act of 'surrender'. Roles were also assigned within the frame with Arthur Scargill, for example, cast in the role of an 'army general':

> (7) The crucial <u>peace talks</u> expected to begin today will be held in Yorkshire. (*Daily Mail*, 31 May 1984)
>
> (8) <u>Surrender</u> came on a tight 98–91 vote by an NUM delegate conference at the TUC headquarters in London. (*The Sun*, 4 March 1985)
>
> (9) Arthur Scargill stood like <u>an army general</u> surveying his warring troops in the bloody battle of Orgreave yesterday. (*Daily Express*, 19 June 1984)

These language usages serve to establish a set of discursive conditions in which images of the strike are readily interpretable in term of the WAR frame. In the case of news photographs, this framing is often further reinforced through immediately accompanying co-text in the form of captions. However, even in the absence of such immediate co-text, the wider co-text and intertextual context act as an anchor or 'attractor' (Gibbs and Cameron 2008), pulling potentially war-framing images firmly into a metaphorical reading.

Press Photographs

News photography is traditionally thought to serve a documentary function, evidencing the realities reported verbally in text (Bednarek and Caple 2012: 112). It is certainly the case that photographs capture real happenings and make at least an implicit claim to truth and objectivity. More recently, however, it is recognised that news photographs construct and evaluate the 'realities' they depict, serving as symbolic representations with emotional appeal (Bednarek and Caple 2012: 112). Images associated with war are especially evocative, standing as symbols of key moments in history capable of conjuring feelings of both national pride and prejudice (Bednarek and Caple 2012: 116). Bednarek and Caple point out that imagery associated with the wars of the twentieth and twenty-first centuries especially is embedded in the national psyche and frequently deployed for propaganda purposes in order 'to galvanize a particular social group to support or resist a particular action' (2012: 116).

In examining press photographs of the miners' strike, centred around violence on the picket line, we find images indexical of World War I in particular with the WORLD WAR I frame accessed via three main elements: PLACE, PARTICIPANTS and INSTRUMENT/MEANS.

PLACE

The locations where violent interactions between police and striking miners took place were depicted as battlefields, reminiscent of World War I. The image in Figure 7.2, for example, suggests the wasteland left by major battles in the First World War. The war framing is reinforced in the caption that accompanied the image:

(10) BATTLEGROUND: Uprooted sign and broken walls (*Daily Mirror*, 19 June 1984)

Similarly, the image in Figure 7.3, which was accompanied by the caption in (11), brings to mind the barbed wire barricades used in World War I, which are symbolic in particular of the Battle of the Somme. Although such barricades were used by both German and Allied forces, in popular British

Figure 7.2 Fallen sign at Orgreave. © Press Association

conception they are associated with German defences. The image together with its caption thus serves an additional perspectivising function, casting the police and the miners in the roles of 'ally' versus 'enemy' respectively. Moreover, where the Battle of the Somme is often taken to epitomise the senseless loss of life suffered in World War I, the framing undermines the strike by presenting it as causing similarly senseless suffering with little to gain:

(11)   BARRICADE: The deadly line of sharpened wooden stakes aimed chest high at police horses (*Daily Mirror*, 19 June 1984)

Figure 7.3 Wooden stakes at Orgreave. © Mirrorpix

While the images in Figures 7.2 and 7.3 remind us of the brutality of war, the image in Figure 7.4 depicts a moment of peace and humanity. The image intertextually references an iconic, much mythologised, image of the 1914

Christmas Day football match played between German and Allied forces on 'No Man's Land'. Thus, although the image depicts a moment of peace, it nevertheless maintains a war framing, via the element of PLACE, by drawing analogies between No Man's Land in World War I and the fields surrounding collieries involved in the strike. This correspondence is made explicit in the caption accompanying the image:

(12) COME ON YOU BLUES: A police officer keeps control as three strikers converge on him in a football match played on <u>no-mans land</u> during a break from picketing at the Bilsthorne colliery. (*The Guardian*, 17 March 1984)

Figure 7.4 Football match played between police and miners. © Guardian News and Media Ltd

PARTICIPANTS

Within the war framing, police and miners were depicted as soldiers. The police in particular were shown in military-like configurations. In Figure 7.5, for example, the police are seen in a configuration suggestive of a military drill or parade. The caption that accompanies the image serves to reinforce this metaphorical reading:

(13) <u>BATTLE FORMATION:</u> The <u>massed ranks</u> of police at Orgreave, confronting pickets trying to stop coal leaving the plant (*The Guardian*, 19 June 1984)

Figure 7.5 Mobilisation of police forces. © Press Association

It is worth noting that the density and uniformity of the police, which itself contributes to the military framing, further legitimates the police by presenting them as disciplined and their actions as coordinated. By contrast, the dispersal of the miners in the image suggests an unorganised rabble rather than a highly trained state army (for similar analyses of real war photographs, see Machin 2007).

While the image in Figure 7.5 shows the police collectivised as an 'army', the image in Figure 7.6 shows a single police officer construed as

Figure 7.6 Front cover of *The Sun*, 4 March 1985. © News UK & Ireland Ltd

an individual 'soldier'. The image, published on the front page of *The Sun* at the end of the strike, is accompanied by the phrase 'lest we forget' in the headline. This phrase comes originally from the poem *Recessional* written by Rudyard Kipling in 1897 and refers to the sacrifice of Christ. However, it is reused in the *Ode of Remembrance* where it is added as a final line to the fourth stanza of Laurence Binyon's poem *For the Fallen*, written in 1914 in honour of British soldiers who had already lost their lives in World War I. The metaphorical framing arises in this instance multimodally, where it relies on an interaction between the figure in the image and the intertextual reference in the headline, which serves to compare the efforts of police officers in the strike to the sacrifices of British soldiers in the First World War.

INSTRUMENT/MEANS

Pictures of police on horseback were a frequent feature of news photography during the strike. Images of police on horseback are reminiscent of mounted forms of warfare associated especially with World War I. Such images thus evoke a WORLD WAR I frame via the element INSTRUMENT/MEANS. Cavalry warfare is often considered more noble than modern forms of warfare, which it is held in contrast to. Thus, while the headline in Figure 7.7 simply reads 'CHARGE', the lead paragraph accompanying the image appraises the police

Figure 7.7 Front cover of the *The Sun*, 30 May 1984. © News UK & Ireland Ltd

action as 'an amazing cavalry charge on picketing miners'. A very similar image was published in the *Daily Express* with the caption 'Into action: Mounted police scatter pickets after officers had faced barrages of bottles, stones and deadly new missiles' (30 May 1984).

Political Cartoons

In contrast to news photography, political cartoons are widely recognised as evaluative and rhetorical, and provide historical records of contemporary attitudes (Swain 2012: 82). A number of studies have now addressed, through the lens of cognitive metaphor theory, metaphorical framings in the visual or visuo-verbal genre of political cartoons (e.g. Bounegru and Forceville 2011; El Refaie 2003, 2009; Schilperoord and Maes 2009).

Gombrich (1971) argues that metaphor is a common and expected device in political cartoons. In cartoons depicting the miners' strike, we find further metaphorical framings of the strike as a war. However, while news photographs, in constructing the strike as a war, appealed mainly to a WORLD WAR I frame, political cartoons exploited a WORLD WAR II frame. Here, the metaphorical construal is evoked primarily through correspondences established between frame elements of PARTICIPANT.

Consider the cartoon in Figure 7.8. The most central and salient feature of the image and thus the one most likely to function as an entry point to the relevant frames is Arthur Scargill. Scargill is depicted, however, in the uniform of a German General in World War II. This textual relation is an example of 'hybridity' in multimodal metaphor theory, showing two distinct entities merged into a single *gestalt* (Forceville 2008). It sets up a conceptual correspondence between Scargill and a Nazi general which, in turn, educes a wider WORLD WAR II framing of the strike.

Figure 7.8 Arthur Scargill as Nazi, *The Sun*, 17 March 1984. © News UK & Ireland Ltd

Correspondences between other frame elements, namely elements of PLACE, can be seen in the image. For example, the winding tower of the mine resembles a watch tower in a Nazi concentration camp. The train tracks and the chimneys in the background are further reminiscent of iconic images of concentration camps. These correspondences support the metaphorical framing but at the same time are established only as a consequence of the metaphorical projection cued by the depiction of Scargill in German military uniform. In other words, they are not metaphorical 'triggers' but take on a metaphorical reading in light of correspondences established explicitly elsewhere in the image.

While the cartoon in Figure 7.8 evokes a WORLD WAR II framing in which Scargill is seen as a Nazi general, the cartoon in Figure 7.9 establishes a WORLD WAR II framing by comparing Margaret Thatcher to Winston Churchill. The construal relies on iconic images of Churchill smoking a cigar as well as the myth of Churchill as a bulldog. The cartoon is in fact a recontextualisation of a famous patriotic cartoon, produced by Sidney Strube and published in the *Daily Express* on 8 June 1940, depicting Churchill as a bulldog (see Figure 7.10). In the same way as Figure 7.8, then, the metaphor is realised as features associated with two distinct figures are fused to create a new hybrid image. The visual metaphor is further reinforced by linguistic co-text in the phrase 'go to it'. This phrase appeared in the same way in Strube's original cartoon and later came to feature on campaign posters produced by the Ministry of Information as a message to 'civilian soldiers' working on the 'home front' in World War II.

Figure 7.9 Margaret Thatcher as Winston Churchill, *The Times*, 6 June 1984.
© News UK & Ireland Ltd

Figure 7.10 Winston Churchill (Sidney Strube), *Daily Express*, 8 June 1940.
© Express Newspapers

Narratives of the Second World War are frequently redeployed by the media as a lens through which to understand contemporary situations (Kelsey 2015). However, as Kelsey points out, following Barthes, when historical moments are mobilised to make sense of contemporary events they are themselves mythologised, reduced to simple, archetypal, narratives. It is this mythologised version of history that gets projected in metaphorical understandings of contemporary situations.

In the cartoons above, the complexities of World War II and thus, as a function of the metaphor, the miners' strike, are compressed in a number of ways. For example, as El Refaie (2003: 88) notes, political cartoons tend to reduce large social groups to one stereotypical image. In these cartoons, the miners' strike, which involved multiple parties and affected large numbers of people, is reduced to a binary opposition between Thatcher and Scargill. This *personification* 'enables the cartoonist to represent complex issues and relationships in a much more simple and easily understandable form' (El Refaie 2003: 91) with a number of ideological consequences. It excludes other possible voices and therefore restricts the debate to only two dichotomous positions. But it also personalises the situation, encouraging judgements based on the characters of two individuals rather than on the issues at stake. The metaphoric projections involved, moreover, construct those characters in particular ways as Thatcher and Scargill inherit qualities associated with their counterpart elements in the WORLD WAR II frame.

In popular memory, Winston Churchill is revered as a national hero and has come to stand as a symbol of defiance, resilience and courage in the face of adversity. His mythical character is frequently exploited in nationalist propagandist discourses (Kelsey 2015). In Figure 7.9, the metaphorical projection serves to bestow Thatcher with traits associated with Churchill. Thatcher is thus characterised as defiant, resilient, valiant, and so on. By contrast, in Figure 7.8, Scargill is attributed personality traits associated with a Nazi general.

In reducing the strike to an opposition between Thatcher and Scargill, caricatured as Churchill and a Nazi general respectively, the war framing retells an archetypal narrative (Lule 2001) of 'Hero versus Villain'. Archetypal narratives are familiar stories with conventional characters, standard plotlines and predictable outcomes. In the Hero versus Villain narrative, the hero fights for the values and ideals of the society in which their story features (Lule 2001: 82). He or she is intelligent, brave and benevolent. The villain is intelligent but irrational, driven by self-interest, and intent on destruction. Crucially, however, the hero is victorious in the end. The metaphorical construal, thus, not only attributes to Thatcher and Scargill the status of 'hero' versus 'villain' respectively, but in so doing makes it seem inevitable that the miners' strike will be defeated.

Conclusion

In this chapter, war framings have been shown as a persistent feature in media representations of the 1984–5 British Miners' Strike. The frequency and systematicity with which these metaphorical framings occur suggests that these examples are not independent framing efforts but rather reflect, reify and reinforce an entrenched worldview, encoded in the form of an underlying conceptual metaphor STRIKE IS WAR. This conceptual metaphor constitutes our understanding of the strike, so that the strike is actually conceived as a war. It forms the basis on which our attitudes and actions towards the strike are developed. Indeed, this media framing created a space for war-based reasoning in government policy. Cabinet documents recently released under the 30-year rule reveal that Thatcher was encouraged by her policy unit, in a paper dated 13 July 1984, to pursue a 'war of attrition, where the perceived way of the strike ending is for miners to go back to work'.

This chapter has shown that the STRIKE IS WAR metaphor is manifested across semiotic modalities, thus further evidencing Forceville's claim that metaphors 'occur non-verbally and multimodally as well as verbally' (2006: 381). Though, as El Refaie notes, visual metaphors are not simply translations into the visual mode of verbal metaphors; rather, in the visual modality, the author may 'give the metaphor a new twist or focus on elements which would otherwise remain unused or unnoticed' (2003: 87). While in the language data, then, the STRIKE IS WAR metaphor is realised through projections of a generic WAR frame, in the visual data, the metaphor is rendered through projections of WORLD WAR I and WORLD WAR II frames specifically. Interestingly, it was found that news photographs tended to appeal to a WORLD WAR I frame while editorial cartoons appealed to a WORLD WAR II frame.

For many images in the data, the metaphorical interpretation is dependent on intertextual references either in the image itself or in accompanying language. In other words, the source frame is accessed as features of texts belonging to WORLD WAR I and WORLD WAR II frames are echoed in the current text. In this way, intertextuality provides a vehicle for metaphorical understanding. As Werner states, the 'echoing of themes, quotations, symbols, storylines, or compositional elements from older images and famous written texts may create visual metaphors' (2004: n.p.). In such cases, of course, the metaphorical interpretation depends on the reader recognising the intertextual references being made. Again, as Werner puts it: 'allusions to historical events and personages, or to past cultural texts (e.g. poems, novels, famous quotations, art), are only successful if the reader is able to access the allusionary base from which the analogies are drawn' (2004: n.p.). When they are not, intertextuality is divisive and serves to create an elite in-group who are able to make the connections and who are held in contrast to those who lack the same cultural capital (Werner 2004).

It is important to note that the media's framing of the strike as a war was not necessarily a deliberate attempt on the part of individual journalists to undermine the strike. For example, the STRIKE IS WAR metaphor may have been motivated by perceived similarities between the WAR frame and scenes in the strike. At the level of event-structure, a VIOLENT ENCOUNTER frame is instantiated in both acts of war and the violent events witnessed on the picket line. The WAR frame, in other words, may have been made available via its entailed VIOLENT ENCOUNTER frame which figures in any literal understating of the target scenes. Similarly, actions of flying pickets bear a structural resemblance to acts of invasion insofar as both involve a group of people entering the 'territory' of another. Moreover, in both the WAR frame and the strike, those large groups are led by powerful individuals. Finally, at a more encyclopaedic level, both World War I and the 'battle of Orgreave' involved horses. What may have begun, then, as a novel, 'situationally triggered' metaphor (Semino 2009), licensed by perceived commonalities with the target situation, became a conventional means of reporting the strike, providing a dominant frame through which the strike could be understood. Nevertheless, alternative metaphors are always available and the particular metaphorical mode of understanding presented achieves a number of ideological effects.

Construing the strike as a war results in particular metaphorical entailments which serve to delegitimate the NUM and the striking miners while legitimating the position and actions of the government and the police. The general WAR frame entails an opposition between two sides, one of which is seen as 'the enemy'. Without exception, it is the striking miners who are cast in this role. From this perspective within the frame, the actions of the government and the police are justified as being in the national interest. This is especially the case in elaborations of the metaphor involving frames for WORLD WAR I and WORLD WAR II. These frames stand mythologically as symbols of national identity, pride and unity. Their invocation in the STRIKE IS WAR metaphor is therefore likely to galvanise support for government policy in the face of 'the enemy' and bestow a conviction that the course of action pursued by the government is morally right and worth 'fighting for'. The metaphor therefore precludes the possibility of compromise and resolution. Framing the British Miners' Strike as a war, then, served to reduce a complex situation to a simple scenario with a restricted set of goals and outcomes. Had the media employed a different metaphor, it might have been possible to imagine the strike taking a different course and, ultimately, having a different outcome.

References

Barthes, R. (1977), *Image Music Text*, London: Fontana Press.

Bednarek, M. and H. Caple (2012), *News Discourse*, London: Continuum.

Beer, F. A. and C. De Landtsheer (eds) (2004), *Metaphorical World Politics*, East Lansing: Michigan State University Press.

Bounegru, L. and C. Forceville (2011), 'Metaphors in editorial cartoons representing the global financial crisis', *Visual Communication*, 10 (2), pp. 209–29.

Charteris-Black, J. (2004), *Corpus Approaches to Critical Metaphor Analysis*, Basingstoke: Palgrave Macmillan.

Chilton, P. (1996), *Security Metaphors: Cold War Discourse from Containment to Common House*, New York: Peter Lang.

Dirven, R., R. Frank and M. Pütz (eds) (2003), *Cognitive Models in Language and Thought: Ideology, Metaphors and Meanings*, Berlin: Mouton de Gruyter.

Dirven, R., F. Polzenhagen and H.-G. Wolf (2007), 'Cognitive linguistics, ideology and critical discourse analysis', in D. Geeraerts and H. Cuckyens (eds), *The Oxford Handbook of Cognitive Linguistics*, Oxford: Oxford University Press, pp. 1222–40.

El Refaie, E. (2003), 'Understanding visual metaphor: The example of newspaper cartoons', *Visual Communication*, 2 (1), pp. 75–96.

El Refaie, E. (2009), 'Metaphor in political cartoons: Exploring audience responses', in C. J. Forceville and E. Urios-Aparisi (eds), *Multimodal Metaphor*, Berlin: Mouton de Gruyter, pp. 173–98.

Fauconnier, G. and M. Turner (2002), *The Way We Think: Conceptual Blending and the Mind's Hidden Complexities*, New York: Basic Books.

Fillmore, C. (1982), 'Frame semantics', in Linguistics Society of Korea (ed.), *Linguistics in the Morning Calm*, Seoul: Hanshin, pp. 111–37.

Fillmore, C. (1985), 'Frames and the semantics of understanding', *Quaderni di Semantica*, 6 (2), pp. 222–54.

Forceville, C. (1996), *Pictorial Metaphor in Advertising*, London: Routledge.

Forceville, C. (2002), 'The identification of target and source in pictorial metaphors', *Journal of Pragmatics*, 34 (1), pp. 1–14.

Forceville, C. (2006), 'Non-verbal and multimodal metaphor in a cognitivist framework: Agendas for research', in G. Kristiansen, M. Achard, R. Dirven and F. J. Ruiz (eds), *Cognitive Linguistics: Current Applications and Future Perspectives*, Berlin: Mouton de Gruyter, pp. 372–402.

Forceville, C. (2008), 'Metaphor in pictures and multimodal representations', in R. W. Gibbs, Jr (ed.), *The Cambridge Handbook of Metaphor and Thought*, Cambridge: Cambridge University Press, pp. 462–82.

Forceville, C. and E. Urios-Aparisi (eds) (2009), *Multimodal Metaphor*, Berlin: Mouton de Gruyter.

Fridolfsson, C. (2008), 'Political protest and metaphor', in T. Carve and J. Pikalo (eds), *Political Language and Metaphor: Interpreting and Changing the World*, London: Routledge, pp. 132–48.

Gibbs, R. and L. Cameron (2008), 'The social cognitive dynamics of metaphor performance', *Journal of Cognitive Systems Research*, 9 (1–2), pp. 64–75.

Glasgow Media Group (1976), *Bad News*, London: Routledge & Kegan Paul.

Glasgow Media Group (1980), *More Bad News*, London: Routledge & Kegan Paul.

Glasgow Media Group (1982), *Really Bad News*, London: Writers and Readers Publishing Cooperative.

Gombrich, E. H. (1971), 'The cartoonist's armoury', in E. H. Gombrich (ed.), *Meditations on a Hobby Horse and Other Essays on the Theory of Art*, 2nd edn, London: Phaidon, pp. 127–42.

Hart, C. (2010), *Critical Discourse and Cognitive Science: New Perspectives on Immigration Discourse*, Basingstoke: Palgrave Macmillan.

Hart, C. (2014a), *Discourse, Grammar and Ideology: Functional and Cognitive Perspectives*, London: Bloomsbury.

Hart, C. (2014b), 'Construal operations in online press reports of political protests', in C. Hart and P. Cap (eds), *Contemporary Critical Discourse Studies*, London: Bloomsbury, pp. 167–88.

Kelsey, D. (2015), *Media, Myth and Terrorism: A Discourse-Mythological Analysis of the 'Blitz Spirit' in British Newspaper Responses to the July 7th Bombings*, Basingstoke: Palgrave Macmillan.

Koller, V. (2002), '"A shotgun wedding": Co-occurrence of war and marriage metaphors in mergers and acquisitions discourse', *Metaphor and Symbol*, 17, pp. 179–203.

Koller, V. (2004), *Metaphor and Gender in Business Media Discourse: A Critical Cognitive Study*, Basingstoke: Palgrave Macmillan.

Koller, V. (2005), 'Designing cognition: Visual metaphor as a design feature in business magazines', *Information Design Journal and Document Design*, 13 (2), pp. 136–50.

Lakoff, G. and M. Johnson (1980), *Metaphors We Live By*, Chicago: University of Chicago Press.

Lakoff, G. and M. Johnson (1999), *Philosophy in the Flesh: The Embodied Mind and its Challenge to Western Thought*, New York: Basic Books.

Lakoff, G. and M. Johnson (2003), *Metaphors We Live By*, 2nd edn, Chicago: University of Chicago Press.

Lule, J. (2001), *Daily News, Eternal Stories: The Mythological Role of Journalism*, New York and London: Guilford Press.

Machin, D. (2007), *An Introduction to Multimodal Analysis*, London: Bloomsbury.

Montgomery, M. (1995), *An Introduction to Language and Society*, 2nd edn, London: Routledge.

Musolff, A. (2004), *Metaphor and Political Discourse: Analogical Reasoning in Debates about Europe*, Basingstoke: Palgrave Macmillan.

Musolff, A. (2006), 'Metaphor scenarios in public discourse', *Metaphor and Symbol*, 21 (1), pp. 23–38.

Musolff, A. (2016), *Political Metaphor Analysis: Discourse and Scenarios*, London: Bloomsbury.

Ruppenhofer, J., M. Ellsworth, M. R. L. Petruck, C. R. Johnson and J. Scheffczyk (2010), *FrameNet II: Extended Theory and Practice*, <https://framenet2.icsi.berkeley.edu/docs/r1.5/book.pdf> (last accessed 1 May 2018).

Schilperoord, J. and A. Maes (2009), 'Visual metaphoric conceptualization in editorial cartoons', in C. Forceville and E. Urios-Aparisi (eds), *Multimodal Metaphor*, Berlin: Mouton de Gruyter, pp. 213–42.

Semino, E. (2008), *Metaphor in Discourse*, Cambridge: Cambridge University Press.

Semino, E. (2009), 'Metaphor and situational motivation', *Quaderns de Filologia: Estudis lingüístics*, 14, pp. 221–33.

Stockwell, P. (1999), 'Towards a critical cognitive linguistics', in A. Combrink and I. Bierman (eds), *Discourses of War and Conflict*, Potchefstroom: Potchefstroom University Press, pp. 510–28.

Swain, E. (2012), 'Analysing evaluation in political cartoons', *Discourse, Context & Media*, 1 (2–3), pp. 82–94.

van Dijk, T. A. (1988), *News as Discourse*, Hillsdale, NJ: Lawrence Erlbaum.

Werner, W. (2004), 'On political cartoons and social studies textbooks: Visual analogies, intertextuality and cultural memory', *Canadian Social Studies*, 38 (2), <https://files.eric.ed.gov/fulltext/EJ1073912.pdf> (last accessed 31 May 2018).

Williams, G. (ed.) (2009), *Shafted: The Media, the Miners' Strike & the Aftermath*, London: Campaign for Press and Broadcasting Freedom.

Williams, G. (ed.) (2014), *Settling Scores: The Media, the Police & and the Miners' Strike*, London: Campaign for Press and Broadcasting Freedom.

Wolf, H. G. and F. Polzenhagen (2003), 'Conceptual metaphor as ideological stylistic means: An exemplary analysis', in R. Dirven, R. Frank and M. Putz (eds), *Cognitive Models in Language and Thought: Ideology, Metaphors and Meanings*, Berlin: Mouton de Gruyter, pp. 247–76.

8

Strategic Manoeuvring in Arab Spring Political Cartoons

Rania Elnakkouzi

Introduction

Scholarly interest in political cartoons seems to stem from the inherent argumentative nature of this genre, on the one hand, and the role that cartoons play in public debate (Groarke 2009), on the other. The widespread discontent and criticisms that the Danish cartoons which ridiculed Prophet Mohammed spurred in the Muslim world is a good example of the impact that cartoons can have worldwide. Blair (2004) ascribes the distinctive nature of political cartoons to the level of explicitness and precision of meaning that this genre permits compared with other visual genres. The genre of political cartoons allows the condensation of historical and cultural events and social relationships within a single frame (Slyomovics 2001). Cartoons can 'recontextualize events and evoke references in ways that a photograph or a film cannot' (Slyomovics 2001: 72).

Visual presentations in cartoons, as Edwards (2004) expounds, create images which define social realities. A number of studies have explored the role of visual metaphors in different multimodal genres, such as advertising (Forceville 1996, 2002; Kjeldsen 2012, 2015), films (Carroll 1996; Wildfeuer 2014) and cartoons (Bounegru and Forceville 2011; El Refaie 2003, 2009; Kennedy 1993; Groarke 1998, 2009). In this chapter, a visual metaphor is not examined from a cognitive point of view, that is, as a framing device that structures and defines social situations and events (El Refaie 2003; Hart 2017). Instead, a visual metaphor is conceived as a visual argument inasmuch as it attempts to convince the audience of a particular political stance or point of view by offering reasons in support of claims (Birdsell and Groarke 2007; Feteris 2013; Feteris et al. 2011; Groarke 1998, 2009). In political or editorial cartoons, the mechanism of offering reasons in support of claims/standpoints is mainly communicated through visual images such as visual metaphors or cultural images.[1] Based on this view, political cartoons are envisaged as an argumentative activity type aimed at convincing the 'audience of a particular critical standpoint by means of argumentation consisting of a visual metaphor, often in combination with text' (Feteris 2013: 416).

From an argumentative point of view, visual images are perceived as indirect speech acts that function as visual arguments advanced to defend standpoints (Feteris et al. 2011).[2] Similarly, other rhetorical figures used in cartoons, as Kjeldsen (2012) elucidates, such as hyperbole, metonymy, exaggeration and visual ellipsis, function as cues that evoke intended meaning and offer patterns of reasoning – argument schemes – to guide the audience to the intended interpretation. It is, therefore, the task of the interpreter to identify the implicit arguments and standpoints that are indirectly conveyed in visual images and to make them verbally explicit.[3] This interpretive process, according to Birdsell and Groarke (2007), is guided by the 'five principles of communication' stipulated by the pragma-dialectical model which govern the interpretation of all speech acts. These principles are reduced to 'three principles of visual communication' (Birdsell and Groarke 2007: 4) which guide the reconstruction of implicit arguments displayed by visuals. Accordingly, visual images have an argumentative function if they can be: (a) understood in principle; (b) interpreted in a manner that takes into account the major visual and verbal elements that the images contain; and (c) interpreted in light of the context in which they are situated, that is, in light of the social and political debates which they are part of.

In the context of the Arab Spring, cartoonists have either sided with oppressive regimes (e.g. the Syrian, Libyan and Yemeni regimes) in their violent crackdown on protesters or supported protesters' demands for freedom, dignity, social justice and recognition.[4] With tension brewing – due to the unprecedented level of violence, such as the use of chemical weapons by the Syrian regime and the sabre-rattling of force by other dictators – the debate which initially focused on siding with or against protesters' demands shifted to calling for foreign intervention to end the cycle of violence. By analysing Arab Spring political cartoons, I aim to examine how Arab cartoonists attempted to defend protesters' legitimate right for equality, freedom and social justice, and in so doing, how they strategically manoeuvred to address their international or western audience to mobilise support.

Following pragma-dialectics, I propose a model for the reconstruction of visual arguments contained in Arab Spring political cartoons. The model is inspired by the works of Feteris and her colleagues (2011), Feteris (2013) and Plug (2013). However, my contention is that the model falls short of identifying the (implicit) final standpoint which cartoonists aim to defend.

Although the model adequately guides the reconstruction of visual arguments conveyed mainly by visual metaphors, the final conclusion or claim attributes a value judgement to support the (un)desirability of a politician's actions or behaviours. In other words, the final conclusion confers an evaluative judgement on the criticised behaviours of a particular politician or public policy. The final standpoint, thus, asserts that the behaviours of a politician/public official (X) must be evaluated negatively (Feteris et al. 2011).

In my view, the negative evaluation of policies or actions is not an end in itself. It is rather too simplistic to limit the objectives of political cartoons – at least as this applies to the analysed cartoons in this chapter – to an evaluation of the status quo. In my view, it is the political implications of perpetuating the status quo which Arab cartoonists wish to emphasise and based on which the decision for future action is justified. These implications are presented in terms of the (positive or negative) consequences of already taken actions which are indirectly conveyed in visual metaphors and other visual properties (visual style and form). I presume that the negative evaluation of a politician's actions insinuates that something should be done to elevate these negative consequences or that other actions or policies have to be adopted. Similarly, the positive evaluation of a politician's actions suggests that similar actions can be adopted in different contexts. Therefore, the (implicit) final conclusion of the visual arguments contained in Arab Spring cartoons can take one of two forms: (1) action (A) should be taken in response to the negatively evaluated actions of a political agent (X); and (2) positively evaluated action (A) of a political agent (X) should be adopted in other contexts.

I argue, therefore, that the main objective of the analysed cartoons is either to promote the adoption of countermeasures as means to circumvent the negative consequences of the violent crackdown on protesters or to support protesters' efforts for social and political change. First, I briefly introduce my data. I then develop the model for reconstructing the visual arguments displayed by Arab Spring cartoons. Finally, I analyse three Arab Spring-related cartoons in order to examine the strategic manoeuvring of Arab cartoonists.

Data

There is a huge number of Arab Spring-related cartoons published in Arab and international newspapers and websites. The majority use visual images and/or visual metaphors to depict the current status quo, ridicule political opponents, and convey the ongoing debates and criticisms related to the Arab Spring. However, three elements determined the criteria for selecting the analysed cartoons. First, the selected cartoons should defend or refute a particular standpoint, that is, the argumentative function of political cartoons. Second, the aim of this chapter is to examine how Arab cartoonists manoeuvre to convince their western audience; therefore, the focus was on cartoons made by Arab cartoonists presented to western audiences. Thus, the selected cartoons are made by Arab cartoonists, are written in English and published on international websites. Finally, only cartoons that contain visual metaphors were selected. This led to a total of eleven cartoons. However, only three of these use visual metaphors that refer to western cultural sources. The selected cartoons are taken from three international websites: *cartoonmovement.com*, *thecanadiancharger.com* and *CagleCartoons.com*. The first and the second cartoons are made by well-known Arab cartoonists, Osama Hajjaj and Khalid Albaih, while the third is made by a less popular cartoonist, Hatem. The selected cartoons are analysed based on the model proposed in the section 'Reconstructing Argumentation in Arab Spring Political Cartoons'.

A Pragma-Dialectical Approach to Arab Spring Political Cartoons

Arab Spring Political Cartoons as an Argumentative Activity

The model of critical discussion stipulated by pragma-dialectical theory outlines the different stages necessary for the resolution of a difference of opinion, on the one hand, and assigns the tasks that participants should perform in every argumentative stage, on the other. According to van Eemeren and Houtlosser (1999, 2000), four stages are pivotal to the resolution of disagreement. These are the *confrontation stage* (externalisation of the difference of opinion), *opening stage* (initiation of discussion), *argumentation stage* (advancement of arguments) and the *concluding stage* where either the antagonist accepts the other side's standpoint or the proponent retracts his or her commitments and changes his or her position.

As mentioned above, Arab Spring cartoonists attempt to convince their audience that a specific action (A) has to be taken in response to the criticised or praised actions of a particular political agent (X). This is the implicit final standpoint put forward in the confrontation stage to which the cartoonist is committed. To justify his political stance, the cartoonist provides reasons that are expressed indirectly through visual metaphors containing images that refer to mythical, fictitious characters or cultural symbols – reasons can be equally invoked through visual style and form. These images allude to literary or cultural sources which are part of the common cultural background (Feteris 2013). From a pragma-dialectical perspective, this means that both cartoonists and the audience share common starting points, or cultural *topoi*, which form the basis of interpreting and reconstructing arguments (Feteris et al. 2011).[5] Establishing agreement concerning common starting points is achieved in the opening stage.

In the argumentation stage, the protagonist defends his or her standpoint by means of argumentation. In the case of Arab Spring political cartoons, the argumentation is multi-layered. First, the images contained in visual metaphors direct the audience to aspects of a politician's actions that the cartoonists want to criticise or extol, which in turn evoke the negative or positive evaluations. The second line of defence is invoked by other visual metaphors and visual properties embedded in a cartoon. Through the strategic choice of colours, lines, texture, arrangement and other visual elements, cartoonists portray the negative or positive consequences of the actions. On equal footing, other elements of visual formatting – for example, contrast and symmetry – also invoke meaning and provide the final inferential step to the standpoint. Finally, the concluding stage establishes the result of the argumentation. This is achieved through the implication that the positions conveyed indirectly in cartoons have withstood criticism and are successfully defended (Feteris et al. 2011).

During an argumentative activity, as van Eemeren and Houtlosser (2006) explicate, participants try to reconcile both dialectical and rhetorical aims. Consequently, the aim of participants is not only to arrive at a reasonable resolution to the disagreement but also to steer the debate to their own advantage. Balancing the attainment of both aims is an instance of strategic manoeuvring. Strategic manoeuvring represents the strategic choices made at the level of putting forward the most advantageous definition of points of disagreement (topical potential), framing the arguments in accordance with audience preferences (adaptation to audience), and choosing the most effective wording or mode of presentation (presentational device). With respect to Arab Spring political cartoons, strategic manoeuvring can be seen in terms of the strategic choices that cartoonists have made from the topical potential of dialectically relevant options, from the stylistic devices used and the way these are adapted to meet the audience's frame of reference.

Analysing strategic manoeuvring at the level of topical potential means identifying the choices made in selecting visual metaphors that allude to certain cultural sources or topoi through which the criticised or praised actions are depicted. Another aspect of strategic manoeuvring is seen in the choice of specific visual properties or elements which invoke patterns of reasoning or argument schemes. At the level of presentational devices, the choices made at the level of visual form and style which cartoonists employ to present their arguments are also aspects of strategic manoeuvring. Finally, cartoonists' adaptation to audiences' frames of reference, in terms of invoking socially shared norms and moral values, is a further aspect of strategic manoeuvring. In the following section, I outline the model for reconstructing visual arguments embedded in Arab Spring political cartoons.

Reconstructing Argumentation in Arab Spring Political Cartoons

According to Feteris et al. (2011) and Plug (2013), visual metaphors form the basis for reconstructing visual arguments. These metaphors are the main visual tools via which reasons in support of standpoints are indirectly expressed (Kjeldsen 2012, 2015). This view of visual metaphors is predominant in multimodal argumentation research. Based on this view, Arab cartoonists select visual metaphors which contain images that refer to cultural or literary sources such as legends, stories, fables, songs or media. These sources represent the common cultural background based on which the elements of the criticised or praised actions of a political agent are interpreted. This means that Arab cartoonists presume that they share with their audiences cultural knowledge, social norms and moral values based on which the classification and evaluation of political action are justified. These visual metaphors that allude to cultural, scientific or literary sources provide the contents of the first part of the complex argumentation deployed in cartoons.

As mentioned in the introduction, the model I am proposing for analysing Arab Spring cartoons partially draws on the model developed by Feteris (2013), Feteris and her colleagues (2011) and Plug (2013). Following this model, the arguments that are conveyed in visual metaphors support the classification and evaluation of the actions of a particular political agent (presented in the diagram as 1.1a and 1.1b). These arguments constitute the first line of providing reasons in support of the implicit final standpoint. The first argumentation (1.1a) consists of symptomatic argumentation which determines the characteristics of the action of a particular political agent (X). This argumentation is supported by the argumentation (1.1b) which is conveyed in visual metaphors that allude to cultural sources or topoi. In other words, the actions of a particular political agent which constitute the target of the metaphor (X) are compared with the negative or positive actions of the source (Z) of the metaphor. Through this analogy the characteristics Y_1, Y_2, etc. of the source (Z) are transferred to the actions of the target of the metaphor (X). This argumentation is presented in the diagram as (1.1a.1a) and (1.1a.1b).

The evaluation of the depicted actions is also invoked through visual images that refer to cultural sources. Plug (2013) maintains that certain visual metaphors that refer to cultural sources are inherently (negatively or positively) evaluated due to their (negative or positive) connotations. These connotations facilitate the transference of the evaluation of the source of the metaphor (Z) to the evaluation of the actions of the target of the metaphor (X). Had the analysis of Arab Spring cartoons limited itself to the role that cultural topoi play in conveying standpoints or arguments (i.e. strictly following Feteris and her colleagues' model), the analysis would not have done justice to what Arab cartoonists endeavour to communicate to their international or western audience.

In my view, to arrive at a positive or a negative evaluation of political actions is a necessary step to suggest that something should be done with respect to these (negatively or positively) evaluated actions. Moreover, restricting the analysis to the function of the main visual metaphors – cultural topoi – means ignoring the function of other visual metaphors, and more importantly, ignoring the function of visual style and form. As mentioned above, visual properties are equally significant in evoking patterns of reasoning and meaning. In this respect, I am in line with scholars who perceive that the choices made in formatting and form are more than just aesthetic devices. They are indeed essential parts of the argument (Kjeldsen 2015). In designing an image, as Tseronis (2013) explicates, choices are made regarding visual properties or elements, such as lines, colours, framing, texture, contrast, symmetry, arrangement, orientation and movement, among others, which also convey meaning and contribute to the ongoing argumentative procedure. It follows that visual style and form in Arab Spring cartoons play a significant role in argument reconstruction. The main role of these visual elements is to direct the audience to assess the consequences of the criticised or praised actions, that is, either exacerbating the political situation or leading to more favourable outcomes. Consequently, visual style and form, as well as visual metaphors (including cultural topoi), provide the contents of argument from consequences and practical reasoning scheme presented in the diagram as 1.2 and 1.3 respectively. In Diagram 8.1, I present a schematic representation of the complex argumentation conveyed indirectly in cartoons (propositions placed within brackets represent implicit premises). I will present an exemplary analysis of two political cartoons in the next section.

Diagram 8.1

1   Action (A) should be taken in response to the criticised or praised actions of a political agent (X)

   1.1 Actions of a political agent (X) should be evaluated negatively or positively

      1.1a. Actions of a political agent (X) have properties/characteristics Y_1, Y_2, etc.

         1.1a.1a. Actions of a political agent (X) are like the actions of (Z)

         1.1a.1b. Z's actions have properties/characteristics Y_1, Y_2, etc.

1.1b. The characteristics Y_1, Y_2, etc. of the actions of a political agent (X) should be evaluated negatively or positively

    1.1b.1a. These characteristics Y_1, Y_2, etc. either do not conform with commonly accepted social values or they conform with these values

    1.1b.1b. (Moral values are accepted common values)

    1.1b.1c. (Actions that are not in conformity with socially accepted values are undesirable while those that conform with socially accepted values are desirable)

1.2 Negatively evaluated actions should not be performed or positively evaluated actions should be performed

    1.2a. (Negative/positive consequences are undesirable/desirable)

1.3 Action (A) is either a means to circumvent the negative consequences or a means to achieve more positive outcomes

    1.3a. (The aim is either to circumvent the negative consequences or to achieve more positive outcomes)

Strategic Manoeuvring in Arab Spring Political Cartoons

The above-mentioned steps for reconstructing the meaning of visual arguments are futile unless the audience draws upon available contextual knowledge. This knowledge is not only related to interpreting visual images that refer to cultural sources which the audience is well acquainted with. A prerequisite for an appropriate decoding of cartoons is the knowledge of the broader social and political context and the familiarity of the audience with the ongoing political debates which cartoons are part of. This means that the audience has to be familiar with the unfolding events of the Arab Spring. The most important of these are the alleged use of chemical weapons by the Syrian regime, which led to the death of thousands, and the use of military force by the Libyan and Yemeni regimes. In the following sections, I analyse Arab cartoonists' argumentative strategies in their attempt to defend protesters' rights and to mobilise international support.

Basharcula the Syrian Vampire

In this cartoon, Osama Hajjaj attempts to convince the audience that something should be done with respect to the use of chemical weapons by the Syrian president, Bashar Al-Assad. This horrific incident compelled the Syrian opposition to call for an immediate foreign intervention to save the lives of innocent people. Assad's regime responded to this call with severe outrage, claiming that such an intervention would amount to an invasion and would represent a threat to the sovereignty of the state. The cartoon should be

Figure 8.1 Basharcula the Syrian vampire (Osama Hajjaj). Reproduced with permission

understood in light of the controversy around the responsibility of Assad's regime for using chemical weapons. The cartoon is, thus, a contribution to critical discussion and an attempt to resolve disagreement by providing reasons to support the cartoonist's standpoint.

It is clear from the outset that the cartoonist takes a critical stance on Assad's actions. The cartoonist's stance is, on the one hand, verbally communicated through the caption 'Basharcula the Syrian vampire', and through the visual metaphor that alludes to the fictitious character of Dracula or vampires, on the other. The strategic choice of this metaphor is seen at the level of referring to a well-known literary source which represents part of the common cultural background (topical potential, cultural topoi) of the international and western audience and based on which the actions of Assad are criticised and evaluated. Dracula's image, thus, serves two functions. On the one hand, Assad's actions (the target of the metaphor, X) are compared to Dracula's actions (the source of the metaphor, Z), that is, Dracula feeds on the blood of the living for sustenance. This implies that Assad's actions – the use of chemical weapons as a means to stay in power – are analogous to Dracula's actions. Therefore, the characteristics (Y_1, Y_2) of Assad's actions are identified (1.1a). On the other hand, the negative connotations that the image of Dracula evokes facilitate the transfer of the negative evaluation of the source of the metaphor (Dracula) to the evaluation of the target of the metaphor, Assad (1.1a.1a, 1.1a.1b).

The negative evaluation of Assad's actions is not only a matter of transferring a negative evaluation from one domain to the other. These actions are also evaluated in terms of commonly shared social norms, values and generally accepted behaviours of presidents (adaptation to audience). A president or public official is expected to serve his own country and meet citizens' demands. It is also an accepted social norm that a president takes the necessary measures to save his country and preserve the lives of his own people. Consequently, Assad's actions are negatively evaluated since they are not in conformity with commonly shared social values and norms. Therefore, Assad's actions are undesirable (1.1b.1a, 1.1b.1b, 1.1b.1c) because they conflict with accepted social norms and values.

Another aspect of strategic manoeuvring is related to the visual elements that the cartoonist selects to present Assad as a vampire (presentational devices). The choice of the colours red, black and grey evokes fear and horror. Undoubtedly, the red refers to the Syrian people. The black and grey refer to death and both propagate a melancholic tone. The caption is presented in contrasting colours of red and black which also contributes to invoke horror and repugnance towards Assad's actions and the use of chemical weapons.

At this stage, Assad's actions are negatively evaluated in light of the strategic choice of cultural topoi, that is, appealing to the audience's socially accepted norms and values. However, to arrive at the implicit final standpoint, attention should be given to other visual metaphors and visual properties. First, the cartoonist presents the Syrian people metaphorically in terms of the Syrian map that Assad is holding tightly between his hands as if it were a piece of meat. Moreover, the way Assad is portrayed looking enthusiastically at the map and the way his fangs are positioned indicates that Assad is determined to kill more Syrians. This supposition is emphasised by the red paint dripping off the first letter of 'Basharcula'. This visual presentation insinuates continuity of action. Second, the presentation of the meat in the colour pink is highly suggestive.[6] This means that the longer Assad continues in power, the more negative consequences in terms of killing more people, specifically young children, are expected (1.2). It goes without saying that these negative consequences are undesirable; therefore, an action of some kind has to be taken to stop Assad from shedding more lives. Since the political debate at the time during which the cartoon appeared revolved around foreign intervention to overthrow Assad, it could be safe to conclude that the final standpoint of the cartoon promotes the adoption of foreign intervention to save Syrian people. The cartoon can be interpreted as an attempt to convince the audience by the argumentation presented in Diagram 8.2.

Diagram 8.2

1 Foreign intervention (A) should be considered as a response to Assad's use of chemical weapons (X)

   1.1 Assad's use of chemical weapons (X) as means to defend his regime or to stay in power should be evaluated negatively

      1.1a. Assad's use of chemical weapons (X) which killed thousands and shed the lives of hundreds of innocent children should be characterised as barbaric, atrocious and horrific (Y_1, Y_2)

         1.1a.1a. Assad's use of chemical weapons in different sites in Syria (X) which killed thousands and shed the lives of many innocent children as means to stay in power are like the actions of Dracula (Z)

         1.1a.1b. Dracula's actions, feeding on blood to survive and moving from one place to another to search for new blood (Z), can be characterised as horrific, brutal and barbaric (Y_1, Y_2)

      1.1b. Assad's use of chemical weapons (X), which is barbaric, horrific and atrocious (Y_1, Y_2), should be evaluated negatively

         1.1b.1a. The use of chemical weapons by Assad (X) against his own people is not in conformity with accepted behaviours of presidents and violates socially shared moral values

         1.1b.1b. (Killing one's own people conflicts with socially accepted norms and values)

         1.1b.1c. (Actions that conflict with socially shared values and norms are undesirable)

   1.2 Assad should not be allowed to shed more lives

      1.2a. (Shedding the lives of innocent people is undesirable)

   1.3 Foreign intervention (A) is a means to prevent Assad from killing more people

      1.3a. (The aim is to prevent the bloodshed in Syria)

Evolution of Gaddafi

In this cartoon, Khalid Albaih attempts to convince the audience of the need to take measures against Gaddafi whose anti-demonstration discourse and response to revolution represent a step backwards to primitive stages of human evolution. The Libyan revolution was met with brutal force where mortars and machine guns were used while airplanes strafed and bombed crowds of protesters. The cartoon should be interpreted in light of the criticisms which Gaddafi's speech spurred in both the Libyan and the pan-Arab world. In his

Evolution of Gaddafi

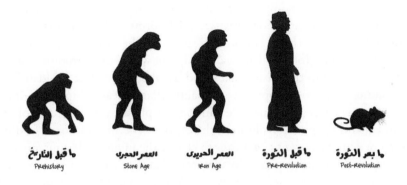

ما قبل التاريخ
PRehistoRy

العصر الحجري
Stone Age

العصر الحديدي
IRon Age

ما قبل الثورة
PRe-Revolution

ما بعر الثورة
Post-Revolution

Khalid Albaih

Figure 8.2 Evolution of Gaddafi (Khalid Albaih). Reproduced with permission

first public response to sweeping demonstrations, Gaddafi described demonstrators as cockroaches and called upon his forces to 'capture the rats', that is,
protestors. Gaddafi's description of demonstrators as rats is recontextualised
via a visual metaphor which promotes the negative evaluation of Gaddafi's
actions and words. In other words, Gaddafi's brutal and barbaric response to
demonstrations as well as his obscene language represent a reversal to a more
primitive, animal-like (rat) stage.

The cartoonist's stance is verbally communicated through the caption
'Evolution of Gaddafi', and through alluding to a scientific theory conveyed
through visual images. The cartoonist exploits the theory of human evolution
presented in the form of the 'March of Progress'. The original cartoon depicts
the progress of the human species through a series of images that summarises
the human evolution from an ape to a man. In this cartoon, however, the
image of a rat is added in order to suggest that Gaddafi's brutal and barbaric
response to demonstrations (X) has the characteristics of an inferior and
primitive species, rat (Z). In fact, the image of the rat suggests that during the
revolution Gaddafi evolved to a more primitive and inferior stage compared
with the initial stage from which humans evolved, the ape (1.1a). In this
respect, the characteristics of Gaddafi's actions are identified which in turn
lead to attributing a negative judgement to these actions (1.1b).

Gaddafi's actions are assessed based on socially accepted norms and values, such as the socially accepted behaviours of heads of state. Moreover, his actions are weighed in terms of their conformity with a scientific theory which represents part of the common cultural background of the western audience. In this respect, the cartoonist strategically manoeuvres by invoking two sources of normativity: social norms and cultural (scientific) sources (1.1b.1a, 1.1b.1b), in order to promote the negative evaluation of Gaddafi's actions. The implicit final standpoint which the cartoonist aims to defend is related to the means that could be taken to prevent Gaddafi from continuing his unwise, oppressive and authoritarian leadership that mimics the primitive stages of human evolution. Inspired by the success of the Tunisian and Egyptian revolutions, the cartoonist seems in favour of calling for more demonstrations as a means to elevate the undesirable consequences of Gaddafi's barbaric regime. This interpretation is promoted by the visual style used. The sharp contrast between the white and black colours as well as the repugnance that the image of the rat invokes suggest that measures should be taken to prevent Gaddafi from leading Libya from a bad to a worse situation, that is, from the pre-revolution to the post-revolution era. Therefore, demonstrations should continue to overthrow Gaddafi. Diagram 8.3 summarises the argumentation put forward by the cartoonist.

Diagram 8.3

    1 More demonstrations (A) are required to overthrow Gaddafi (X)

        1.1 Gaddafi's discourse and response to protests (X) as a means to defend his regime or to stay in power should be evaluated negatively

            1.1a. Gaddafi's response to demonstrations which led to the death of hundreds of innocent civilians (X) should be characterised as barbaric and brutal (Y_1, Y_2)

                1.1a.1a. Gaddafi's response to protests (X) is like the primitive stages of the human evolution (Z)/ the rat

                1.1a.1b. The first stages of the human evolution are characterised by being primitive and barbaric (Y_1, Y_2)

            1.1b. Gaddafi's response to protests which is characterised as being unwise, primitive and barbaric (Y_1, Y_2) should be evaluated negatively

                1.1b.1a. Gaddafi's use of brutal force (X) against his own people is not in conformity with accepted behaviours of presidents and conflicts with the scientific theory of human evolution

1.1b.1b. (Killing one's own people conflicts with socially accepted norms and values; Gaddafi's evolution represents a reversal to human progress)

1.1b.1c. (Actions that conflict with socially shared values, norms and cultural sources are undesirable)

1.2 Gaddafi should not be allowed to stay in power for his actions represent a step backwards to a more primitive stage of human evolution

1.2a. (Moving backwards to a primitive stage of evolution is undesirable)

1.3 Demonstrations (A) are a means to prevent Gaddafi from staying in power

1.3a. (The aim is to end Gaddafi's reign)

Arab Spring: Democracy, Liberty and Social Justice

In this cartoon, Hatem attempts to convince the audience that the violent crackdown on protesters by the Libyan regime should not discourage protesters in Yemen to continue with their sit-ins and demonstrations. The revolution in Yemen started shortly after the Libyan revolution and was equally met with violence where hundreds were killed, injured or detained. The cartoon has to be understood in light of the debate about whether demonstrations should be brought to an end to save the lives of protesters and the Yemeni people, or demonstrations should spread to other cities to force the Yemeni dictator to resign. The cartoonist seems in favour of the latter. The cartoonist seems to suggest that the lesson learnt from the Tunisian, Egyptian and Libyan revolutions shows that despite enormous sacrifices, revolutions succeeded in toppling dictators – presented in the form of the domino effect.

Figure 8.3 Democracy, liberty and social justice (Hatem)

In contrast to the previous cartoons in which Osama Hajj (Figure 8.1) and Khalid Albaih (Figure 8.2) criticise the actions of a dictator, this cartoon seems to advance a positive standpoint with respect to protesters' role in bringing about social and political change. The positive attitude is partially invoked through the title of the cartoon, which summarises the main objectives of the Arab Spring. This is further emphasised through the words scribbled on the blowing winds (the slogan of the Arab Spring). The aim of the verbal message is to dismiss any scepticism related to protesters' genuine political motivations and aspirations.[7] The Arab Spring's objectives are not only presented verbally but are also re-emphasised metaphorically in the form of blowing winds of change.

To put it differently, it is through revolutions that succeeded in toppling regimes, such as those in Tunisia, Egypt and Libya, that Arab citizens enjoy fair, liberal and democratic societies. The cartoon presents winds of change which metaphorically refer to the Arab Spring as the main reason for toppling oppressive regimes.[8] Therefore, the evaluation of the Arab Spring demonstrations or protesters' actions is indirectly invoked through a visual metaphor that alludes to a famous song which taps into the common cultural background of the targeted audience (topical potential, cultural topoi). Through this metaphor, protesters' actions and their political aspirations (the target of the metaphor, X) are compared to the actions and the political achievements to which the song refers (the source of the metaphor, Z), that is, the positive consequences of ending the Cold War. This suggests that the political changes which the actions of the demonstrators are expected to bring to the Arab political arena are analogous to the political achievements and changes brought by western people. In this respect, the characteristics (Y_1, Y_2) of Arab revolutions are identified (1.1a).

Moreover, the positive connotations that the song 'Wind of Change' evokes facilitate the transfer of the positive evaluation from the source of the metaphor (Z) to the actions of protesters – the target of the metaphor (X) (1.1a.1a, 1.1a.1b). Protesters' actions are positively evaluated in light of the socially shared norms and common values (adaptation to audience) that are invoked by reference to the song. This means that protesters' demands for justice, liberty and democracy are in conformity with the value hierarchy of the audience. Therefore, the classification of protesters' actions and the subsequent positive evaluation of these actions are conveyed through the strategic choice of a visual metaphor that alludes to a cultural source and the shared social norms and common values that form the basis of the audience's evaluation. On this view, the visual metaphor 'wind of change' provides the contents of the arguments that support the first argumentation (1.1).

To arrive at the implicit final standpoint, a careful examination of other visual metaphors and visual properties seems necessary. The domino effect of the blowing winds of change suggests that lessons should be learnt from countries where these revolutions succeeded in toppling dictators. This metaphorical representation can be interpreted as pointing to the positive consequences that these revolutions brought. This interpretation is emphasised through visual properties presented in terms of colour gradation. That is, with the successive fall of dictators, the grey and black colours of the whirlwind change to lighter and clearer grey-white. Another visual portrayal that feeds into emphasising the positive consequences is the change of the yellow colour of the background. The greyish yellow which prevails in the background with the beginning of the Tunisian and Egyptian revolutions changes to a brighter and clearer yellow with the fall of dictators' statues. These positive consequences constitute the second argumentation which is conveyed primarily through visual style (1.2).

The portrayal of the last statue, which represents the Yemeni president, as just starting to move indicates that the revolution in Yemen is in its early stages. Therefore, to boost the morale of Yemeni protesters and to encourage them to continue in their revolution despite obvious risks, the cartoonist selects another visual metaphor to indirectly communicate to protesters that it is only a matter of time before the Yemeni dictator will be toppled. The cartoonist presents the time interval that each revolution took to overthrow a dictator in terms of distance: the distance between the falling statues and the ground represents the time that each demonstration took. The longer the distance, the more time it took protesters to overthrow the dictator.[9] As a consequence, this leaves the Yemeni dictator contemplating how much time will it take protesters to topple him – presented in dark grey silhouette.

Guided by the positive spirits gained from revolutions that took place in other Arab countries, the cartoonist seems to encourage protesters in Yemen to continue their struggle through more demonstrations (1.3) despite sacrifices. The final standpoint of the cartoon seems to mobilise support for more demonstrations. Consequently, the cartoon can be interpreted as an attempt to convince the audience by the argumentation presented in Diagram 8.4.

Diagram 8.4

1 More protests and sit-ins (X) are required in Yemen to overthrow the regime

    1.1 Protesters' actions/demonstrations (X) which succeeded in overthrowing the Tunisian, Egyptian and Libyan dictators should be evaluated positively

1.1a. Protesters' actions/demonstrations (X) in Tunisia, Egypt and Libya which aimed to bring democracy, liberty and social justice after long years of oppression should be characterised as being emancipatory, peaceful and consolidating (Y_1, Y_2)

    1.1a.1a. Protesters' actions/demonstrations (X) in Tunisia, Egypt and Libya which aimed at social and political changes are like the political actions and achievements celebrated in the song 'Wind of Change' (Z)

    1.1a.1b. The political actions and achievements celebrated in 'Wind of Change', such as the end of the Cold War and the fall of the Berlin Wall (Z), are characterised as being peaceful, emancipatory and consolidating (Y_1, Y_2)

1.1b. Protesters' actions or Arab revolutions which are peaceful, emancipatory and consolidatory (Y_1, Y_2) should be positively evaluated

    1.1b.1a. Protesters' actions (X) which aim for democracy, liberty and social justice are in accordance with commonly accepted norms or socially shared values

    1.1b.1b. (Liberty, social justice and democracy are accepted values)

    1.1b.1c. (Actions that are in conformity with socially shared values and norms are desirable)

Conclusion

In this chapter, I have demonstrated how political cartoons in the context of the Arab Spring served as an argumentative tool to defend a positive stance towards protesters while defending a negative position towards oppressive regimes and their representatives. As for the former, protestors' motivations underlying their aspirations for political change (such as liberty, freedom and social equality) are highlighted. In the second and third cartoons, the authors are in favour of having more demonstrations as a means to bring about the expected change. As for the latter, dictators' barbaric and brutal responses to protestors are underscored (first and second cartoons) with emphasis on finding the means to topple oppressive and totalitarian regimes. I have shown how political cartoonists operate argumentatively not only to convince the audience that a particular action should be taken to protect protesters from atrocities but also to mobilise and galvanise support for protesters' efforts to attain basic human rights.

In their attempt to defend their political position in front of an international or western audience, Arab cartoonists strategically manoeuvred by framing the arguments to be in conformity with their western audience's values and common cultural background. In this respect, Arab cartoonists have exploited endoxa in the form of cultural topoi in constructing their visual arguments (Feteris 2013; Feteris et al. 2011; Plug 2013).[10] At the level of topical potential, the strategic choice of cultural topoi – in terms of a well-known western horror tale, *Dracula* (first cartoon); a popular scientific theory, the 'theory of evolution' (second cartoon); and a famous song, 'Wind of Change' (third cartoon) – served as common starting points and as premises for visual arguments. Reference to these cultural sources formed the basis against which the criticised or praised actions were evaluated and (de)legitimised.

The analyses showed that Arab cartoonists also strategically manoeuvred by appealing to moral values and social norms that an international or western audience cherishes, such as freedom of speech, justice, liberty and democracy, or those that the audience disfavour, for example the brutal crackdown on protestors. This means that Arab cartoonists are aware of their audience's background knowledge and value hierarchy, and therefore, framed their visual arguments accordingly. The results of the analyses showed that visual arguments are not only conveyed through visual metaphors and images, but also through visual style and form (Kjeldsen 2012, 2015; Tseronis 2013). Finally, the selected cartoons convey a positive standpoint on the Arab Spring. Thus, it might be interesting to see whether Arab cartoonists who support oppressive regimes use similar argumentative strategies.

Notes

1. Blair (1996) argues that many visual images, particularly in advertisements, are instances of persuasion rather than argumentation. In Birdsell and Groarke's (2007) typology of visual meaning, images are used as flags, demonstrations, metaphors, symbols and archetypes. In their view, visual images used as flags do not necessarily have an argumentative function because they are used either to draw viewers' attention or for purely aesthetic purposes. Roque (2015) has a similar view with respect to visual flags.
2. Birdsell and Groarke (1996, 2007) maintain that the implicit or the indirect propositions conveyed in visuals can be made explicit in a manner similar to verbal claims or premises conveyed in figurative and metaphorical expressions.
3. Blair (1996) asserts that the indirect propositions or arguments conveyed in visuals can be made linguistically explicable, that is, to express in words the indirect arguments conveyed in visuals.
4. On 18 December 2010, the 'Freedom and Dignity Revolution' started in Tunisia and within a few weeks it succeeded in overthrowing the Tunisian president. This inspired the downtrodden in Egypt, Libya, Yemen and Syria to revolt against oppression, tyranny, corruption, poverty, unemployment, and the unequal distribution of power and wealth. A common theme in 'Arab Spring Revolutions' is people's demand for equality, freedom of speech, social recognition and justice. However, protesters were seen as a threat to national unity and

were subsequently represented in anti-demonstration discourse as rioters, traitors, conspirators and saboteurs whose primary goal was to disintegrate the state and inflame civil strife.

5. In argumentation theory, the concept of topoi is highly controversial. There is no agreement over the definition of a topos as well as its characterisation and function. In a nutshell, argumentation scholars follow either Aristotle's conceptualisation of topoi – as general and abstract formulas – or Cicero who views topoi as subject matter indicators and as argument schemes (Rubinelli 2009).

6. An internet search related to the meaning of different meat colours reveals that the meat of younger birds shows the most pink because their thinner skins permit oven gases to reach the flesh.

7. Arab regimes have repeatedly represented protesters as saboteurs or as a bunch of defectors.

8. 'Wind of Change' is a famous song by the German band, Scorpions. This song, as declared by its writer, is a celebration of the end of the Cold War and the reforms that were brought by Gorbachev. The song later on became the unofficial anthem of the fall of the Berlin Wall and German reunification. It celebrates change and evokes sentiments of hope and peace.

9. The Tunisian revolution lasted about 3 weeks and the Egyptian one lasted 4 weeks, while the Libyan revolution lasted for almost 9 months.

10. Endoxa are commonly held views, beliefs and values that are culture-specific (van Eemeren 2010).

References

Birdsell, D. S. and L. Groarke (1996), 'Towards a theory of visual argument', *Argumentation and Advocacy*, 33 (1), pp. 1–10.

Birdsell, D. S. and L. Groarke (2007), 'Outlines of a theory of visual argument', *Argumentation and Advocacy*, 43, pp. 103–13.

Blair, J. A. (1996), 'The possibility and actuality of visual argument', *Argumentation and Advocacy*, 33 (1), pp. 23–39.

Blair, J. A. (2004), 'The rhetoric of visual arguments', in C. A. Hill and M. Helmers (eds), *Defining Visual Rhetorics*, Mahwah, NJ: Lawrence Erlbaum Associates, pp. 137–51.

Bounegru, L. and C. Forceville (2011), 'Metaphors in editorial cartoons representing the global financial crisis', *Visual Communication*, 10 (2), pp. 209–29.

Carroll, N. (1996), 'A note on film metaphor', *Journal of Pragmatics*, 26 (6), pp. 809–22.

Edwards, J. L. (2004), 'Echoes of Camelot: How images construct cultural memory through rhetorical framing', in C. A. Hill and M. Helmers (eds), *Defining Visual Rhetorics*, Mahwah, NJ: Lawrence Erlbaum Associates, pp. 179–94.

El Refaie, E. (2003), 'Understanding visual metaphor: The example of newspaper cartoons', *Visual Communication*, 2 (1), pp. 75–96.

El Refaie, E. (2009), 'Metaphor in political cartoons: Exploring audience responses', in C Forceville and E. Urios-Aparisi (eds), *Multimodal Metaphor*, Berlin: Mouton de Gruyter, pp. 173–96.

Feteris, E. (2013), 'The use of allusions to literary and cultural sources in argumentation in political cartoons', in H. van Belle, P. Gillearts, B. van Gorp, D. van de Mieroop and K. Rutten (eds), *Verbal and Visual Rhetoric in a Media World*, Leiden: Leiden University Press, pp. 415–27.

Feteris, E., L. Groarke and J. Plug (2011), 'Strategic maneuvering with visual arguments in political cartoons. A pragma-dialectical analysis of the use of topoi that are based on common cultural heritage', in E. Feteris, B. Garssen and F. Snoeck Henkemans (eds), *Keeping in Touch with Pragma-Dialectics: In Honor of Frans H. van Eemeren*, Amsterdam: John Benjamins, pp. 59–74.

Forceville, C. (1996), *Pictorial Metaphor in Advertising*, London: Routledge.

Forceville, C. (2002), 'The identification of target and source in pictorial metaphors', *Journal of Pragmatics*, 34 (1), pp. 1–14.

Groarke, L. (1998), 'The pragma-dialectics of visual argument', in F. H. van Eemeren, J. A. Blair and B. Garssen (eds), *Proceedings of the International Society for the Study of Argumentation*, Amsterdam: Sic Sat.

Groarke, L. (2009), 'Five theses on Toulmin and visual argument', in F. H. van Eemeren and B. Garssen (eds), *Pondering on Problems of Argumentation: Twenty Essays on Theoretical Issues*, Amsterdam: Springer, pp. 229–39.

Hart, C. (2017), 'Metaphor and intertextuality in media framings of the (1984–1985) British Miners' Strike: A multimodal analysis', *Discourse & Communication*, 11 (1), pp. 3–30.

Kennedy, V. (1993), 'Mystery! Unraveling Edward Gorey's tangled web of visual metaphor', *Metaphor and Symbolic Activity*, 8 (3), pp. 181–93.

Kjeldsen, J. E. (2012), 'Pictorial argumentation in advertising: Visual tropes and figures as a way of creating visual argumentation', in F. H. van Eemeren and B. Garssen (eds), *Topical Themes in Argumentation Theory: Twenty Exploratory Studies*, Dordrecht: Springer, pp. 239–55.

Kjeldsen, J. E. (2015), 'The rhetoric of thick representation: How pictures render the importance and strength of an argument salient', *Argumentation*, 29, pp. 197–215.

Plug, H. J. (2013), 'Manoeuvring strategically in political cartoons: Transforming visualizations of metaphors', in H. van Belle, P. Gillearts, B. van Gorp, D. van de Mieroop and K. Rutten (eds), *Verbal and Visual Rhetoric in a Media World*, Leiden: Leiden University Press, pp. 429–39.

Roque, G. (2015), 'Should visual arguments be propositional in order to be arguments?', *Argumentation*, 29, pp. 177–95.

Rubinelli, S. (2009), *Ars Topica: The Classical Technique of Constructing Arguments from Aristotle to Cicero*, Berlin: Springer.

Slyomovics, S. (2001), 'Sex, lies and television: Algerian and Moroccan caricatures of the Gulf War', in S. Joseph and S. Slyomovics (eds), *Women and Power in the Middle East*, Philadelphia: University of Pennsylvania Press, pp. 72–97.

Tseronis, A. (2013), 'Argumentative functions of visuals: Beyond claiming and justifying', in D. Mohammed and M. Lewinski (eds), *Virtues of Argumentation: Proceedings of the 10th International Conference of the Ontario Society for the Study of Argumentation (OSSA)*, Windsor, ON: OSSA, pp. 1–17.

van Eemeren, F. H. (2010), *Strategic Maneuvering in Argumentative Discourse: Extending the Pragma-Dialectical Theory of Argumentation*, Amsterdam: Benjamin.

van Eemeren, F. H. and P. Houtlosser (1999), 'Strategic manoeuvring in argumentative discourse', *Discourse Studies*, 1 (4), pp. 479–97.

van Eemeren, F. H. and P. Houtlosser (2000), 'Rhetorical analysis within a pragma-dialectical framework', *Argumentation*, 14, pp. 293–305.

van Eemeren, F. H. and P. Houtlosser (2006), 'Strategic maneuvering: A synthetic recapitulation', *Argumentation*, 20, pp. 381–92.

Wildfeuer, J. (2014), *Film Discourse Interpretation: Towards a New Paradigm for Multimodal Film Analysis*, New York: Routledge.

9

Social Media Activism by Favela Youth in Rio de Janeiro

Andrea Mayr

Introduction

This chapter looks at the use of social media as a tool of protest by the urban poor of Rio de Janeiro and its incorporation into the mainstream press. Internet access and use of social media has been steadily rising in Brazil's favelas (self-built communities of the urban poor) over the past years, reflecting the increase in internet use in the country as a whole, particularly in urban areas, where it has become an important instrument for civic engagement (see, for example, Holmes 2012). The mass demonstrations of 2013 were perhaps the best example of how large crowds all over Brazil could be mobilised on online platforms such as Facebook and Twitter for large-scale street protests against the state, in this case against corruption and mismanagement of the 2014 World Cup and the 2016 Olympics.

The focus of this chapter, however, is not on massive internet campaigns, but on one example of the many small-scale online protests initiated by young favela residents against human rights violations, some of which have occurred in the wake of the Rio state government's policy of favela 'pacification' and the city's preparation for the two mega events. The case reported here is of a Facebook campaign that was launched by favela youth after the fatal shooting of a young man by military police in a 'pacified' favela.[1]

This 'favela online media activism' (Custódio 2016) is a recent development of Latin American traditions of communication for social change (Gumucio-Dagron and Tufte 2006) and participatory media (Peruzzo 1996; Rodriguez 2011). Recent research from Brazil has pointed to the potential of often youth-led media collectives from favelas to act as a democratising force that helps to mobilise 'off-line activism' (Custódio 2014) in the form of street protests or photographic documentation and exhibition of social issues (see Souza 2013; Custódio 2014; Willis et al. 2014). Importantly, some of this user-created content is increasingly incorporated into Rio's mainstream press. By interacting with mainstream media in this way, favela activists take an import step towards being recognised as civic actors rather than being regarded as threats or mere victims of state violence.

Sociological research has amply demonstrated that it is mainly black and mixed-race males between the ages of 15 and 29 years who are the main victims of this violence and who are often treated as mere casualties in a war on drugs that has been waged by the state and its police forces for decades.[2] The violent crackdown on young people who may or may not be involved in drug trafficking has in part been fuelled by popular support for police violence, including police massacres of street children and favela residents (Gay 2005; Holston and Caldeira 1998; Huggins 2000). This persistent victimisation of (young) people of Afro-Brazilian descent can also be seen as the legacy of the country's violent history of colonialism and slavery.

Background

Roughly 20 per cent of Rio's 6.2 million residents live in favelas, while many others are consigned to the poorer northern and western parts of the city, which are largely cut off from the vibrant and economically successful parts of the city's South Zone. Throughout their history, favelas have been seen as dangerous and violent places that threaten the sometimes adjacent wealthier neighbourhoods of the city (see Perlman 1976, 2010). This social construction of favelas as areas of lawlessness and neglect has entrenched their militarisation and given rise to media discourses and public security approaches which consider favelas first and foremost as social and spatial threats that need to be controlled and disciplined (see, for example, Dias and Eslava 2013; Mayr 2015).

The city's most significant public security policy to combat urban violence has been favela 'pacification', an ambitious proximity policing approach that was introduced in 2008. Led by a 'new' military police force, the Pacifying Police Units or UPPs (Unidades de Polícia Pacificadora), its stated intention has been to create conditions for the social, economic and political integration of favelas into the city. The main strategy, however, has been re-establishing state control in favelas by driving out drug-trafficking groups who have controlled them almost undisputedly since the early 1990s.[3]

Despite its success in reducing the number of police killings, the Pacification Programme has suffered a number of setbacks in the form of very serious human rights abuses committed by members of its own police forces. One high-profile case, which is the subject of this chapter, was the fatal shooting of 25-year-old Douglas Rafael Pereira da Silva on 22 April 2014 by UPP police in a 'pacified' favela near Copacabana.[4] The case received intense national as well as international media coverage because da Silva (also known as 'DG') was an aspiring dancer on the television show 'Esquenta' for Rede Globo, Brazil's largest television network, and because the event happened close to the staging of the 2014 World Cup in a famous tourist area.

The favela where the fatal shooting of da Silva occurred, Pavão-Pavãozinho, is situated above Ipanema and Copacabana in Rio's South Zone and has been pacified since 2009.[5] Its UPP unit has been accused of many forms of mismanagement since its implementation, which has led to distrust between residents and police.[6] After da Silva was found dead in the favela on the morning of 22 April 2014 in the backyard of a children's daycare centre, the initial military police report stated that his death was caused by a fall as he attempted to climb over the daycare centre wall, fleeing from the police who were engaged in a shootout with drug traffickers. The medical forensic assessment, however, concluded that he had died from a shot in the back, which perforated his lung. The killing sparked protests by favela residents, in which they demanded a proper explanation for da Silva's death. In violent clashes with police which lasted all night, yet another young man, Edilson dos Santos, was shot dead by a member of the UPP as he stepped outside a house to take part in the protest. A young man with learning difficulties, his death was reported by the media, but it did not nearly receive as much attention as da Silva's death.

It was during these protests that a well-known blogger from the Complexo do Alemão favela complex in Rio's North Zone, René Silva, posted an image of himself with a piece of paper bearing the inscription *Eu não mereço morrer assassinado* ('I don't deserve to be killed') on the website of his own online community journal *Voz da Comunidade* – 'Voice of the Community' (see Figure 9.2 for a cropped version of this post).[7] In the post he mourned da Silva's death and called upon young people from favelas to do the same. The post was subsequently uploaded on the Facebook page of *Maré Vive* ('Maré lives'). *Maré Vive* is yet another online channel, which was created for and by residents of the Maré favela so they can register and denounce acts of violence by military police, especially after the favela was occupied by the army in 2014.

The campaign was widely publicised on online channels and subsequently covered in Rio's mainstream print and broadcast media. This chapter looks at its coverage in Rio's popular newspaper *Extra*, which has a track record of campaigning against human rights violations, perhaps more so than other newspapers in Rio. In the interview the author conducted with *Extra*'s editor, Fabio Gusmão, he confirmed that the paper's main motivation for publicising the campaign was precisely to give it greater visibility and to create more impact. In the context of Rio, with its high incidence of lethal police violence against favela residents, it is particularly important for the local press to highlight human rights abuses. Media reports of execution-style killings by police are commonplace, but it is usually only when incidents are photographed or filmed that justice is done and officers face trial.

The Newspaper *Extra*

Created in 1998, *Extra* belongs to the *O Globo* newspaper, itself part of Brazil's largest news conglomerate of the same name. A popular newspaper for the class B and class C sectors of the Brazilian lower-middle classes,[8] it has a print and an online version. It was also the first newspaper in Rio to introduce the smartphone messaging application WhatsApp to its readers in 2013 so they can report human rights issues and contribute to the news production process.[9]

WhatsApp did indeed become a decisive tool in bringing da Silva's case to court. According to Gusmão, it was a UPP policewoman who sent an image of da Silva's body via WhatsApp to *Extra*, saying she wanted the truth to be known. The image revealed that da Silva was originally found slumped on the ground of the daycare centre. It also clearly showed that he had been shot in the back (see Figure 9.1).

Extra used this image on its front page together with the headline *Não foi bala perdida* ('It wasn't a stray bullet'), which refuted the official version of events issued by the military police. According to Gusmão, an earlier photo that had been sent by UPP police to TV Globo showed da Silva lying on his back with his arms spread out to make it look as if he had died in confrontation with the police. Changing the crime scene by moving the body is a common strategy used by Rio police to manipulate evidence. The investigation of the case, which was conducted by the civil police (who deal with criminal offences), came to a close in March 2015.[10] The Public Prosecution Service charged one UPP officer with murder and another six with fraudulent manipulation.

Methodology

This chapter uses a combined ethnographic and discourse-analytical approach. After collecting a small corpus of newspaper articles about da Siva's case, the author conducted two interviews with two editors from the Rio newspaper *Extra* (May 2015), which revealed important details about the newspaper's coverage of the internet campaign and which informed the analysis of its linguistic and pictorial strategies. The discourse paradigm employed for the analysis is in the tradition of multimodal critical discourse

Figure 9.1 *Extra* front page, 25 April 2014. Courtesy of Humberto Tziolas

analysis (Machin and Mayr 2012) and uses Kress and van Leeuwen's (2006) image analysis framework in combination with Martin's (2001) interpersonal system of evaluation, 'Appraisal'. Appraisal is primarily a system of semantic resources for describing emotional reactions ('Affect') and moral assessments ('Judgement') and for making aesthetic evaluations ('Appreciation'), but it has more recently also been applied to media images and journalistic discourse analysis (e.g. Economou 2006, 2008; Caple and Knox 2012). The reason for this combined approach is that Kress and van Leeuwen's interpersonal categories of viewer–image social relations are limited to interaction and modality. Martin (2001), on the other hand, expands on these with another interpersonal category. According to Martin, the primary function of a prominent image in a multimodal text is to provoke a *desired* audience evaluation of the text that follows. The system of Appraisal is useful here because it is concerned with 'how writers/speakers approve and disapprove, enthuse and abhor, applaud and criticise, and with how they position their readers/listeners to do likewise' (Martin and White 2005: 1). Appraisal therefore allows the speaker or writer to comment on the world. Like all forms of evaluation, it also plays an important role in legitimation.

This chapter seeks to apply this combined approach to online (newspaper) communication, thereby contributing to more recent research in critical discourse analysis of digital media as 'emerging sites of discursive struggles' (KhosraviNik 2014; see also Wodak and Wright 2006; Unger 2012; Kelsey and Bennett 2014). The following section analyses *Extra*'s coverage of da Silva's case from 24 April 2014 in terms of Kress and van Leeuwen's categories of Social Relations (Interaction and Modality) and Martin's (2001) Appraisal categories – (Affect, Appreciation and Judgement). I will also use Appraisal to show how the Facebook campaign was evaluated in the fifty-three reader comments sent to the newspaper's online version.

Analysis

Kress and van Leeuwen's model has three main categories that allow for three types of meaning choices in constructing images: content, interaction (i.e. social relations between viewer and image) and composition, based on Halliday's (1978) three linguistic metafunctions, the ideational, interpersonal and textual meanings, respectively. These allow for a systematic analysis of the original campaign images as well as of their coverage in *Extra*'s online version.

In its online page from 24 April 2014 (see Figure 9.2), *Extra* reports on the Facebook campaign. Below the headline, which translates as 'After DG's

Figure 9.2 *Extra* online page. Courtesy of Humberto Tziolas

death, young people demand an end to killings in favelas in a social media campaign', the main image is a cropped version of the original Facebook post, featuring the initiator of the campaign, René Silva. The visual composition of the online page can be said to be structured along what Kress and van Leeuwen (2006) call 'centre' and 'margin' dimensions, where one element, in this case the main image of the Facebook campaign, is made the central element of the page, with two smaller images, one of da Silva's mother holding up a family photo with her dead son, and one of his funeral, being placed in the top left-hand margin. Fabio Gusmão explained that *Extra* always uses one large image (the centre element) to create reader impact, while the elements in the margins are positioned so that the reader stays on the site for longer. This is also indicated by the rather weak framing between all the items, which links them together. The reader comments are unusually placed at the top right-hand corner of the page and are highlighted by a small white arrow that directs the reader from the headline straight to them.

Moving on to the images of the Facebook campaign in *Extra*'s online version, which depict some of the young people who initiated the campaign, these may be classed as both 'narrative' and 'conceptual', following Kress and van Leeuwen's (2006) classification. Narrative images represent social actors and their action(s), while conceptual images symbolise and represent social actors more in terms of their attributes. The narrative quality in the images here derives from the social actors being engaged in the material action of standing and holding a piece of paper bearing a message. At the same time, we also learn about their mental states from the expressions on their mute faces, whereby readers/viewers are encouraged to feel empathy for them. The images are also narrative in that they are 'high-modality', that is, they are naturalistic, contain details and depth, natural shading and a background in the form of windows or walls.

The interaction or social relationship between viewer and image is set up by camera angle and shot type. The main image showing René Silva is a very close frontal shot taken from a horizontal angle and largely occupying the frame of the image, all of which results in what Kress and van Leeuwen (2006) call 'intimate social distance' between viewer and represented participant. The rest of the images chosen in *Extra*'s online article (see Figures 9.3–9.6 below) are medium frontal shots, where we see the participants from the waist upwards. They still occupy the frame, but the shot type puts them at a perhaps slightly greater social and personal distance from the viewer. All but one of the represented participants look straight at the viewer. These 'demand' shots usually ask viewers to feel 'social affinity' for the represented participants (Kress and van Leeuwen 2006: 118). Only one image (Figure 9.6) is an 'offer' image, where the social actor's gaze is directed

Figure 9.3 Dancer Hilton Fantástico. Courtesy of Humberto Tziolas

Figure 9.4 Fernando Barcellos from City of God. Courtesy of Humberto Tziolas

downwards and off-frame, presenting her as an object of contemplation for the viewer to be drawn into her mental world. Frontal angles usually generate greater involvement of the viewer with the represented participant(s) through their direct gaze. All the images here are taken from a horizontal angle, which suggests they are on an equal level with the viewer.

Figure 9.5 Elesandra Santos showing her own version of the original campaign message: 'Nobody deserves to be killed, he did not deserve it . . . Peace'. Courtesy of Humberto Tziolas

Figure 9.6 Unknown girl. Courtesy of Humberto Tziolas

Appraisal

We now turn to examine which of Martin's three kinds of Appraisal may be provoked by the choices of content, interaction and composition in the *Extra* online page discussed so far. Affect is inscribed in the campaign images by showing the social actors' facial expressions and body language. Their gaze could be said to express vulnerability, suffering and defiance (Figures 9.3, 9.4 and 9.5). Affect can therefore be said to be provoked by the direct gaze of the social actors and their mute faces. Other features, such as colour, also provoke Affect. The red droplets in Figure 9.6, connoting the spilling of blood, are particularly evocative. The three images in black and white (Figures 9.2, 9.3 and 9.4), on the other hand, have a more documentary 'feel' of authenticity.

While the images are all interpersonally charged with Affect, they alone may not necessarily align the viewer for or against the social actors in the images. The linguistic message itself, which contains strong negative Judgement ('I don't deserve to be killed'), is equally important. Fernando Barcellos from City of God (Figure 9.4) is quoted by *Extra*, expressing further strong negative Judgement of da Silva's killing: 'We cannot remain silent with so many black people in favelas being killed. Enough!' In most images the message is hand-written, which adds a personal touch, except for Figure 9.5, where it is printed in capitals in a sans serif font. Even the hashtag in Figures 9.3 and 9.4, '#Luto DG' ('I mourn DG'), is evaluative as it is used to signal the emotionally charged comment and can be said to construe Affect in terms of sadness (see Zappavigna 2015). All participants shown here were creative in their use of fonts, capitals and exclamation marks. That means that their messages are clearly also *aesthetic* interventions; their Appreciation value is therefore quite high. For example, the young woman in Figure 9.5 changed the entire wording of the original message to 'Nobody deserves to die. He did not deserve it. Peace'; she also added an image of da Silva. Therefore, the 'semiotic burden' in communicating 'affective resonance' (Wade, quoted in Caple and Knox 2012: 222) also comes from the linguistic message. This is borne out by the reader comments, some of which reacted very negatively to the actual message ('Eu não mereço . . .'). The following comments from *Extra*'s page clearly illustrate this through inversions of the original message (original capitals retained in translation):

(1) I DON'T DESERVE TO LIVE WITH DOPEHEADS!!!
    [EU NÃO MEREÇO CONVIVER COM MACONHEIROS!!!!]

(2) #IDon'tDeserveToLiveWithDrugdealers
    [#EuNãoMereçoConviverComTraficantes]

(3) I don't deserve to have drug dealers in my area.
    [Eu não mereço ter traficantes de droga de meu bairro.]

(4) I also don't deserve to be killed, therefore help to get rid of the drug dealers here, who kill, corrupt and torture everybody who crosses their path and only then will we have peace.
    [Nem eu mereço morrer assassinado, então ajude acabar com os traficantes que aí estão, já que eles matam, viciam e torturam todos que cruzarem por seus caminhos e só assim teremos paz.]

All three posts also contain negative Judgement of drug dealers and drug consumers ('dopeheads') and their actions ('kill, corrupt and torture', 'killed').
Interestingly, there is no condemnation of the police, who after all were
responsible for da Silva's death. Instead, some readers criticised the campaigners for failing to challenge drug dealers:

(5) None of these young people make campaigns that say 'No to drugs'
of which they are the main consumers. None of these young people
respect authorities, society, their parents and what the State produces
with our taxes.
[Ninguem ve esses jovens fazendo manifestacao para dizer Nao as
drogas, onde eles sao os grandes consumidores. Nao se ve esses jovens
respeitar as autoridades, a sociedade, os pais, o que o Estado produz
com os nossos impostos.]

(6) I want to see them make this demand to drug dealers and addicts who
are the real contributors to this violence!
[Quero ver eles pedirem isso aos traficantes e viciados, os verdadeiros
financiadores desta violência!]

What these commentators ignore is that favela residents cannot criticise drug
dealers openly, let alone on social media. They could be quite severely punished by them if they did that. Going back to the *Extra* online page, the
headline 'After DG's death, young people demand an end to killings in favelas
in a social media campaign' contains negative Judgement ('killings'), but no
Affect, which is produced primarily by the main image, the cropped version
of René Silva's Facebook post. The Affect produced by the image *positions* the
reader to accept the negative Judgement in the headline and the rest of the
text, which is interspersed with four pictures of young people who took part
in the campaign (see Figures 9.3–9.6 above). However, as we can see from the
reader responses, although headline and image together certainly position the
reader to feel empathy, affectual responses do not necessarily lead to empathy
in readers. Domke et al. (2003) found that images have the ability to 'trigger' people's pre-existing values, cognitions and feelings. These pre-existing
ideas can reflect and influence how an image is interpreted and talked about.
Economou (2008: 258) suggests that the depiction of emotion on people's
faces produces Affect, while Judgement is more likely to be produced by the
stance and gesture of social actors. Figures 9.2, 9.3 and 9.4 in particular may
have produced strong negative Judgement in some readers. Visually, the dark-
skinned, bare-chested youth with the baseball cap (Figure 9.3) is a potent cultural and class symbol in Brazil and taken as an indication of favela residence
and hence criminality. None of the fifty-three reader comments referred to

the fact that two young men had been tragically killed by police. Instead, they revolved around the activities of drug dealers in favelas and negative evaluation of the dead da Silva and those who took part in the online campaign.

Affect is the most basic of Attidude types, so a provocation of strong Affect caused by an image may trigger personal or cultural Judgement. This may have provoked the negative linguistic Judgement of da Silva, who was categorised by some readers as a 'Sympathiser of drug traffickers' (*Simpatisante do trafico*) and as a 'Friend of "Big Dog"' (*Amigo de Cachorão*, 'Cachorão' being the name of a drug dealer). Da Silva's status as an artist was also doubted by putting inverted commas around the word ('artista'). Many of the fifty-three reader comments were preoccupied with drug dealers. The word *bandido/bandidos*[11] ('bandit') was used sixteen times, *traficante* ('drug dealer') thirteen times and *vagabundo* ('vagabond') three times in these fifty-three comments. All these terms contain negative Judgement that serves to implicate da Silva in the drug trade, a common strategy used by the popular media and the police to justify killing 'suspects'. Although only a small fraction of favela residents have direct connections to crimes such as drug trafficking, there is a common assumption in Brazilian popular culture, fed by some media, that favela residents are either potential or actual criminals (Machado da Silva 2008). Terms such as 'bandido' are not only negative evaluations, but also amount to what van Leeuwen (2000) calls an 'impersonalisation' and 'objectivisation' of these social actors, turning them into generic types and reducing them to the status of criminals. Goldstein points out that the racialised figure of the 'bandido' and 'marginal'[12] has been described as 'back-ward, aggressive, and primitive or uncivilised in nature, qualities that their geographical position on the urban periphery supposedly reflects' (2004: 12). This collapsing of location and character is further exacerbated through race-based fears about the people who inhabit these marginal spaces. That is why it is mainly young, darker-skinned males who are criminalised and dehumanised as second-class citizens in discourses that Penglase (2007) has called 'neo-racist'.[13] Darker people have historically been understood as more 'animalistic', and threats of dark, masculine bodies and spaces become naturalised through these linguistic and visual media discourses (Prouse 2012).

Discussion

Some scholars suggest that online media activism of the kind discussed here may indeed have its greatest impact when it is incorporated into mainstream news media culture, as it is often perceived by professional journalists as possessing greater 'discursive authority' (Andén-Papadopoulos and Pantti 2011: 100). Content like that analysed here provides a sense of authenticity and personal intimacy with events, often in an unpolished form that supporters and some audiences appreciate (Bock 2012; Holton et al. 2013; Williams et al. 2011). At the same time, campaigns of this nature are ephemeral and tend to be forgotten soon. They are also highly selective in that some cases travel from 'digital subcultures' (Mortensen 2011) to mainstream media, whereas others, which might be equally worthy of attention, do not. In the case study analysed here, two young men were shot and killed by the police, one a well-known aspiring television star for *O Globo* (da Silva), the other a homeless man with learning difficulties (dos Santos). The latter had been released from a mental institution and ended up in the Pavão-Pavãozinho favela, where he was cared for by residents.

Perhaps the main problem with an online campaign like this and its newspaper coverage is, as Mortensen points out, that even if violence is 'exhibited pedagogically to prevent further violence' and to engage the viewer, as the Facebook campaign and its reporting in *Extra* did, 'the spectator is enrolled in the logics of violence and needs to position him- or herself in a difficult process of identification and distancing' (2011: 11). We also have to bear in mind that images hardly ever convey a fixed message, as they are 'polysemous': they contain what Barthes (1977) calls a 'floating chain' of signifieds from which the viewer can choose some and ignore others. They literally ask readers to 'see for themselves' and may limit critical enquiry of the story they are presented with. Therefore, the presumption that images like the ones analysed here will afford a heightened sense of emotional identification is never guaranteed (see Chouliaraki 2008). The reader comments analysed above appear to confirm this.

In the context of today's 'participatory' networked communication it is also important to note that internet campaigns like the one reported may be a 'superficial mode of paticipation' (Moubray 2015: 24), where participation is limited to circulating contributions on the net, helping to perpetuate a 'fantasy of participation' (Dean 2008: 109–10). This acts as a substitute for real political engagement in the form of 'off-line' activism (Custódio 2014), such as street protests. Favela photographer and activist Luiz Baltar expressed this dilemma to the author very well:

> These campaigns irritate me a lot, where people demand peace in a generic way, such as 'we want peace in Alemão' [a favela], 'we want peace in I don't know where' , as if anybody didn't want peace whether they be drug traffickers or the Governor [of Rio State]. It also has a lot to do with vanity to show and say 'look I am in the trendings topic of Twitter and Facebook, my post was one of the most commented ones. Every time there is a shootout, we will make a hastag, peace in Alemão, what will you change? There are other campaigns that are more political, more incisive.[14]

Conclusion

There are now numerous examples in Brazil of the use of the internet and social media by the poor for denouncing human rights violations (see Custódio 2013), such as the online sharing of photo essays on the forced evictions of favela residents to make room for the Olympic village, to name just one. Mobile phone footage of human rights abuses by the police are another important tool to challenge the official version of events, and are increasingly incorporated into and disclosed by Rio's mainstream press, making police more accountable for their violent actions.

By interacting with mainstream media in this way, favela activists take an important step against media that stigmatise favela residents. Activists use both old (e.g. radio, newspapers) and new media (e.g. internet, smartphone applications) combined with artistic, pedagogic and journalistic techniques to promote political mobilisation in- and outside favelas.[15] Another example of media activism from Rio's favelas in 2016 is the launch of an app, Nós por Nós ('For us by us') by the Rio de Janeiro Youth Forum, which is specifically designed for favela residents to denounce police brutality in real time and to demand justice for those who have fallen victim to abuse.

Despite the concerns about online media campaigns of the kind discussed above, the significance of this social media favela activism is that favela residents are increasingly taking control of (online) communication channels and platforms to raise their own voices and demands (see van Mastrigt and Reist 2016). So far much of the 'everyday life politics' in favelas has been mediated by NGOs, academics and the police. Favela media activism is therefore an important bottom-up reaction to the way favela residents have historically been represented. It has provided a broader platform for favela residents' 'voices' and increasingly also features positive stories about these communities. As Custódio (2013) has pointed out, favela residents' visible online actions have been important steps towards creative collective action. They are one way in which favela residents enact, mobilise, articulate and publicise citizenship within, across and beyond favelas.

Notes

1. The residents of Brazil's favelas and other poor communities are the victims of the security forces, but they are also at risk of violence from the gangs who control many of the poorest areas of Brazil's cities. These gangs derive a large part of their income from trafficking drugs and weapons (some of which they obtain from the army and police). More recently, militia in the form of off-duty police, firefighters, prison officers and soldiers have also begun to impose themselves on poor areas by pretending to provide services and 'security' to the residents.

The militia in particular engage in the extortion of residents and businesses, and both they and the gangs impose their own 'laws', meting out their own forms of justice.

2. According to data published in 2016 by Rio's Institute for Public Security (Instituto de Segurança Pública, ISP), of the 644 people killed in violent clashes with police in 2015 across the state of Rio de Janeiro, 497 (77 per cent) were black or mixed race.

3. The installation of UPPs in thirty-eight favelas so far has produced tangible results, with some research suggesting that the number of violent deaths of favela residents as well as police has been dramatically reduced (see Cano and Borges 2012).

4. The most publicised case of police violence in Rio's recent history, both nationally and internationally, was the killing of Amarildo de Souza, a bricklayer from the Rocinha favela in Rio's South Zone. Suspected of being involved in drug trafficking, Amarildo was tortured to death at the UPP police station in the favela. About twenty-five police officers, some of whom stood trial, were involved in this crime. The case coincided with the mass protests in Brazil against the government in 2013, and Amarildo's case was taken up by the protest movement who turned him into an icon. People from all over the world showed placards with the bricklayer's image, asking, 'Where is Amarildo?' Amarildo's body was never found, but there were strong suspicions, based on CCTV footage obtained from the favela, that his body was removed at night by BOPE, Rio's Special Police Operations Batallion. The commanding officer of the UPP in Rocinha, who ordered and took part in Amarildo's torture, was a former BOPE captain.

5. Pavão-Pavãozinho suffers from the incomplete public works promised by the previous government through its Growth Acceleration Programme (PAC). R$43 million was set aside for public works in the community, but the area still lacks investment to improve mobility and basic services such as sanitation and electricity.

6. Amnesty International has received reports of the use of excessive force and other abuses by UPP police officers against residents. According to one report, only two days before the fatal shooting of da Silva, 'a 27-year-old man coming back from a family gathering was reportedly approached by two police officers from the UPP, who then shot twice at a wall next to his head and fired three more shots into the air as a form of intimidation' (Amnesty International 2014: n.p.).

7. The campaign *Eu não mereço morrer assassinado* is not the first of its kind, but linked to a previous campaign entitled *Eu não mereço ser estuprada/Ninguem mereçe ser estuprada* ('I don't deserve to be raped/Nobody deserves to be raped') which was started by a Rio journalist after the publication of a survey which erroneously claimed that 65 per cent of the Brazilians surveyed said that if a woman dresses in a revealing way, she 'deserves to be attacked'. The correct figure was actually 26 per cent. The campaign featured women in varying states of undress holding a poster condemning the survey's (wrong) results with the above message.

8. The gross monthly salary range for class C remains very low at R$300–1,000, which is US$ 150–500 (see <http://thebrazilbusiness.com/article/social-classes-in-brazil-1453802521>, last accessed 31 May 2018). It also reduces class status

to pure economics. Many class C people live in favelas and under the scarcely disputed control of drug trafficking groups. While they may be able to afford television sets, that does not mean that the social prejudice they suffer has disappeared just because of their slightly elevated consumer status.

9. There are now more than 72,000 people who use WhatsApp to communicate with *Extra* (Fabio Gusmão; personal communication).
10. Brazil has two main types of police, military and civil, both of which are subordinate to the state governments. While the military police are responsible for maintaining public order, the civil police perform the role of judicial police and are responsible for criminal offences.
11. The term 'bandido' is also used by drug traffickers to refer to themselves, as it has romantic connotations of the outlaw and social bandit, an image some drug traffickers like to project (Penglase 2014: 31).
12. 'Marginal' is now a common expression for the poor black male criminal (Roth-Gordon 2013; see also Perlman 2004).
13. These ongoing processes of both 'dehumanisation' and criminalisation' in popular media also partly explain the fact that many Brazilians see the United Nations Convention against Torture and Other Cruel, Inhuman or Degrading Treatment or Punishment as a hindrance to police operations. Many see the Convention as being lenient on criminals (Caldeira 2000: 157).
14. Luiz Baltar; personal communication.
15. Activism in Rio's favelas is nothing new. Already in the 1970s and 1980s favela residents initiated movements to bridge the gap between the formal city and themselves, challenging unsecure land tenure, limited access to formal employment and education, and routine harassment by the forces of law and order (McCann 2014).

References

Amnesty International (2014), 'Urgent action: Call for inquiries into two killings in Rio Brazil', *Amnesty International*, 11 September, <http://www.amnesty.org.uk/resources/urgent-action-call-inquiries-two-killings-rio-brazil#.VcJFnI6UC0c> (last accessed 8 May 2018).

Andén-Papadopoulos, K. and M. Pantti (eds) (2011), *Amateur Images and Global News*, Bristol: Intellect; Chicago: University of Chicago Press.

Barthes, R. (1977), *Image Music Text*, London: Fontana Press.

Bock, M. (2012), 'Citizen video journalists and authority in narrative: Reviving the role of the witness', *Journalism*, 13 (5), pp. 639–53.

Caldeira, P. R. T. (2000), *City of Walls: Crime, Segregation, and Citizenship in São Paulo*, Berkeley, CA: University of California Press.

Cano, I. and D. Borges (eds) (2012), *Os donos do morro: Uma análise exploratória do impacto das unidades de polícia pacificadora (UPPs) no Rio de Janeiro* [The Owners of the Hill: An Exploratory Study of the Impact of the Police Pacifying Units (UPPs) in Rio de Janeiro], São Paulo: Fundo Brasileiro de Segurança Pública.

Caple, H. and J. Knox (2012), 'Online news galleries, photojournalism and the photo essay', *Visual Communication*, 11 (2), pp. 207–36.

Chouliaraki, L. (2008), 'The symbolic power of transnational media: Managing the visibility of suffering', *Global Media and Communication*, 4 (3), pp. 329–51.

Custódio, L. (2013), 'Offline dimensions of online favela youth reactions to human rights violations before the 2016 Olympics in Rio de Janeiro', in N. P. Wood (ed.), *Brazil in Twenty-First Century Popular Media: Culture, Politics, and Nationalism on the World Stage*, Lanham, MD: Lexington Books, pp. 139–56.

Custódio, L. (2014), 'Offline dimensions of online favela youth reactions to human rights violations before the 2016 Olympics in Rio de Janeiro', in N. Wood (ed.), *Brazil in Twenty-First Century Popular Media: Culture, Politics and Nationalism on the World Stage*, Lanham, MD: Lexington Books, pp. 139–56.

Custódio, L. (2016), *Favela Media Activism: Political Trajectories of Low-Income Brazilian Youth*, Tampere: Tampere University Press.

Dean, J. (2008), 'Communicative capitalism: Circulation and the foreclosure of politics', in M. Boler (ed.), *Digital Media and Democracy: Tactics in Hard Times*, Cambridge, MA: MIT Press, pp. 101–23.

Dias, M. C. and L. Eslava (2013), 'Horizons of inclusion: Life between laws and developments in Rio de Janeiro', *University of Miami Inter-American Law Review*, 44 (2), pp. 177–218.

Domke, D., D. Perlmutter and M. Spratt (2003), 'The primes of our times? An examination of the "power" of visual images', *Journalism*, 3, pp. 131–59.

Economou, D. (2006), 'The big picture: The role of the lead image in print feature stories', in I. Lassen, J. Strunck and T. Vestergaard (eds), *Mediating Ideology in Text and Image: Ten Critical Studies*, London: Continuum, pp. 211–33.

Economou, D. (2008), 'Pulling readers in: News photographs in Greek and Australian broadsheets', in P. R. R. White and E. A. Thomson (eds), *Communicating Conflict: Multilingual Case Studies of the News Media*, London: Continuum, pp. 253–80.

Gay, R. (2005), *Lucia: Testimonies of a Brazilian Drug Dealer's Woman*, Philadelphia: Temple University Press.

Goldstein, D. M. (2004), *The Spectacular City: Violence and Performance in Urban Bolivia*, Durham, NC: Duke University Press.

Gumucio-Dagron, A. and T. Tufte (eds) (2006), *Communication for Social Change Anthology: Historical and Contemporary Readings*, South Orange, NJ: Communication for Social Change Consortium.

Halliday, M. (1978), *Language as Social Semiotic*, Baltimore, MD: University Park Press.

Holmes, T. (2012), 'The traveling texts of local content: Following content creation, communication and dissemination via internet platforms in a Brazilian favela', *Hispanic Issues On Line*, 9, pp. 263–88.

Holston, J. and T. Caldeira (1998), 'Democracy, law, and violence: Disjunctions of Brazilian citizenship', in F. Aguero and J. Stark (eds), *Fault Lines of Democracy in Post-Transition Latin America*, Miami, FL: University of Miami North-South Center Press, pp. 263–96.

Holton, A., M. Coddington and H. Gil de Zúñiga (2013), 'Whose news? Whose values? Citizen journalism and journalistic values through the lens of content creators and consumers', *Journalism Practice*, 7 (6), pp. 720–37.

Huggins, M. K. (2000), 'Urban violence and police privatization in Brazil: Blended invisibility', *Social Justice*, 27 (2), pp. 113–34.

Kelsey, D. and L. Bennett (2014), 'Discipline and resistance on social media: Discourse, power and context in the Paul Chambers "Twitter Joke Trial"', *Discourse, Context, Media*, 3, pp. 37–45.

KhosraviNik, M. (2014), 'Critical discourse analysis, power, and new media discourse', in M. Kopytowska and Y. Kalyango (eds), *Why Discourse Matters: Negotiating Identity in the Mediatized World*, New York: Peter Lang, pp. 287–306.

Kress, G. and T. van Leeuwen (2006), *Reading Images: The Grammar of Visual Design*, 2nd edn, London: Routledge.

McCann, B. (2014), *Hard Times in the Marvelous City: From Dictatorship to Democracy in the Favelas of Rio de Janeiro*, Durham, NC: Duke University Press.

Machado da Silva, L. A. (2008), *Vida sob cerco: Violência e rotina nas favelas do Rio de Janeiro*, Rio de Janeiro: Nova Fronteira.

Machin, D. and A. Mayr (2012), *How to Do Critical Discourse Analysis: A Multimodal Approach*, London: Sage.

Martin, J. R. (2001), 'Fair trade: Negotiating meaning in multimodal texts', in P. Coppock (ed.), *The Semiotics of Writing: Transdisciplinary Perspectives on the Technology of Writing*, Turnhout: Brepols, pp. 311–38.

Martin, J. R. and P. R. R. White (2005), *The Language of Evaluation: Appraisal in English*, Basingstoke: Palgrave Macmillan.

Mayr, A. (2015), 'The social semiotics of military urbanism: Spectacles of online representations of the Elite Squad of the military police of Rio de Janeiro', *Social Semiotics*, 25 (5), pp. 533–57.

Mortensen, M. (2011), 'When citizen photojournalism sets the news agenda: Neda Agha Soltan as a Web 2.0 icon of post-election unrest in Iran', *Global Media and Communication*, 7 (1), pp. 4–16.

Moubray, M. (2015), 'Alternative logics? Parsing the literature on alternative media', in C. Atton (ed.), *The Routledge Companion to Alternative and Community Media*, London: Routledge, pp. 21–31.

Penglase, B. (2007), 'Barbarians on the beach: Media narratives of violence in Rio de Janeiro, Brazil', *Crime, Media, Culture*, 3 (3), pp. 305–25.

Penglase, B. (2014), *Living with Insecurity in a Brazilian Favela: Urban Violence and Daily Life*, New Brunswick, NJ: Rutgers University Press.

Perlman, J. (1976), *The Myth of Marginality: Urban Poverty and Politics in Rio de Janeiro*, Berkeley, CA: University of California Press.

Perlman, J. (2004), 'Marginality: From myth to reality in the favelas of Rio de Janeiro: 1969–2002', in A. Roy and N. AlSayyad (eds), *Urban Informality: Transnational Perspectives from the Middle East, Latin America, and South Asia*, Lanham, MD: Lexington Books, pp. 105–46.

Perlman, J. (2010), *Favela: Four Decades of Living on the Edge in Rio de Janeiro*, Oxford: Oxford University Press.

Peruzzo, C. (1996), 'Participation in community communication', in J. Servaes, T. Jacobson and S. White (eds), *Participatory Communication for Social Change*, London: Sage, pp. 162–79.

Prouse, C. (2012), 'Framing the World cUPP: Competing discourses of favela pacification as a mega-event legacy in Brazil', *Recreation and Society in Africa, Asia and Latin America (RSAALA)*, Special Issue on Sports Events Legacies, 3 (2), pp. 1–17.

Rodriguez, C. (2011), *Citizens' Media against Armed Conflict: Disrupting Violence in Colombia*, Minnesota: University of Minnesota Press.

Roth-Gordon, J. (2013), 'Racial malleability and the sensory regime of politically conscious Brazilian hip-hop', *The Journal of Latin American and Caribbean Anthropology*, 18 (2), pp. 294–313.

Souza, P. (2013), *Relatório estudo de caso dentidade favelada e novas tecnologias – pesquisa jovens pobres e o uso das NTICs na criação de novas esferas públicas democráticas*, Rio de Janeiro: Ibase.

Unger, J. (2012), 'New tools for critical discourse studies in new media contexts', Paper presented at Critical Approaches to Discourse Analysis across Disciplines conference, University of Minho, Braga, Portugal, 4–6 July 2012.

van Leeuwen, T. (2000), 'Visual racism', in M. Reisigl and R. Wodak (eds), *The Semiotics of Racism: Approaches in Critical Discourse Analysis*, Vienna: Passagen Verlag, pp. 333–50.

van Mastrigt, J. and S. Reist (2016), 'Youth forum launches "Nós por Nós" application to denounce police violence', *RioOnWatch*, 24 March, <http://www.rioonwatch.org/?p=27670> (last accessed 8 May 2018).

Williams, A., K. Wahl-Jorgensen and C. Wardle (2011), '"More real, less packaged": Audience discourses on amateur news content and their effects on journalism practice', in K. Andén-Papadopoulos and M. Pantti (eds), *Amateur Images and Global News*, Bristol: Intellect; Chicago: University of Chicago Press, pp. 193–209.

Willis, G., R. Muggah, J. Kosslyn and F. Leusin (2014), 'The changing face of technology use in pacified communities', Strategic note 13, February 2014, Rio de Janeiro: Igarape Institute.

Wodak, R. and S. Wright (2006), 'The European Union in cyberspace. Multilingual democratic participation in a virtual public sphere?', *Journal of Language and Politics*, 5 (2), pp. 251–75.

Zappavigna, M. (2015), 'Searchable talk: The linguistic functions of hashtags', *Social Semiotics*, 25 (3), pp. 274–91.

10

Rioting and Disorderly Behaviour as Political Media Practice: Body Postures on the Streets of L.A. during the Riots of 1992

Serjoscha Ostermeyer and David Sittler

Introduction

The 1992 L.A. riots were the first riots to be extensively covered live on television. Since then, a considerable number of scholarly studies have been undertaken around the questions of how and why the riots occurred (Abu-Lughod 2007; Baldassare 1994; Davis 2006; Gale 1996; Hunt 1996, 2012). However, most research has exclusively dealt with the discourse about the riots, not the actual violent actions themselves. Therefore, most texts feature what people thought about the riots, not how they acted during the event. It is an open question how to incorporate bodily action into discourse analysis. In this chapter, we scrutinise stills from live television coverage and a video filmed on-site of one prominent attack. Due to the already existing studies on the discursive context, we are able to add further understanding by analysing bodily actions. An approach like this complements discourse analysis and thereby achieves innovative insights. Our hypothesis is that the deciphering of bodily expressions adds a significant layer to the way actions are incorporated in discourse analyses.

We briefly outline the historical context of the events and the setting of the television coverage. A description of the theoretical background connecting rioting and visual body analysis follows. Along our adaptation of the concept of a moral economy of rioting, we concentrate on references to social and cognitive reservoirs and repertoires to show how the violent actions can be seen as media practices. Therefore, the analysis of exemplary body postures in the video material itself forms the main part of the chapter.

Theoretical Background

Rioting always means to act concretely or bodily and at the same time to articulate yourself symbolically and towards a wider social and political public. Even the denial of this political dimension by commentators – for example, politicians through simple criminalisation of this behaviour – underlines this symbolic potential. Without this discursive dimension riot practices seem absurd. Riots are directly connected to already existing, emotionally loaded conflicts and often persist afterwards. Riots address questions of access to and participation in the city and its publics (Harvey 2008; Lefèbvre 2003). To speak of riots means to group very heterogeneous actors and events into one framing macro-narrative.

Rioting on the street cannot sufficiently be understood as merely criminal or racist acts. Neither is it just a 'valve' for destructive frustration by marginalised social groups in 'problematic' neighbourhoods. Beside its destructive effects rioting addresses a public and therefore is a political media practice embedded in other discourses, like mass media political discourse. We use a wide conception of the term 'media practice', going beyond mass media and including the body. Acts of rioting become utterances in a larger discursive ecology.

Therefore, riots need to be studied with a discourse analysis method that is complemented by a study of the non-verbal forms of articulation and body language of rioters. Rioters use the street as their stage to perpetuate messages in a spectacular form. Thus riots should also be understood as a media practice with its own aesthetic codes. During riots 'emotional energies' (Collins 2008; Greenblatt 1997) which are normally less visible are set free. Historically, it can be argued that – at least since the 1919 Race Riots in Chicago – not only are race riots accompanied by mass media, but these media are part of the phenomenon (Sittler 2011: 197–210). The 1992 Los Angeles riots even started with the television broadcast of a video showing police violence. Riot practices use the media of the street: feet, hands, stones, guns, cars, and so on. Simultaneously, rioters interact with classical media like television cameras. Violent acts on the street have to be scrutinised as symbolic performative acts on the street as a stage (Reiss 2007). Even though we highlight the communicative function of rioting, we do not want to legitimise violence or argue that every violent act is mass communication to the same degree.

The 'message' of rioters will always be reduced to letting out irrational aggression, if the expressive posture in rioting is not taken into account. Rioting as a media practice can therefore not gain a discursive state and remains misrepresented as a non-communicative phenomenon. We want to take a closer look into the details of violence in action. It is hoped that the scrutinised haptic quality and material aesthetics of this behaviour can be used to prevent such behaviour in the future.

Richard Sennett reminded us of the role of material aesthetics when thinking about cities (Sennett 1994). The bodily learned 'code of the street' (Anderson 1999) acquired by being raised and living in an urban habitat influences such violent performances of rioters during riot scenes. Furthermore, mass media like television are transporting images of rioting behaviour. As with other actions, rioters draw on implicit scripts for proper conduct of their actions with an underlying intertextual 'image-grammar' (Weigel 2015; Kress and van Leeuwen 2006; Newbold 1998). Everyday life and popular culture – from sports, photography and film to popular music – serve as a stock of recognisable riot-iconographic frames. They give perpetrators, victims, bystanders, as well as bodily absent audiences a means to make sense of rioting behaviour. The rioters use body moves from gang life, American football, breakdance and capoeira and thereby prove the perpetrators' skills with regard to demonstrative violence.

Accordingly, violent gestures and postures have to be decoded in a media-aesthetical perspective. From this perspective it becomes a relevant fact in what manner someone is attacked, with what device and how spectacularly it is presented and broadcasted to a wider audience. These frames, clichés, icons and pathos formulas can support moral economic (Randall and Charlesworth 2000) claims to legitimacy of self-asserted 'executive' power and violent display.

Such a 'logic of the riot' (Farge and Revel 1991) violently breaks up the presumed societal consensus (Habermas 1984). The quest for individual motives is not eligible to answer our questions, because it diversifies and highlights individual improvisation in actions, not cultural patterns:

> Even before establishing a comprehensive interpretation of the episode, these seemingly random actions suggest that a scenario of conflict already existed. All involved in the events act out their particular roles as though they are simply improvising on a very familiar situation. (Farge and Revel 1991: 4)

On the one hand, there is a role to act out and, on the other hand, there is space for improvisation. Rioting articulates underlying conflicts between urban dwellers explicitly and para-discursively. It acts out what rioters feel to be the 'real' reality in place of official misrepresentations of reality by the media or state institutions (Althusser 1994). Instead of romanticising disorderly behaviour via an over-rationalisation or its opposite in pure othering and criminalisation, we scrutinise iconic qualities and logics of bodily performances on the street.

Some rioting acts take onlookers and media coverage explicitly into account. Being watched changes the behaviour of the protagonists and might make violence even more likely to occur (Collins 2008). Whereas African Americans are normally constructed as America's 'other' (Anderson 1994; Fiske 1998; Brenkman 1995), they become more publicly visible in the media during the riots due to the mass media surveillance and reports. The lives of generally ignored persons (like gang members) are put on television and their actions suddenly matter. Culture is public, as Geertz (1973) puts it; one has to be able to articulate oneself (Laclau and Mouffe 2001) to be heard (Bhabha 1994; Clifford and Marcus 1986) and to participate in the power struggle for cultural dominance (Thompson 1959).

We exemplify our concept of the logic of the riot and its icono-logistics for rioting as a media practice with a case study of a short excerpt from live television broadcasting as a widely accessible cut-out from the 'circulation of images' (Mitchell 2005: 294–6) that we call 'image traffic'. The live broadcast originally ran on KTTV Los Angeles and was recorded from a helicopter. A 49-minute-long, low-quality version can be found on YouTube (Tur 1992). The printed video stills have a higher resolution and stem from the original tape material provided by Tur directly. Goldman recorded another video standing on the ground at the same intersection (Mydans 1992). Some of the material can be seen online (Goldman 1992) but he provided us with stills from the original tape. We chose the most prominent scene of the 1992 Los Angeles riots, not because it is representative, but because of its iconic status in the discourse. Within the analysis of this media representation we further concentrate on the intertextual context (Pollak 2008: 93), for example, references of the body postures to sports, media representations, gangsta rap, gangs, typical violent settings, all found in globally disseminated cultural patterns or postures. Therefore, we disregard the broader context of the unfolding media scene and especially the institutional, historic or political context.

Situating the Los Angeles Riots

Traditionally, riot research names crime, poverty and racism as reasons for the L.A. riots (Abu-Lughod 2007: ch. 7; Baldassare 1994; Gale 1996). Of course, these factors matter, but they are no convincing explanation, if they are not combined with a closer look (Hunt 1996, 2012). On 3 March 1991 the African American Rodney King had been brutally beaten for several minutes by police officers after a car chase, and the scene was filmed. When the jury verdict announced the officers innocent in 1992, things turned violent. The outbreak had long been in the making (Davis 2006). The perceived injustice was enough to push the atmosphere in L.A. over the edge. At 4:15 p.m. on 29 April 1992 the looting of a liquor store started the riot on the intersection of Florence and Normandie in South Central Los Angeles (Dunphy 2010). The intersection made for a central node of the riot (Haddock and Polsby 1994). It became an 'ideal' stage, because it guaranteed attention and offered the opportunity to seriously interrupt the traffic.

At 6:45 p.m. the truck driver Reginald Denny tried to cross the intersection with his truck and was stopped by several rioters. At the same time a news helicopter arrived at the spot and broadcasted the events live. At that time the television audience was used neither to helicopter-filmed live footage, nor to a live broadcast of violence. The attack on Reginald Denny became emblematic visual material (Hunt 2012: x). It achieved a status similar to Geertz's (1973) cockfight in cultural studies for interpreting the riots (Tur 2007). However, as a 'white' male, truck driver Denny was no typical victim.

Minutes before the attack on Reginald Denny the police had withdrawn from the area, leaving a power vacuum. The power literally lay on the streets (Arendt 1970: 47). As there was 'no winter palace to be seized', as Manuel Castells (2010: 388) puts it, the outbreak turned violent against people driving by. Contrary to popular belief, even during the riot and its heated emotional atmosphere this did not result in a completely moral-free zone. Looters do not loot from other looters (Collins 2008: 249). Collins also points out that almost no rapes were reported during the riot. Therefore, we propose to differentiate his term of a 'moral holiday' (Collins 2008: 243–6) with a concept reflecting the shift of morals. Building on Thompson (1991: 63–6), we understand this legitimisation of collaborative violent behaviour as a 'moral economy'. After the verdict was announced the rioters felt justified to strike back and set accounts straight (Kawalerowicz and Biggs 2015; Randall and Charlesworth 2000). Additionally, Hispanic, Caucasian and black race groups from L.A. perceived the moral justification differently (Hunt 1996). Hall (1999) has argued for a long time that varying publics do not decode television material equally.

At Florence and Normandie the looting prepared the setting for a more violent spectacle. It charged the necessary emotional energy for a violent 'forward panic' (Collins 2008: ch. 3). Typically, four or more attackers take part in an attack, such as the random assault on Reginald Denny:

> This is the most typical scenario where serious injury is done. Very commonly photos of this kind of crowd event show a group attacking a single individual, who is usually down on the ground and unable to defend him or herself. Examples include numerous incidents photographed or described during the riots in Los Angeles and elsewhere in 1992, following the acquittal verdict in the Rodney King beating trial, showing individuals—white or Asian—being attacked by groups of young black men. (Collins 2008: 128)

For rioting to occur there needs to be a situation of social support or at least the feeling of having it, a lack of police control, and a weak victim that is outnumbered (Collins 2008: 368) and can be attacked with almost no risk of sanctions. Only the specific situational make-up of the scene and the tension explain the sudden outbreak of violence. The background of the moral economy helps to explain why there is more going on than a simple beating and why this spectacle fuelled an intensified rioting elsewhere in the city. By interweaving the findings of discourse analyses of the L.A. riots with body postures and image inventory (Mitchell 2005; Warburg 2008), we suggest that a 'thicker' understanding of the violent acts is possible. Drawing upon this repository, mass media and personal experiences provide us with background scripts for situationally appropriate actions to carry out, as shown in the works of Goffman (1956, 1986), Berger and Luckmann (1967) and Mauss (1973). Thus, combining action frames and image inventories creates a material 'riot aesthetic' (Farge and Revel 1991).

Method

Our procedure consists of four steps. (1) We incorporate the body in the beforehand predominant analysis of language in critical discourse analysis. (2) We interweave discourse analysis and media analysis. (3) We elaborate on our sample choice. (4) We give a brief background of our approach to video analysis.

Discourse analysis tends to draw connections from language to cognition as well as its social embedding (Fairclough 2003, 2005, 2006; Foucault 2007). Scholars of discourse analysis noted that actions are conventionalised similarly to language (van Dijk 1977: 182), that verbal and visual semiotics overlap (Pollak 2008: 84), that practices precede discourses as social action and power struggle (Scollon 2001: 141), and that experience builds the ground for meaning, being culturally and bodily embedded (Hart 2014: 109). Body analysis in discourse analysis is most elaborated in the analysis of hand gestures (Goodwin 2003a, 2003b, 2007; McNeill 2005). All these approaches share the idea of language grounded in action. The analysis needs to take 'the whole interconnected pattern of activity in which [signs] are embedded' (McNeill 2005: 100) into account. The body is a publicly visible display with a semiotic structure (Goodwin 2000: 1490). We draw these body genres, frames or social scripts (van Dyk 2013) for our analysis from the cultural backgrounds and situational surroundings in which the attackers were involved (cf. Singal 2007).

So far, discourse analysis has tended to use media analysis only in connection with the question of how media represent their content (Hall et al. 2000; van Dijk 1989, 1995). The same is true for discourse analyses dealing with the L.A. riots. They concentrate primarily on (biased) representations of the events and do not include the protagonists and their action patterns directly. The research remains limited to speaking about riots. There is, however, a difference between writing discourse and doing discourse.

Using live media coverage comes with certain advantages compared with ethnographic analysis on-site. On the one hand, we miss the local embedding and, on the other hand, we gain the advantage of repeated viewings and are therefore able to realise a very detailed analysis of individual body postures (Collins 2008: 4). The live coverage allows for a perspective similar to that of the witnesses on-site as well as the media public. It has long been argued that an overt observer changes the actions at the scene. This is obviously true for the occurrence of the news helicopter at the intersection. Due to the angle from the helicopter the viewer has a bird's or god's eye view. The camera angle puts the viewer in a position of power, as she or he watches from above and for the same reason can stay more distanced from the events (van Leeuwen 2008: 141). Even though everything is live and ultra-violent, the observer does not get 'all involved' (Gattis 2015) like the people in the situation. The coverage from the helicopter became iconic, but the media coverage remained that of a surveillance camera, highlighting disjointed events and heating the atmosphere even further (Abu-Lughod 2007: 235).

The main reason we chose stills from video footage of the 'Denny Beating' is its iconic status in the image inventory and discursive landscape around the riots. As we have argued, the L.A. riots have a prime tier in media coverage. Within the flow of circulating pictures the attack on Reginald Denny is by far the most prominent media coverage during and after the event, the process and even around anniversaries. Because of this social relevance, profound discourse analyses exist. They build a secure background for our interpretation of the body postures with regard to their moral economic effectiveness. Therefore, we concentrate on an emblematic, exemplary and thick sample and not on a typical scene in the sense of quantitative representativeness (Maxwell 1998). As we focus on showing that single actions differ from a written account of them in the way they made sense in situ and on television, we do not follow a sequence-by-sequence analysis, as commonly undertaken in language or film analysis. Instead, we try to separate artificially frozen individual postures with their rough-grained iconicity. We took scenes with emblematic poses, communicating clear references to other contexts of similar actions.

The attackers' postures became staged performances, instantly recognised by the mass media publics. In the selection of video stills we repeat our sample strategy and concentrate on the most iconic actions out of the 45-minute live video taken by the helicopter crew (Tur 1992) and the video taken by a bystander (Goldman 1992). Those stills represent a sequence of movements with their corresponding connectors, forming them into actions (Kress and van Leeuwen 2006: 261). In this tragedy of injustice we find a spectacular scenography, with undirected, real suffering and crime and at the same time a coarse-grained call for revenge or justice. The analysis focuses on four postures: kneeling, a flying kick, stone throwing and celebration.

Analysis

The video stills convey extreme points from the emotionally charged situation. Reginald Denny and his attackers appear in opposing postures of helplessness versus dominance. The figuration of bodies gains the quality of a pathos formula in the sense of Warburg (Fabbri 2011) that can be recognised especially in these images. On the one hand, Denny kneels on the ground after being dragged from his truck, and is hit several times; and on the other hand, the attackers perform triumphant poses. Both postures are deeply habitualised within all major religions and cultures around the globe. The power asymmetry of this figuration and its deep cultural roots and wide dissemination as implicit knowledge make the postures highly effective for the moral economy of riots. Their potential is realised by the iconic state of the moves. The single victim comes to represent his 'race' (the whites) due to the iconic form of the attack and its logic in the image inventory. The living image is produced by the interaction of several people using what they find on the street and investing their bodily and performative skills shaped by iconologic repertoires learned from sports and other central social realms of culture.

Kneeling

In the still from the video camera footage from the bystander Timothy Goldman (Figure 10.1), we can see what people on the street saw (Goldman 1992; Mydans 1992). As he did several times, Denny kneels on the street in front of his truck. The camera is slightly out of focus on a white man in white clothes on the street, trying to get up and raise his arms, but failing to do so. On the right side we see part of a truck and in the centre of the background five dark figures on the sidewalk in front of a wall. The arm of the white man forms no vector to the camera or the bystanders; he points out of the frame to the left.

Reading the still like a position on a triptych puts the kneeling Denny in the area of the image standing for the 'new real' order, the space for things to come (Kress and van Leeuwen 2006: 197). Kneeling provides an entry point for further action (Dow 2014: 62) and demonstrates powerless subordination towards an executive power (Teissier 1996: 114). Certainly, kneeling can be understood as functional: Denny tries to get up. But it can also be interpreted

Figure 10.1 Truck driver Reginald Denny kneeling in front of his truck after the first attack (Goldman 1992: 6:50 p.m.). © Timothy Goldman

along the iconographic conventions from religious traditions of depicting a god's worshippers and rulers with the ruled. These action scripts of power asymmetry help explain why the scene became so powerful and the attackers felt so comfortable with their actions.

Kneeling can also be an act of reverence (in Greek *proskynesis*), asking for forgiveness for sins. Denny is made to look like he is asking for forgiveness for the sins of the police and 'the whites', as if admitting being guilty and therefore legitimising 'punishment' by the 'people's trial' or vigilantism (Kirkpatrick 2008). He is attacked as a representation of the hated persons and groups not at hand in the local riot situation. In art history this symbolic other is called an effigy (Weigel 2015: 208–12). Rioters could not get their hands on the responsible police officers for the King beating, but they were able to take their anger out on somebody else instead. Denny was certainly not begging for forgiveness and of course he would not have thought to sacrifice himself, but these considerations help to make sense of the scene's moral economic functioning. The rioters and other highly emotionalised people filled with rage and taking part in the disorder would have wished for someone begging for forgiveness. The court decision was widely seen as a symptom of the police regularly and brutally attacking black people without proper cause. The power asymmetry is almost an inverted re-enactment of the beating of Rodney King. It thereby helps to justify violent action and adds understanding to what is going on. Nonetheless, understanding causes does not mean justifying them.

Flying Kick

The audience watching the attack was informed simultaneously about what had become obvious on-site: 'Here is the information, here is the

(a) First part of the move   (b) Second part of the move

Figure 10.2 Flying kick at Reginald Denny (Goldman 1992: 3:33/6:49 p.m.).
© Timothy Goldman

scoop: LAPD has just told me that they have ordered all police helicopters and all LAPD cruisers out of this area' (Tur 1992: 14:31:03–14:41:23, 6:50 p.m.), comments Robert A. Tur on the live broadcast his wife Marika Tur shoots from the news helicopter for Los Angeles News Service. Robert Tur also informs the audience about the discursive framing of the situation by the police at that point: 'This is a riot area, this is a term the LAPD is using at this point' (Tur 1992: 17:50:16). At that moment an attacker jumps very skilfully and kicks Denny in the head (Tur 1992: 18:33:05). While Denny is already kneeling as a consequence of having been violently torn from the truck, he is attacked again with this 'flying kick' (Goldman 1992). The performance of this attack shows considerable sportsman skills and supports the image of a warrior 'defending' his 'turf' or territory seen from a gang-related perspective (Brumble 2000: 166; Collins 2008: 233; Garot 2007; Lee 2009). The attacker, a former Marine, takes a run-up, jumps and kicks the kneeling Denny in the head, while still flying through the air (Figure 10.2). This action goes far beyond the physically necessary movements to achieve the violent result. Taking a run-up or performing a capoeira martial arts move (Caldas-Coulthard 2007: 290; Kimminich 2003) indeed transforms the beating into a performance with show character. The beating remains a crime, but its style becomes an argument on reputation (Anderson 1994), knowingly staged for bystanders and supposed to result in mass media coverage.

Brick in the Head

The brick is a widely known, pertinent weapon of opportunity from workers protest history – since at least the 1870s in Chicago (Smith 2007; Sittler 2015). It represents the defence of the suppressed against the hegemonic capitalists and bureaucratic class. In riots and uprisings it is a typical instrument of violent articulation of the working class. It is also known from the iconography of David versus Goliath (De Girolami Cheney 1998: 404). The material aesthetic of stone used to attack and punish is crucial. Using a brick as a (defensive) weapon adds to a self-concept of righteousness in a moral economy.

Shortly after the kick one attacker comes close to the kneeling Denny and hits him on the head with a brick. The attacker does not react to an imminent threat; if the kick does not yet remind us of severe bodily punishment, this attack does. Stoning a defenceless, kneeling opponent is both an ancient ritual punishment and something we can witness today with ISIS or in Saudi Arabia. The repeated beating prepares the scene for the culmination in the stoning. It brings Denny's body down and lets the attackers triumph. Even though the means of violence during the attack are constantly modified, the scene almost appears to be scripted. Like the performed kick, this is made possible as a part of the forward panic caused by the confrontational tension in combination with the encouraging power asymmetry. Throwing stones is a typical symptom of ballistic inferiority. The outgunned party usually uses stones. In this situation the symbolic power asymmetry of stone throwing is reversed – the stone being thrown by the stronger party. Considering the larger moral economy, the choice of the brick adds to the feeling of justification and self-empowerment.

Celebrating Victory

The attackers repeatedly perform postures of celebration and assurance of their superiority. This includes a victory dance, a hunkering down and powering up pose like in American football, making gang signs with the hands, and pointing or shooting at the helicopter. To keep the argument brief, we only give video stills for the victory dance and the hunkering down.

After one of the assaults one attacker – a former semi-professional American football player – raises his arms triumphantly, while Denny lies on the ground again (Figure 10.3). His movements are agile and enthusiastic, indicated by the strong up and down direction. There is in fact a strong genre similarity between sports victory and combat victory, both being competitive, highly emotional and physically active in the moment (Fairclough 2003: 33). Again, this takes time and is only possible as a part of the situational dynamic of a forward panic (Collins 2008) or an interactive vigilance ritual (Kirkpatrick 2008). The movement remains comparatively slow and exposes the attacker to counter-attacks. At the same time, raising one's arms symbolises power, exactly because it is not defensive but enlarges the body, intimidates the opponent and opens the chest for attacks, signalling a feeling of self-security. The exaggerated leg movement makes it seem like the attacker

Figure 10.3 An attacker performing a victory dance (Tur 1992: 15:05). © Zoey and Marika Tur, Los Angeles News Service

Figure 10.4 An attacker celebrating his assault and powering up (Tur 1992: 15:12). © Zoey and Marika Tur, Los Angeles News Service

is stomping on someone. This furthers the emotional energy and thus the feeling of justification in the attacker's perception of his moral economic capital.

In contrast to Denny kneeling in front of his attackers, kneeling can also be done as hunkering down, like one of the attackers does (Figure 10.4). The attacker bends his knees, keeping them in motion and bobs up and down. His knees remain in the air, their angle still allows for a jump, he remains prepared. The hunkering down and the up and down movements are similar to American football pre-game charging. The posture serves to build up power. Video stills give action vectors, but to distinguish postures an analysis cannot rely on video stills alone. Singular postures need to be regarded as part of a longer action sequence.

When the attackers point at the news helicopter and make the Crip gang sign, they claim authorship (McNeill 2005: 10), they add an explicit iconic signature and involve the viewer via the camera (Goodwin 2003a). The gestures are also part of the culture of gangsta rap promoted by Hollywood imagery (Hagedorn 2008; Davis 2006: 87). While otherwise feeling somehow distanced by the bird's eye view, in these short moments of being directly addressed we realise the connection between the ongoing attack and us as spectators. The attackers break our technologically mediated distance and try to drag us into the action. Respect is gained through hailing outsiders on gang territory. This is exactly what happens at the intersection of Florence and Normandie. Being watched increases the protagonists' opportunity for earning respect.

In spite of the gangsta repertoire present, the attack is no typical gang crime. Gangs generally attack males of the same age, not older adults, and limit their violence to ritualistic forms of fights over territory. In spontaneous mob confrontations like riots this is not the case (Collins 2008: 355). Violent attacks like the ones here are also part of attempts to claim the streets (Garot 2007). Stopping someone from another territory evokes a pre-noted script leading to violence. The set-up of this situation is similar to several others where trucks were stopped and the drivers dragged out during the L.A. riots (Collins 2008: 233).

Conclusion

Instead of concluding on motives, we examined the violent behaviour and postures of the protagonists as articulations within social frames shifting during cooperative interaction on the street. During riots, the street becomes a stage functioning as a media environment for the violent mob. Therefore, postures should be integrated into discourse analyses as meaningful articulations of rioters. Embedding bodily articulations in discourse analysis of rioting offers the possibility of understanding them as producing disorder as a message – but not total chaos. The discursive framing and actions are interconnected; however, body postures should not be treated as language but as a visual equivalent. We propose an understanding of frames for actions and visual repertoires for conventionalising actions during spontaneously unfolding situations like riots. Such a visual analysis can highlight probable meaning and emotional energies connected to such meaning within situations. This is the moral economy of a riot setting. A visual complement of discourse analysis is helpful wherever the actors articulate themselves with symbolically loaded bodily action instead of spoken language. Including postures as political articulations allows us to critically include the voices of otherwise unheard social groups.

References

Abu-Lughod, J. L. (2007), *Race, Space, and Riots in Chicago, New York, and Los Angeles*, Oxford: Oxford University Press.

Althusser, L. (1994), 'Ideology and ideological state apparatuses [1971]', in J. Storey (ed.), *Cultural Theory and Popular Culture: A Reader*, New York: Harvester Wheatsheaf, pp. 151–62.

Anderson, E. (1994), 'The code of the streets', *The Atlantic* (May), <http://www.theatlantic.com/magazine/archive/1994/05/the-code-of-the-streets/306601/> (last accessed 9 May 2016).

Anderson, E. (1999), *The Code of the Street: Decency, Violence and the Moral Life of the Inner City*, New York: W. W. Norton.

Arendt, H. (1970), *On Violence*, San Diego: Harcourt.

Baldassare, M. (ed.) (1994), *The Los Angeles Riots: Lessons for the Urban Future*, Boulder, CO: Westview Press.

Berger, P. L. and T. Luckmann (1967), *The Social Construction of Reality: A Treatise in the Sociology of Knowledge*, London: Penguin Books.

Bhabha, H. K. (1994), *The Location of Culture*, London and New York: Routledge.

Brenkman, J. (1995), 'Race publics', *Transition*, 66, pp. 4–36.

Brumble, H. D. (2000), 'The gangbanger autobiography of Monster Kody (Aka Sanyika Shakur) and warrior literature', *American Literature History*, 12 (1/2), pp. 158–86.

Caldas-Coulthard, C. R. (2007), 'Cross-cultural representations of "otherness" in media discourse', in G. Weiss and R. Wodak (eds), *Critical Discourse Analysis: Theory and Interdisciplinarity*, New York: Palgrave Macmillan, pp. 272–96.

Castells, M. (2010), *The Information Age: Economy, Society, and Culture*, 2nd edn, Chichester: Wiley-Blackwell.

Clifford, J. and G. E. Marcus (eds) (1986), *Writing Culture: The Poetics and Politics of Ethnography*, Berkeley, CA: University of California Press.

Collins, R. (2008), *Violence: A Micro-sociological Theory*, Princeton, NJ and Oxford: Princeton University Press.

Davis, M. (2006), *City of Quartz: Excavating the Future in Los Angeles*, London: Verso.

De Girolami Cheney, L. (1998), 'Honor/Honoring', in H. E. Roberts (ed.), *Encyclopaedia of Comparative Iconography: Themes Depicted in Works of Art*, vol. 1, Chicago: Fitzroy Dearborn, pp. 401–9.

Dow, D. N. (2014), *Apostolic Iconography and Florentine Confraternities in the Age of Reform*, Burlington, VT: Ashgate.

Dunphy, J. (2010), 'Controversy over Rodney King beating and L.A. riots reignites', *Los Angeles Police Protective League*, <http://lapd.com/news/headlines/contro versy_over_rodney_king_beating_and_la_riots_reignites/> (last accessed 10 May 2016).

Fabbri, P. (2011), 'Beyond Gombrich: The recrudescence of visual semiotics', *Journal of Art Historiography*, 5 (December), pp. 1–9.

Fairclough, N. (2003), *Analysing Discourse: Textual Analysis for Social Research*, London: Routledge.

Fairclough, N. (2005), 'Critical discourse analysis in transdisciplinary research', in R. Wodak and P. Chilton (eds), *A New Agenda in (Critical) Discourse Analysis: Theory, Methodology and Interdisciplinarity*, Amsterdam and Philadelphia: John Benjamins, pp. 53–70.

Fairclough, N. (2006), *Discourse and Social Change*, Malden, MA: Polity Press.

Farge, A. and J. Revel (1991), *The Vanishing Children of Paris: Rumor and Politics before the French Revolution* [*Logiques de la foule*, 1988], Cambridge, MA: Harvard University Press.

Fiske, J. (1998), 'Surveilling the city, whiteness, the black man and democratic totalitarianism', *Theory, Culture & Society*, 15 (2), pp. 67–88.

Foucault, M. (2007), *Security, Territory, Population: Lectures at the Collège de France 1977–1978*, New York: Palgrave Macmillan.

Gale, D. E. (1996), *Understanding Urban Unrest: From Reverend King to Rodney King*, Thousand Oaks, CA: Sage.

Garot, R. (2007), '"Where you from!": Gang identity as performance', *Journal of Contemporary Ethnography*, 36 (1), pp. 50–84.

Gattis, R. (2015), *All Involved*, New York: HarperCollins.

Geertz, C. (1973), *Thick Description: Toward an Interpretive Theory of Culture*, New York: Basic Books.

Goffman, E. (1956), *The Presentation of Self in Everyday Life*, Edinburgh: University of Edinburgh Social Science Research Centre.

Goffman, E. (1986), *Frame-Analysis: An Essay on the Organization of Experience*, Boston: Northeastern University Press.

Goldman, T. (1992), 'Florence and Normandie LA riots beatings, Los Angeles, CA', *YouTube*, <https://www.youtube.com/watch?v=UymAKaUquzs> (last accessed 6 June 2016).

Goodwin, C. (2000), 'Action and embodiment within situated human interaction', *Journal of Pragmatics*, 32, pp. 1489–522.

Goodwin, C. (2003a), 'Pointing as situated practice', in S. Kita (ed.), *Pointing: Where Language, Culture and Cognition Meet*, Mahwah, NJ: Lawrence Erlbaum Associates, pp. 217–41.

Goodwin, C. (2003b), 'The body in action', in J. Coupland and R. Gwyn (eds), *Discourse, the Body and Identity*, Basingstoke: Palgrave Macmillan, pp. 19–42.

Goodwin, C. (2007), 'Environmentally coupled gestures', in S. D. Duncan, J. Cassell and E. T. Levy (eds), *Gesture and the Dynamic Dimension of Language: Essays in Honor of David McNeill*, Amsterdam and Philadelphia: John Benjamins, pp. 195–212.

Greenblatt, S. (1997), *Shakespearean Negotiations: The Circulation of Social Energy in Renaissance England*, Oxford: Clarendon Press.

Habermas, J. (1984), *The Theory of Communicative Action: Reason and the Rationalization of Society*, Boston: Beacon Press.

Haddock, D. D. and D. D. Polsby (1994), 'Understanding riots', *Cato Journal*, 14 (1), pp. 147–57.

Hagedorn, J. M. (2008), *The World of Gangs: Armed Young Men and Gangsta Culture*, Minneapolis, MN: University of Minnesota Press.

Hall, S. (1999), 'Encoding/Decoding', in P. Marris and S. Thornham (eds), *Media Studies: A Reader*, 2nd edn, Edinburgh: Edinburgh University Press, pp. 51–61.

Hall, S., C. Critcher, T. Jefferson, J. Clarke and B. Roberts (2000), 'The social production of news', in P. Marris and S. Thornham (eds), *Media Studies: A Reader*, 2nd edn, New York: New York University Press, pp. 645–52.

Hart, C. (2014), *Discourse, Grammar and Ideology: Functional and Cognitive Perspectives*, London: Bloomsbury.

Harvey, D. (2008), 'The right to the city', *New Left Review*, 53 (September/October), pp. 23–40.

Hunt, D. M. (1996), *Screening the Los Angeles Riots: Race, Seeing, and Resistance*, New York: Cambridge University Press.

Hunt, D. M. (2012), 'American toxicity: Twenty years after the 1992 Los Angeles "riots"', *Amerasia Journal*, 38 (1), pp. ix–xviii.

Kawalerowicz, J. and M. Biggs (2015), 'Anarchy in the UK: Economic deprivation, social disorganization, and political grievances in the London riot of 2011', *Social Forces*, 94 (2), pp. 673–98.

Kimminich, E. (2003), 'Tanzstile der Hip Hop Kultur: Bewegungskult und Körperkommunikation', *Kulturen im Fokus*, <http://www.kulturenfokus.de> (last accessed 13 June 2016).

Kirkpatrick, J. (2008), *Uncivil Disobedience: Studies in Violence and Democratic Politics*, Princeton, NJ and Oxford: Princeton University Press.

Kress, G. and T. van Leeuwen (2006), *Reading Images: The Grammar of Visual Design*, 2nd edn, London and New York: Routledge.

Laclau, E. and C. Mouffe (2001), *Hegemony and Socialist Strategy: Towards a Radical Democratic Politics*, 2nd edn, London and New York: Verso.

Lee, J. (2009), 'Battlin' on the corner: Techniques for sustaining play', *Social Problems*, 56 (3), pp. 578–98.

Lefèbvre, H. (2003), *The Urban Revolution*, Minneapolis, MN: University of Minnesota Press.

McNeill, D. (2005), *Gesture and Thought*, Chicago: University of Chicago Press.

Mauss, M. (1973), 'The techniques of the body (Les techniques du corps. 1934)', *Economy and Society*, 2 (1), pp. 70–88.

Maxwell, J. (1998), 'Designing a qualitative study', in L. Bickmann and D. Rogs (eds), *Handbook of Applied Social Research Methods*, Thousand Oaks, CA: Sage, pp. 69–100.

Mitchell, W. J. T. (2005), *What Do Pictures Want? The Lives and Loves of Images*, Chicago: University of Chicago Press.

Mydans, S. (1992), 'In Los Angeles riots, a witness with videotapes', *The New York Times*, <http://www.nytimes.com/1992/07/31/news/in-los-angeles-riots-a-witness-with-videotapes.html> (last accessed 6 June 2016).

Newbold, C. (1998), 'Analysing visuals: Still and moving images', in A. Hansen, S. Cottle, R. Negrine and C. Newbold (eds), *Mass Communication Research Methods*, New York: New York University Press, pp. 198–224.

Pollak, A. (2008), 'Analyzing TV documentaries', in R. Wodak and M. Krzyzanowski (eds), *Qualitative Discourse Analysis in the Social Sciences*, New York: Palgrave Macmillan, pp. 77–95.

Randall, A. and A. Charlesworth (eds) (2000), *Moral Economy and Popular Protest: Crowds, Conflict and Authority*, Basingstoke: Palgrave Macmillan.

Reiss, M. (ed.) (2007), *The Street as Stage: Protest Marches and Public Rallies since the Nineteenth Century*, Princeton, NJ and Oxford: Oxford University Press.

Scollon, R. (2001), 'Action and text: Towards an integrated understanding of the place of text in social (inter)action, mediated discourse analysis and the problem of social action', in R. Wodak and M. Meyer (eds), *Methods of Critical Discourse Analysis*, London: Sage, pp. 139–83.

Sennett, R. (1994), *Flesh and Stone: The Body and the City in Western Civilization*, New York: W. W. Norton.

Singal, J. (2007), 'Damian Williams: The L.A. riots: 15 years after Rodney King', *Time*, <http://content.time.com/time/specials/2007/la_riot/article/0,28804,1614 117_1614084_1614510,00.html> (last accessed 6 June 2016).

Sittler, D. (2011), 'Tat-Ort und Schau-Platz? 1919', in A. Häusler and J. Henschen (eds), *Topos Tatort, Fiktionen des Realen*, Bielefeld: Transcript, pp. 197–210.

Sittler, D. (2015), *Die Geschichte der Metropolitanen Straße als Massenmedium: Chicago 1870–1930*, Dissertation, University of Erfurt.

Smith, C. (2007), *Urban Disorder and the Shape of Belief: The Great Chicago Fire, the Haymarket Bomb, and the Model Town of Pullman*, 2nd edn, Chicago: Chicago University Press.

Teissier, B. (1996), *Egyptian Iconography on Syro-Palestinian Cylinder Seals of the Middle Bronze Age*, Göttingen: Vandenhoeck & Ruprecht.

Thompson, E. P. (1959), 'Commitment in politics', *Universities & Left Review*, Spring (6), pp. 50–5.

Thompson, E. P. (1991), *The Making of the English Working Class*, New York: Penguin.

Tur, B. (2007), 'The L.A. riots: 15 years after Rodney King (interview)', *Time*, <http://content.time.com/time/specials/2007/la_riot/article/0,28804,161 4117_1615206,00.html> (last accessed 6 June 2016).

Tur, Z. A. (1992), 'LA riots, raw footage of Reginald Denny beatings – April 29, 1992, Los Angeles, CA', *YouTube*, <https://www.youtube.com/watch?v=kzuWr0 FYe5Y> (last accessed 6 June 2016).

van Dijk, T. A. (1977), *Text and Context: Explorations in the Semantics and Pragmatics of Discourse*, London and New York: Longman.

van Dijk, T. A. (1989), 'Race, riots and the press: An analysis of editorials in the British press about the 1985 disorders', *Gazette*, 43, pp. 229–53.

van Dijk, T. A. (1995), 'Power and the news media', in D. Paletz (ed.), *Political Communication and Action*, Cresskill, NJ: Hampton Press, pp. 9–36.

van Dyk, S. (2013), 'Was die Welt zusammenhält', *Zeitschrift für Diskursforschung*, 1, pp. 46–66.

van Leeuwen, T. (2008), *Discourse and Practice: New Tools for Critical Discourse Analysis*, Oxford: Oxford University Press.

Warburg, A. (2008), 'Einleitung [zum Mnemosyne-Bildatlas]', in U. Wirth (ed.), *Kulturwissenschaft: Eine Auswahl grundlegender Texte*, Frankfurt am Main: Suhrkamp, pp. 137–45.

Weigel, S. (2015), *Grammatologie der Bilder*, Berlin: Suhrkamp.

Index